Encyclopedia of Food Science Technology, Health & Nutrition

Encyclopedia of Food Science Technology, Health & Nutrition

Viniti Sharma

AMIGA PRESS INC.

DELHI (INDIA)

AMIGA PRESS INC.
H.O.: 28-A, Indra Park, Chander Nagar
Delhi-110051 (India)
Tel.: 011-22504028, +91-98736-57000
E-mail: amigapub@gmail.com
Website : www.amigapress.co.in

This edition is published by Amiga Press Inc.

ISBN: 978-93- 87295-02- 5

First Published 2019

Printed and bound India by Replika Press Pvt. Ltd.

Preface

The invention of vitamins is a long story that started with observations made centuries ago in China where the disease now recognised as Beriberi was essentially known. It is perhaps also that liver was used in very early times for the treatment of diseases which may have been related to a vitamin deficiency. Experience in the middle ages showed that certain foods were definitely connected with the prevention and cure of Scurvy. All these and other observations led ultimately to the scientific investigations of the present century.

Food Science is a highly inter-disciplinary applied science. It incorporates concepts from many different fields including microbiology, chemical engineering, and biochemistry. Nutrition science investigates the metabolic and physio-logical responses of the body to diet. With advances in the field of molecular biology, biochemistry, and genetics, the study of nutrition is increasingly concerned with metabolism and metabolic pathways: the sequences of biochemical steps through which substances in living things change from one form to another.

Food scientists at universities may study more fundamental phenomena that are directly linked to the production of a particular food product and its properties. This book makes a thorough and comprehensive examination of all these details, giving insightful information to the readers on nearly every dimension of the subject. It then proceeds on to the discussion of nutrition, making sure that the needs of current times are kept in mind with regard to this issue.

– Author

Contents

1

Introduction

The nutritional status of a population depends on the availability of food, its consumption, and its biological utilization. A natural disaster may affect the nutritional status of the population by affecting one or more components of the food chain depending on the type, duration, and extent of the disaster, as well as the food and nutritional conditions existing in the area before the catastrophe.

Slow-onset disasters such as drought are more likely to affect long-term nutritional status than sudden-onset disasters such as earthquakes and hurricanes. Not all sudden-onset disasters produce food shortages severe enough to cause harmful changes in the nutritional status of the population. The effect of any type of disaster on the nutritional status of the affected population is never immediate. Large scale food distribution is not always an immediate relief priority, and its long-term implementation may, in fact, produce undesired effects.

To plan and implement successful food relief operations, nutrition workers responsible for humanitarian operations must be familiar with the possible nutritional outcomes of specific types of natural disasters, as well as the food and nutrition situation in the affected area prior to the disaster. A nutrition officer trained in emergency management must be part of the disaster planning and response teams.

The immediate steps for ensuring that a food relief programme will be effective include:

- Assessing the food supplies available after the disaster;
- Gauging the nutritional needs of the affected population;
- Calculating daily food rations and needs for large population groups; and
- Monitoring the nutritional status of the affected population.

EXPECTED CONSEQUENCES OF DISASTERS ON THE FOOD CHAIN

Hurricanes, floods, land- or mud-slides, volcanic eruptions, and sea surges directly affect food availability. Standing crops may be completely destroyed, and seed stores and family food stocks may be lost, especially if there is no warning period. Volcanic eruptions can cause widespread crop destruction: food crops may be burned, defoliated, and buried under ashfall; reduced photosynthesis resulting from ash clouds limits subsequent production.

Earthquakes, on the other hand, generally have little direct impact on the long-term total availability of food. Standing crops are unaffected, and food stocks can often be salvaged from family, wholesale, and retail stores. However, temporary food problems may result as a consequence of the breakdown of the transportation and marketing systems. If an earthquake strikes during a labour-intensive period such as harvest, the loss of labour from death or its diversion from agriculture may cause short-term scarcities. The most likely consequence of any kind of sudden-impact disaster will be the disruption of transportation and communications systems and upheavals in routine social and economic activities. Even when food stocks exist, they may be inaccessible due to disruptions in the distribution system or the loss of income with which to buy food.

Destruction of cash crops also will have an effect on the economy of families. When destruction of a greater magnitude occurs, leading to the death of livestock and the loss of crops and stored foodstuffs, the short-term dilemma can leave a more severe, long-term crisis in its wake. Moreover, evacuation and resettlement of communities during the post-disaster period are often necessary, creating foci in which total food supplies will have to be provided for the duration of the encampment.

Hospitals and other institutions may require emergency food supplies as well. Livestock may have to be sacrificed if they cannot be fed, and they are likely to die when vast tracts of land are flooded for long periods. While the meat can be used immediately for distribution among the affected population, or salted for later distribution, in the long run it results in food and economic shortfalls. The effect of disasters on the biological utilization of food, that is, intestinal absorption and subsequent utilization of nutrients, is indirect, and dependent on factors such as the impact of the disaster on the environment, particularly on water supply and sanitation.

Other infectious diseases increase the demand for nutrients. These effects are more likely to occur among the young and vulnerable groups. If there is an increase in undernutrition rates among young children soon after a disaster, it will most likely be the effect of gastrointestinal illness rather than actual food shortages. This is something to keep in mind in the implementation of surveillance mechanisms. Outbreaks of infectious diseases are uncommon after natural disasters, especially in the Americas.

POSSIBLE ADVERSE EFFECTS OF LARGE-SCALE FOOD DISTRIBUTION

The decision to distribute large amounts of food, although made at the political level, should be based on the most accurate information available. If unnecessarily large quantities of food are brought into an area, this may hinder recovery. Food distribution requires transport and personnel that may be better employed in other ways, and small farmers may face hardship due to depressed market prices.

Perhaps the most serious side effect is that maintaining a population by free food distribution, if not accompanied by essentials such as seeds and tools needed to restart the local economy, may create dependence on relief.

SETTING PRIORITIES

The priorities in alleviating food problems are to:

- Supply food immediately where there appears to be an urgent need, namely to isolated populations, institutions, and relief workers;
- Make an initial estimate of likely food needs in the area, so that steps can be taken towards procurement, transport, storage, and distribution;
- Locate or procure stocks of food and assess their fitness for local consumption; and
- Monitor information on food needs so that procurement, distribution, and other programmes can be modified as the situation changes.

IMMEDIATE RELIEF

During the first, usually chaotic, days after a disaster strikes, the exact extent of the damage is unknown, communications are difficult, and the number of people affected seems to double by the hour. Food distribution must start as soon as possible to keep people fed, rather than prevent clinical malnutrition. Given the large variety and small stocks of commodities sent in as aid by governments, agencies, private organizations, and individuals, however, food distribution is initially a day-to-day exercise.

Planning nutritionally sensible food rations during this period is impossible. What matters during this "chaotic stage" is to provide a minimum of 6.7 to 8.4 Megajoules (1,600 to 2,000 kcal) per day, per person. As an immediate relief step, available food should be distributed in sufficient quantity to any group that is at high risk or appears to be wanting, to ensure survival for one week (3 or 4 kg per person). Food may be included automatically, for example, in supplies sent to communities isolated by earthquake or displaced by flooding.

Where fuel shortages are likely, it may be better to distribute cooked food such as boiled rice or bread rather than dry food. No detailed calculations need be made of the precise vitamin, mineral, or protein content of the food distributed in the initial phase, but supplies should be acceptable and palatable. The most important thing to be provided is sufficient energy. If no other items can be obtained, distribution of a cereal alone will be sufficient to meet basic nutritional requirements. When a population can find some of its own food, it may be possible to supply only part of the ration, or one food item that complements the basic or staple food lacking in their available supplies.

ESTIMATING FOOD REQUIREMENTS

As soon as possible after a disaster, a rapid assessment of the food and nutrition situation should be made to get a rough estimate of likely bulk food items needed. This is based on the population affected, its composition, distribution (for example, isolated villages, refugee camps), and locally available foods.

This will enable managers to take the necessary steps to locate and procure stocks, storage, and transport. Hoarding is not uncommon and leads to over- response.

In the absence of detailed information, an estimate of food requirements must be based to some extent on judgement in the light of the initial assessment, but it should take into account the following factors:

- The probable effect of the disaster on food availability (e.g., a tsunami may have destroyed all household supplies);
- The approximate size of the population affected;
- The impact of seasonal factors. In subsistence areas just before the harvest, for instance, household and traders' stocks may be depleted and the population may be more dependent on the market.

The nutrition officer should prepare estimates of foods on the basis of a family unit (usually considered to consist of five people) for one week and one month.

Logistically, food distribution on a family basis for one month may be considered the most practical approach. The nutrition officer also should prepare estimates of commodities required by large population groups, for instance, on the basis of 1,000 people for one month.Two simple and useful rules of thumb are:

- 16 metric tonnes of food sustain 1,000 people for one month,
- To store one metric tonne of food, about two cubic metres of space are needed.

Proper storage is extremely important to avoid food losses due to rain, pests, or looting.

When calculating the composition of daily rations, the following points should be kept in mind:

- The ration should be kept as simple as possible;
- To facilitate storage and distribution, nonperishable food commodities that are not bulky should be chosen;
- Substitution of items within food groups should be allowed for.

The food ration should be based on three food groups: a staple, preferably a cereal; a concentrated energy source such as a fat; and a concentrated source of protein, such as salted or dried fish or meat. In practice, the diets will be dictated by the availability of ingredients.

A standardized ration may be impractical as availability will change daily and according to areas. Whenever possible, vulnerable groups should receive a food supplement in addition to the basic diet.

Among these groups we include children under 5 years old, who are growing very fast and may suffer permanent damage if malnourished, and pregnant and lactating women, who require more nutrients. Breastmilk is the best food for infants under six months of age, and Health Disaster Coordinators should not allow the emergency situation to become an excuse for flooding the country with infant formula.

PROCUREMENT

If the calculated amount of food required exceeds immediate local availability, and if it is anticipated that food will have to be distributed for several months, steps must be taken to obtain food from elsewhere in the country or abroad. A rough estimate of local food transport requirements should also be made for this contingency. Food for the initial emergency distribution phase should be obtained from national government or wholesaler stocks, or from bilateral or international development agencies (e.g., World Food Programme, NGOs). If large quantities of food are required from abroad, procurement and shipping may require several months.

Approaches to suitable agencies should hence be made at the earliest possible date. It is critical that Health Disaster Coordinators advise potential donors of the eating habits and preferences of their populations. Food not eaten is of no nutritional benefit. The need for special infant foods ("baby foods") immediately after disasters is often exaggerated.

Improving maternal nutrition and assisting mothers economically is more cost-effective and safer than airlifting strained baby foods. Since vitamin requirements are of little concern during the acute emergency phase after sudden-impact natural disasters, multivitamin tablets should not be requested as a separate relief item. The population's specific vitamin and mineral needs will have to be assessed for the long-term.

SURVEILLANCE

If long-term food supply problems seem likely, as in areas with subsistence agriculture and poor communications, the nutritional status of the community should be monitored. This can be accomplished by making regular physical measurements of a suitable sample of the population. Since young children are the most sensitive to nutritional changes, the surveillance system should be based on them, remembering that the most serious malnutrition results from an acute exacerbation of chronic under nutrition.

In emergency situations, weight-for-height will provide the best indicator of acute changes in nutritional status. If height and weight cannot be measured, arm circumference, which is simple and easy to measure, may be used to gauge changes in communities. As the results of the first needs assessments become available, more accurate information will make it possible to adjust preliminary estimates of the proportion of the population most in need of long-term food distribution.

Surveys of need should make sure to cover not only food availability, but also identify areas where problems of labour, tools, marketing, and other variables affecting distribution have arisen. As soon as an area is able to return to normal consumption patterns, distribution should be phased out.

□

2

Food Preservation

You are familiar with perishability of food and importance of selection as well as storage of food to prevent its spoilage. Do you know how you can actually prevent food from getting spoilt? Yes, by preserving it. You must have seen it at your homes-potato wafers being dried, raw mango being cut and dried, tomato sauce, chutneys, dal wadi and papads being made. Preserved food not only adds variety to our meals but also helps in utilizing excess produce at harvest time.

MEANING AND NEED FOR PRESERVATION

Food preservation is to treat food to keep it in good condition for a long time. Why do we do that? Let us take a simple example of boiling milk. Why do we boil milk? So that we can use it for a longer period. You know that boiling delays milk from getting sour.

You can say you have processed milk and preserved it, even if it is for a short duration. It may be as simple as boiling of milk or complicated like pickling of mango or lemon. By preserving foods, we are also increasing their shelf life. You already know what shelf life of food means. Yes, it means the time period for which a food can remain fit for human consumption at optimum temperature.

Need for Preservation

- To increase the shelf 1ife of foods.
- To prepare new products like jams, papads, pickles, etc. Such products are enjoyed by everyone and all the year round.
- Processing reduces the bulk of fruits and vegetables. The storage and transportation becomes easier, e.g., 1 kg of carrots wouId take more space than 1 kg of carrot murraba.
- Helps in ulilizing the food stuffs when available in excess.

PRINCIPLES OF FOOD PRESERVATION

You have learnt earlier that by boiling milk we are preserving it for a longer time. But, what are you actually doing by boiling? You are killing the microorganisms by raising the temperature of milk. Microorganisms cannot survive at very high temperature. This is one of the principles of food preservation. Let us now learn about the principles of food preservation:

- By killing the microorganisms.
- By preventing or delaying the action of micro-organisms.
- By stopping the action of enzymes.

By Killing the Micro-Organisms

You already know that boiling of milk kills micro-organisms. Sometimes, heat is applied for a shorter duration to kill only undesirable microorganisms, that is those which can spoil the food stuff. It is done while pasteurizing milk. The cooking that you do at home also keeps food free from microorganisms. In canning, food is heated to high temperature to prevent growth of microorganisms in food.

Preventing or Delaying the Action of Microorganisms

You all know that a peeled apple spoils faster than one with intact skin. Do you know why? This is because the apple has its skin as a protective covering which prevents the entry of microorganisms. Similarly, the shell of nuts and eggs, skin of fruits and vegetables serve as a protective coating and delays the action of microorganisms. Food packed in polythene bags and aluminium foils are also protected against microorganisms. You have read earlier that microorganisms need air and water to grow. But if these are removed, you can prevent the action of microorganisms and ensure that food does not get spoilt.

Lowering temperature or freezing a food also helps in delaying the action of microorganisms and thus in food preservation. You must have come across frozen foods. Frozen food can be kept for a longer time than fresh food. This is because microorganisms cannot act at low temperatures. Thus, when you are putting food in the refrigerator or freezer, you are preventing the microorganism from growing. Lastly, certain chemicals like sodium benzoate and potassium metabisulphite also help in preventing the growth of micro-organisms. These chemicals are called "preservatives".

Thus you have learnt that the action of microorganisms can be delayed or prevented in many ways:

- By providing a protective covering.
- By raising the temperature.
- By lowering the temperature.
- By adding chemicals.

By Stopping the Action of Enzymes

Enzymes also cause food spoilage. They are naturally present in food. Take the example of fruits. Keep a raw banana for a few days and observe what happens to it. Yes, the banana will turn ripe, become yellow and then start decaying and browning.

All this happens due to presence of enzymes. What will happen if the action of enzymes is stopped? The foodstuff will be prevented from spoiling. Enzyme action can be prevented by giving a mild heat treatment. Before canning or freezing, vegetables are dipped in hot water or exposed to steam for a few minutes. This is known as blanching. When you heat milk, you are not only killing microorganisms present in it but also stopping the action of enzymes. This extends its shelf life.

HOUSEHOLD METHODS OF FOOD PRESERVATION

Some of the practical methods which can be used for preserving food at home are:

- Dehydration.
- Pickling with salt, spices and/or oil.
- Making jams, jellies, murabbas.
- Bottling of squashes and juices.
- Freezing.

CANNING

Canning is a method of preserving food in which the food is processed and sealed in an airtight container. The process was first developed as a French military discovery by Nicolas Appert in 1810. The packaging prevents microorganisms from entering and proliferating inside. To prevent the food from being spoiled before and during containment, quite a number of methods are used: pasteurization, boiling, refrigeration, freezing, drying, vacuum treatment, antimicrobial agents that are natural to the recipe of the foods being preserved, a sufficient dose of ionizing radiation, submersion in a strong saline solution, acid, base, osmotically extreme or other microbe-challenging environments. Other than sterilization, no method is perfectly dependable as a preservative. For example, the microorganism Clostridium botulinum can only be eliminated at temperatures above the boiling point.

From a public safety point of view, foods with low acidity need sterilization under high temperature. To achieve temperatures above the boiling point requires the use of a pressure canner. Foods that must be pressure canned include most vegetables, meats, seafood, poultry, and dairy products. The only foods that may be safely canned in an ordinary boiling water bath are highly acidic ones with a pH below 4.6, such as fruits, pickled vegetables, or other foods to which acidic additives have been added.

History and Development of Canning

During the first years of the Napoleonic Wars, the French government offered a hefty cash award of 12,000 francs to any inventor who could devise a cheap and effective method of preserving large amounts of food. The larger armies of the period required increased, regular supplies of quality food. Limited food availability was among the factors limiting military campaigns to the summer and autumn months.

In 1809, a French confectioner and brewer, Nicolas Appert, observed that food cooked inside a jar did not spoil unless the seals leaked, and developed a method of sealing food in glass jars. The reason for lack of spoilage was unknown at the time, since it would be another 50 years before Louis Pasteur demonstrated the role of microbes in food spoilage. However, glass containers presented challenges for transportation. Glass jars were largely replaced in commercial canneries with cylindrical tin or wrought-iron canisters following the work of Peter Durand.

Cans are cheaper and quicker to make, and much less fragile than glass jars. Glass jars have remained popular for some high-value products and in home canning. Can-openers were not invented for another thirty years—at first, soldiers had to cut the cans open with bayonets or smash them open with rocks. The French Army began experimenting with issuing canned foods to its soldiers, but the slow process of canning foods and the even slower development and transport stages prevented the army from shipping large amounts across the French Empire, and the war ended before the process was perfected.

Unfortunately for Appert, the factory which he had built with his prize money was razed in 1814 by Allied soldiers invading France. Following the end of the Napoleonic Wars, the canning process was gradually employed in other European countries and in the US. Based on Appert's methods of food preservation, Peter Durand patented a process in the United Kingdom in 1810. He did not develop the process, selling his patent in 1811 to Bryan Donkin and John Hall, who were in business as Donkin Hall and Gamble, of Bermondsey.

Bryan Donkin developed the process of packaging food in sealed airtight cans, made of tinned wrought iron. Initially, the canning process was slow and labour-intensive, as each large can had to be hand-made, and took up to six hours to cook, making canned food too expensive for ordinary people. The main market for the food at this stage was the Army and Navy. By 1817 Donkin recorded that he had sold £3000 worth of canned meat in six months. In 1824

Sir William Edward Parry took canned beef and pea soup with him on his voyage to the Arctic in HMS Fury, during his search for a northwestern passage to India. In 1829, Admiral Sir James Ross also took canned food to the Arctic, as did Sir John Franklin in 1845.

Some of his stores were found by the search expedition led by Captain Leopold McLintock in 1857. One of these cans was opened in 1939, and was edible and nutritious, though it was not analyzed for contamination by the lead solder used in its manufacture. Throughout the mid-19th century, canned food became a status symbol amongst middle-class households in Europe, becoming something of a frivolous novelty. Early methods of manufacture employed poisonous lead solder for sealing the cans, which may have worsened the disastrous outcome of the 1845 Franklin expedition to chart and navigate the Northwest Passage.

Increasing mechanisation of the canning process, coupled with a huge increase in urban populations across Europe, resulted in a rising demand for canned food. A number of inventions and improvements followed, and by the 1860s smaller machine-made steel cans were possible, and the time to cook food in sealed cans had been reduced from around six hours to thirty minutes. Canned food also began to spread beyond Europe—Robert Ayars established the first American canning factory in New York City in 1812, using improved tin-plated wrought-iron cans for preserving oysters, meats, fruits and vegetables.

Demand for canned food greatly increased during wars. Large-scale wars in the nineteenth century, such as the Crimean War, American Civil War, and Franco-Prussian War introduced increasing numbers of working-class men to canned food, and allowed canning companies to expand their businesses to meet military demands for non-perishable food, allowing companies to manufacture in bulk and sell to wider civilian markets after wars ended. Urban populations in Victorian era Britain demanded ever-increasing quantities of cheap, varied, quality food that they could keep at home without having to go shopping daily.

In response, companies such as Nestlé, Heinz, and others emerged to provide quality canned food for sale to working class city-dwellers. In particular, Crosse and Blackwell took over the concern of Donkin Hall and Gamble. The late 19th century saw the range of canned food available to urban populations greatly increase, as canners competed with each other using novel foodstuffs, highly decorated printed labels, and lower prices.

Demand for canned food skyrocketed during World War I, as military commanders sought vast quantities of cheap, high-calorie food to feed their millions of soldiers, which could be transported safely, survive trench conditions, and not spoil in transport. Throughout the war, soldiers generally subsisted on low-quality canned foodstuffs, such as the British "Bully Beef", pork and beans and Maconochies Irish Stew, but by 1916 widespread boredom with cheap canned food amongst soldiers resulted in militaries purchasing better-quality food to improve morale, and the complete meals in a can began to appear. In 1917 the French Army began issuing canned French cuisine, such as coq au vin, while the Italian Army experimented with canned ravioli and spaghetti bolognese.

Shortages of canned food in the British Army in 1917 led to the government issuing cigarettes and amphetamines to soldiers to suppress their appetites. After the war, companies that had supplied military canned food improved the quality of their goods for civilian sale. Today, tin-coated steel is the material most commonly used. Laminate vacuum pouches are also used for canning, such as used in MREs and Capri Sun drinks.

Double Seams

Invented in 1888 by Max Ams, modern double seams provide an airtight seal to the tin can. This airtight nature is crucial to keeping bacteria out of the can and keeping its contents sealed inside. Thus, double seamed cans are also known as Sanitary Cans. Developed in 1900 in Europe, this sort of can was made of the traditional cylindrical body made with tin plate. The two ends were attached using what is now called a double seam. A can thus sealed is impervious to the contamination by creating two tight continuous folds between the can's cylindrical body and the lids.

This eliminated the need for solder and allowed improvements in manufacturing speed, reducing cost. Double seaming uses rollers to shape the can, lid and the final double seam. To make a sanitary can and lid suitable for double seaming, manufacture begins with a sheet of coated tin plate. To create the can body, rectangles are cut and curled around a die, and welded together creating a cylinder with a side seam. Rollers are then used to flare out one or both ends of the cylinder to create a quarter circle flange around the circumference. Precision is required to ensure that the welded sides are perfectly aligned, as any misalignment will cause inconsistent flange shape, compromising its integrity. A circle is then cut from the sheet using a die cutter. The circle is shaped in a stamping press to create a downward countersink to fit snugly in to the can body. The result can be compared to an upside down and very flat top hat. The outer edge is then curled down and around about 140 degrees using rollers to create the end curl. The result is a steel tube with a flanged edge, and a countersunk steel disc with a curled edge. A rubber compound is put inside the curl.

Seaming

The body and end are brought together in a seamer and held in place by the base plate and chuck, respectively. The base plate provides a sure footing for the can body during the seaming operation and the chuck fits snugly in to the end. The result is the countersink of the end sits inside the top of the can body just below the flange. The end curl protrudes slightly beyond the flange.

First Operation

Once brought together in the seamer, the seaming head presses a first operation roller against the end curl. The end curl is pressed against the flange curling it in towards the body and under the flange. The flange is also bent downward, and the end and body are now loosely joined together. The first operation roller is then retracted. At this point five thicknesses of steel exist in the seam.

From the outside in they are:

- End,
- Flange,
- End Curl,
- Body,
- Countersink.

This is the first seam. All the parts of the seam are now aligned and readyfor the final stage.

Second Operation

The seaming head then engages the second operation roller against the partly formed seam. The second operation presses all five steel components together tightly to form the final seal.

The five layers in the final seam are then called:

1. End,
2. Body Hook,
3. Cover Hook,
4. Body,
5. Countersink.

All sanitary cans require a filling medium within the seam because otherwise the metal-to-metal contact will not maintain a hermetic seal. In most cases, a rubberized compound is placed inside the end curl radius, forming the critical seal between the end and the body.

Probably the most important innovation since the introduction of double seams is the welded side seam. Prior to the welded side seam, the can body was folded and/or soldered together, leaving a relatively thick side seam. The thick side seam required that the side seam end juncture at the end curl to have more metal to curl around before closing in behind the Body Hook or flange, with a greater opportunity for error.

Seamer Setup and Quality Assurance

Many different parts during the seaming process are critical in ensuring that a can is airtight and vacuum sealed. The dangers of a can that is not hermetically sealed are contamination by foreign objects or that the can could leak or spoil. One important part is the seamer setup. This process is usually performed by an experienced technician. Amongst the parts that need setup are seamer rolls and chucks which have to be set in their exact position.

The lifter pressure and position, roll and chuck designs, tooling wear, and bearing wear all contribute to a good double seam. Incorrect setups can be non-intuitive. For example, due to the springback effect, a seam can appear loose, when in reality it was closed too tight and has opened up like a spring. For this reason, experienced operators and good seamer setup are critical to ensure that double seams are properly closed. Quality control usually involves taking full cans from the line—one per seamer head, at least once or twice per shift, and performing a teardown operation, mechanical tests as well as cutting the seam open with a twin blade saw and measuring with a double seam inspection system.

The combination of these measurements will determine the seam's quality. Use of a or software in conjunction with a manual double seam monitor, computerized double seam scanner, or even a fully-automatic double seam inspection system makes the laborious process of double seam inspection faster and much more accurate.

Statistically tracking the performance of each head or seaming station of the allows for better prediction of can seamer issues, and may be used to plan maintenance when convenient: rather that to simply react after bad or unsafe cans have been produced.

Nutrition Value

Canning is a way of processing food to extend its shelf life. The idea is to make food available and edible long after the processing time. A 1997 study found that canned fruits and vegetables provide as much dietary fibre and vitamins as the same corresponding fresh or frozen foods, and in some cases, even more. The heating process during canning appears to make dietary fibre more soluble, and therefore more readily fermented in the colon into gases and physiologically active byproducts. Canned tomatoes have a higher available lycopene content.

Potential Hazards

To improve food safety for those who eat canned food, governments have enacted laws requiring alphanumeric codes being put on food cans during manufacture indicating information relevant to health, such as the date of canning, etc.

Migration of Can Components

In canning toxicology, migration is the movement of substances from the can itself into the contents. Potential toxic substances that can migrate are lead, causing lead poisoning, or bisphenol A, a potential endocrine disruptor that is an ingredient in the epoxy commonly used to coat the inner surface of cans.

Salt Content

Canned food can be a major source of dietary salt. Too much salt increases the risk of health problems, including high blood pressure. Therefore, health authorities have recommended limitations of dietary sodium. Many canned products are available in low-salt and no-salt alternatives.

Botulism

Foodborne botulism results from contaminated foodstuffs in which C. botulinum spores have been allowed to germinate and produce botulism toxin, and this typically occurs in canned non-acidic food substances. C. botulinum prefers low oxygen environments, and can therefore grow in canned foods. Botulism is a rare but serious paralytic illness, leading to paralysis that typically starts with the muscles of the face and then spreads towards the limbs. In severe forms, it leads to paralysis of the breathing muscles and causes respiratory failure. In view of this life-threatening complication, all suspected cases of botulism are treated as medical emergencies, and public health officials are usually involved to prevent further cases from the same source.

Canning and the Recession

Canned goods sell particularly well in times of recession due to the tendency of financially-stressed individuals to engage in cocooning, a term used by retail analysts to describe the phenomenon in which people actively avoid straying from their houses. In February 2009, the recession-laden United States saw an 11.5 per cent rise in sales of canning-related items.

CURING

Curing refers to various food preservation and flavouring processes, especially of meat or fish, by the addition of a combination of salt, sugar, nitrates or nitrite. Many curing processes also involve smoking.

Chemical Actions

The chemical actions of curing are highly complex with slow reactions of proteins and fats through autolysis and oxidation. These reactions can be driven by auto-oxidation alone though it is typically accompanied by enzymes in the curing food as well as beneficial fungi and bacteria.

To enable these slow curing reactions and prevent rapid decomposition through rotting, water is extracted from the food and the food is made inhospitable to microorganisms. This is usually done by applying salt and a combination of other ingredients to cure the food.

SaltTable salt, which consists primarily of sodium chloride, is the most important ingredient for curing food and is used in relatively large quantities. Salt kills and inhibits the growth of microorganisms by drawing water out of the cells of both microbe and food alike through osmosis. Cell growth for most species of unwanted bacteria ceases when the water activity is reduced below 0.91. For meat cured with salt alone, without drying, salt at 5 to 10 per cent may be required. Country ham is an example. With drying or use of other solutes, the salt level may be lowered considerably. Once properly salted, the food's interior contains enough salt to exert osmotic pressures that prevent or retard the growth of many undesirable microbes.

Sugar

Although often used in curing to give a pleasant taste, sugar can also be used to encourage the growth of beneficial bacteria such as those of the Lactobacillus genus. Dextrose or sucrose used as the food source ferments the food. As the unwanted bacterial growth is delayed, the salt-tolerant lactobacilli outcompete them, and further growth is prevented by generating an acidic environment through production of lactic acid. This inhibits the growth of other microbes and accounts for the tangy flavour of some cured products. Pepperoni is an example.

Nitrates and Nitrites

Nitrates and nitrites not only help kill bacteria, but also produce a characteristic flavour and give meat a pink or red colour. Nitrate, generally supplied by sodium nitrate or potassium nitrate, is used as a source for nitrite. The nitrite further breaks down in the meat into nitric oxide, which then binds to the iron atom in the centre of myoglobin's heme group, reducing oxidation and causing a reddish-brown colour when raw, and the characteristic cooked- ham pink colour when cooked.

The addition of ascorbate to cured meat reduces formation of nitrosamines, but increases the nitrosylation of iron. The use of nitrates in food preservation is controversial, though, due to the potential for the formation of nitrosamines when the preserved food is cooked at high temperature. The usage of either compound is therefore carefully regulated; for example, in the United States, the concentration of nitrates and nitrites is generally limited to 200 ppm or lower. However, they are considered irreplaceable in the prevention of botulinum poisoning from consumption of cured dry sausages by preventing spore germination. A

2007 study by Columbia University suggests a link between eating cured meats and chronic obstructive pulmonary disease. Nitrites were posited as a possible cause.

Smoke

Although more frequently used for flavour than preservation, smoke is an antimicrobial and antioxidant. Some of the smoke molecules adhere to the outer surfaces of food, inhibiting bacterial growth and oxidation, while the others provide the characteristic colour. Both provide the flavour. Smoke particles are undesirable and avoided by controlling the temperature and humidity in the smoking environment.

FERMENTATION

Fermentation in food processing typically is the conversion of carbohydrates to alcohols and carbon dioxide or organic acids using yeasts, bacteria, or a combination thereof, under anaerobic conditions. A more restricted definition of fermentation is the chemical conversion of sugars into ethanol. The science of fermentation is known as zymurgy. Fermentation usually implies that the action of microorganisms is desirable, and the process is used to produce alcoholic beverages such as wine, beer, and cider. Fermentation is also employed in the leavening of bread, and for preservation techniques to create lactic acid in sour foods such as sauerkraut, dry sausages, kimchi and yogurt, or vinegar for use in pickling foods.

History

Since fruits ferment naturally, fermentation precedes human history. Since ancient times, however, humans have been controlling the fermentation process. The earliest evidence of winemaking dates from eight thousand years ago, in Georgia, in the Caucasus area. Seven-thousand-year-old jars containing the remains of wine have been excavated in the Zagros Mountains in Iran, which are now on display at the University of Pennsylvania.

There is strong evidence that people were fermenting beverages in Babylon circa 5000 BC, ancient Egypt circa 3150 BC, pre-Hispanic Mexico circa 2000 BC, and Sudan circa 1500 BC. There is also evidence of leavened bread in ancient Egypt circa 1500 BC and of milk fermentation in Babylon circa 3000 BC. French chemist Louis Pasteur was the first known zymologist, when in 1854 he connected yeast to fermentation. Pasteur originally defined fermentation as "respiration without air". Pasteur performed careful research and concluded:

- "I am of the opinion that alcoholic fermentation never occurs without simultaneous organization, development and multiplication of cells.... If asked, in what consists the chemical act whereby the sugar is decomposed... I am completely ignorant of it."

Contributions to Biochemistry

When studying the fermentation of sugar to alcohol by yeast, Louis Pasteur concluded that the fermentation was catalyzed by a vital force, called "ferments", within the yeast cells. The "ferments" were thought to function only within living organisms. "Alcoholic fermentation is an act correlated with the life and organization of the yeast cells, not with the death or putrefaction of the cells", he wrote. Nevertheless, it was known that yeast extracts ferment sugar even in the absence of living yeast cells. While studying this process in 1897, Eduard Buchner of Humboldt University of Berlin, Germany, found that sugar was fermented even when there were no living yeast cells in the mixture, by a yeast secretion that he termed zymase. In 1907 he received the Nobel Prize in Chemistry for his research and discovery of "cell-free fermentation". One year prior, in 1906, ethanol fermentation studies led to the early discovery of NAD^+.

Uses

The primary benefit of fermentation is the conversion of sugars and other carbohydrates, e.g., converting juice into wine, grains into beer, carbohydrates into carbon dioxide to leaven bread, and sugars in vegetables into preservative organic acids.

Food fermentation has been said to serve five main purposes:

- Enrichment of the diet through development of a diversity of flavours, aromas, and textures in food substrates.
- Preservation of substantial amounts of food through lactic acid, alcohol, acetic acid and alkaline fermentations.
- Biological enrichment of food substrates with protein, essential amino acids, essential fatty acids, and vitamins.
- Elimination of antinutrients.
- A decrease in cooking times and fuel requirements. Some fermentation products are deleterious.

Risks of Consuming Fermented Foods

Alaska has witnessed a steady increase of cases of botulism since 1985. Despite its small population, it has more cases of botulism than any other state in the United States of America.

This is caused by the traditional Eskimo practice of allowing animal products such as whole fish, fish heads, walrus, sea lion and whale flippers, beaver tails, seal oil, birds, etc., to ferment for an extended period of time before being consumed.

The risk is exacerbated when a plastic container is used for this purpose instead of the old-fashioned method, a grass-lined hole, as the botulinum bacteria thrive in the anaerobic conditions created by the air-tight enclosure in plastic.

FROZEN FOOD

Freezing food preserves food from the time it is prepared to the time it is eaten. Since early times, farmers, fishermen, and trappers have preserved their game in unheated buildings during the winter season. Freezing food slows down decomposition by turning water to ice, making it unavailable for most bacterial growth.

Process

History: Clarence Birdseye, an American inventor, developed the quick-freezing system. He discovered that the combination of ice, wind, and low temperatures in the Arctic froze anything left exposed almost instantly. Birdseye soon realized that the quick freezing effectively kept large crystals from forming. Other attempts had resulted in the formation of large crystals, destroying the delicate cellular structure of the food. With only an electric fan, a few buckets of brine, and cakes of ice, Clarence Birdseye perfected his system of packing fresh food into waxed cardboard boxes and flash-freezing them under high pressure. He sold the patent to the Goldman-Sachs Trading Corporation and the Postum Company. In 1929 the first quick frozen vegetables were sold to the public.

Modern Techniques

Today manufacturers freeze foods by immersion in very cold liquids. Liquid nitrogen is the preferred medium to use. Liquid nitrogen is about-320°F, making it very useful to quickly freeze foods. The moment the food is submerged in liquid nitrogen, it rapidly begins to freeze. The faster something freezes, the smaller the crystals are that form. High-Pressure Shift Freezing is another method used today to manufacture frozen food. At a very high pressure, 900MPa, ice may be formed at room temperature. This is not an efficient way to create frozen foods, but it is being researched for use in later years. Dehydrofreezing is a commercial method used to reduce the cost of shipping, handling, and storage of fruits and vegetables. During dehydrofreezing, food is first dehydrated to the desirable moisture level and then frozen. Fruits and vegetables contain more water than meats. More water makes the fruits and vegetables more susceptible to the formation of large ice crystals. Dehydrofreezing gives the manufacturer peace of mind and keeps produce fresher.

Preservatives

Frozen foods don't require many preservatives because the process of preparing the food for freezing kills much of the bacteria living on the food. Carboxymethylcellulose is used as a stabilizer in frozen foods because of its tasteless and odorless properties.

Packaging

Frozen food packaging must maintain its integrity throughout machine filling, sealing, freezing, storage, transportation, thawing, and often cooking. Most frozen foods are cooked in a microwave oven. To make it easier for the consumer, manufacturers have developed packaging that can go straight from freezer to microwave. In 1974, the first differential heating container was sold to the public. A DHC is a sleeve of metal designed to allow frozen foods to receive the correct amount of heat. Various sized apertures were positioned around the sleeve. The consumer would put the frozen dinner into the sleeve just as to what needed the most heat. This ensured proper cooking.

Today there are multiple options for packaging frozen foods. Boxes, cartons, bags, pouches, heat-in-bag pouches, lidded trays and pans, crystallized PET trays, and composite and plastic cans. Scientists are continually researching new aspects of frozen food packaging. Active packaging offers a host of new technologies that can actively sense and then neutralize the presence of bacteria or other harmful sepcies. Active packaging can extend shelf-life, maintain product safety, and help preserve the food over a longer period of time.

There are currently several functions of active packaging currently being researched:

- Oxygen scavengers
- Time temperature indicators and digital temperature dataloggers
- Antimicrobials
- Carbon dioxide controllers
- Microwave susceptors
- Moisture control: water activity, moisture vapour transmission rate, etc
- Flavour enhancers
- Oder generators
- Oxygen-permeable films
- Oxygen generators
- Validation of cold chain.

With these new technologies, food may last longer and our knowledge about its safety will increase.

Effects on Nutrients

Vitamin Content of Frozen Foods

- Vitamin C: Usually lost in a higher concentration than any other vitamin. A study was performed on peas to determine the cause of blanching phase with the rest of the loss occurring during the cooling and washing stages. The vitamin loss was not actually accredited to the freezing process. Another experiment was performed involving peas and lima beans. Frozen and canned vegetables were both used in the experiment. The frozen vegetable were stored at -10 °F and the canned vegetables were stored at room temperature. After 0, 3, 6, and 12 months of storage, the vegetables were analyzed with and without cooking. O'Hara, the scientist performing the experiment said, "From the view point of the vitamin content of the two vegetables when they were ready for the plate of the consumer, there did not appear to be any marked advantages attributable to method of preservation, frozen storage, processed in a tin, or processed in glass."

- Vitamin B1: A vitamin loss of 25 per cent is normal. Thiamin is easily soluble in water and is destroyed by heat.
- Vitamin B2: Not much research has been done to see how much freezing affects Riboflavin levels. One study found an 18 per cent vitamin loss in green vegetables while another found a 4 per cent loss. It is commonly accepted that the loss of Riboflavin has to do with the preparation for freezing rather than the actual freezing process itself.
- Vitamin A: There is little loss of Carotene during preparation for freezing and freezing of most vegetables. However, there is a danger of losing the vitamin during a long-continued storage period.

Efficiency

Freezing is an effective form of food preservation because the pathogens that cause food spoilage are killed or do not grow very rapidly at reduced temperatures.

The process is less effective in food preservation than are thermal techniques, such as boiling, because pathogens are more likely to be able to survive cold temperatures rather than hot temperatures. One of the problems surrounding the use of freezing as a method of food preservation is the danger that pathogens deactivated by the process will once again become active when the frozen food thaws.

Foods may be preserved for several months by freezing. Long-term frozen storage requires a constant temperature of -18°C or less. Some freezers cannot achieve such a low temperature. The time food can be kept in the freezer is reduced considerably if the temperature in a freezer fluctuates; small ice crystals thaw as the temperature moves up, and refreeze onto larger crystals as the temperature declines. Fluctuations can occur by a small gap in the freezer door or adding a large amount of unfrozen food.

FREEZE-DRYING

Freeze-drying is a dehydration process typically used to preserve a perishable material or make the material more convenient for transport. Freeze- drying works by freezing the material and then reducing the surrounding pressure and adding enough heat to allow the frozen water in the material to sublime directly from the solid phase to the gas phase.

The Origins of Freeze-Drying

Freeze-drying was first actively developed during WW II. Serum being sent to Europe for medical treatment of the wounded required refrigeration. Due to the lack of available refrigeration, many serum supplies were spoiling before reaching the intended recipients. The freeze-drying process was developed as a commercial technique that enabled serum to be rendered chemically stable and viable without having to be refrigerated. Shortly thereafter, the freeze dry process was applied to penicillin and bone, and lyophilization became recognized as an important scientific technique for preservation of biologicals. Since that time, freeze-drying has been used as a preservation or processing technique for a wide variety of products. Some of the applications include the processing of pharmaceuticals, diagnostic kits, restoration of water damaged documents, river bottom sludge prepared for hydrocarbon analysis, ceramics used in the semiconductor industry, viral or bacterial cultures, tissues prepared for analysis, the production of synthetic skins and restoration of historic/ reclaimed boat hulls.

The Freeze-Drying Process

There are four stages in the complete drying process: pretreatment, freezing, primary drying, and secondary drying.

Pretreatment

Pretreatment includes any method of treating the product prior to freezing. This may include concentrating the product, formulation revision, decreasing a high vapour pressure solvent or increasing the surface area. In many instances the decision to pretreat a product is based on theoretical knowledge of freeze- drying and its requirements, or is demanded by cycle time or product quality considerations. Methods of pretreatment include: Freeze Concentration, Solution Phase Concentration, Formulation to Preserve Product Appearance, Formulation to Stabilize Reactive Products, Formulation to Increase the Surface Area, and Decreasing High Vapour Pressure Solvents.

Freezing

In a lab, this is often done by placing the material in a freeze-drying flask and rotating the flask in a bath, called a shell freezer, which is cooled by mechanical refrigration, dry ice and methanol, or liquid nitrogen. On large scale, freezing is usually done using a freeze-drying machine. In this step, it is important to cool the material below its triple point, the lowest temperature at which the solid and liquid phases of the material can coexist. Larger crystals are easier to freeze-dry. To produce larger crystals, the product should be frozen slowly or can be cycled up and down in temperature. This cycling process is called annealing. However, in the case of food, or objects with formerly-living cells, large ice crystals will break the cell walls, resulting in the destruction of more cells, which can result in increasingly poor texture and nutritive content. In this case, the freezing is done rapidly, in order to lower the material to below its eutectic point quickly, thus avoiding the formation of ice crystals. Usually, the freezing temperatures are between 50°C and 80°C. The freezing phase is the most critical in the whole freeze-drying process, because the product can be spoiled if badly done. Amorphous materials do not have a eutectic point, but they do have a critical point, below which the product must be maintained to prevent melt-back or collapse during primary and secondary drying.

Primary Drying

During the primary drying phase, the pressure is lowered and enough heat is supplied to the material for the water to sublimate. The amount of heat necessary can be calculated using the sublimating molecules' latent heat of sublimation. In this initial drying phase, about 95 per cent of the water in the material is sublimated. This phase may be slow because, if too much heat is added, the material's structure could be altered. In this phase, pressure is controlled through the application of partial vacuum.

The vacuum speeds sublimation, making it useful as a deliberate drying process. Furthermore, a cold condenser chamber and/or condenser plates provide a surface(s) for the water vapour to re-solidify on. This condenser plays no role in keeping the material frozen; rather, it prevents water vapour from reaching the vacuum pump, which could degrade the pump's performance. Condenser temperatures are typically below 50°C. It is important to note that, in this range of pressure, the heat is brought mainly by conduction or radiation; the convection effect is considered to be inefficient.

Secondary Drying

The secondary drying phase aims to remove unfrozen water molecules, since the ice was removed in the primary drying phase. This part of the freeze- drying process is governed by the material's adsorption isotherms. In this phase, the temperature is raised higher than in the primary drying phase, and can even be above 0°C, to break any physico-chemical interactions that have formed between the water molecules and the frozen material. Usually the pressure is also lowered in this stage to encourage desorption. However, there are products that benefit from increased pressure as well. After the freeze- drying process is complete, the vacuum is usually broken with an inert gas, such as nitrogen, before the material is sealed. At the end of the operation, the final residual water content in the product is extremely low, around 1 per cent to 4 per cent.

Properties of Freeze-Dried Products

If a freeze-dried substance is sealed to prevent the reabsorption of moisture, the substance may be stored at room temperature without refrigeration, and be protected against spoilage for many years. Preservation is possible because the greatly reduced water content inhibits the action of microorganisms and enzymes that would normally spoil or degrade the substance.

Freeze-drying also causes less damage to the substance than other dehydration methods using higher temperatures. Freeze-drying does not usually cause shrinkage or toughening of the material being dried.

In addition, flavours, smells and nutritional content generally remain unchanged, making the process popular for preserving food. However, water is not the only chemical capable of sublimation, and the loss of other volatile compounds such as acetic acid and alcohols can yield undesirable results. Freeze-dried products can be rehydrated much more quickly and easily because the process leaves microscopic pores.

The pores are created by the ice crystals that sublimate, leaving gaps or pores in their place. This is especially important when it comes to pharmaceutical uses. Freeze-drying can also be used to increase the shelf life of some pharmaceuticals for many years.

Freeze-Drying Protectants

Similar to cryoprotectants, some molecules protect freeze-dried material. Known as lyoprotectants, these molecules are typically polyhydroxy compounds such as sugars, polyalcohols, and their derivatives. Trehalose and sucrose are natural lyoprotectants.

Applications of Freeze-Drying

Pharmaceutical and Biotechnology: Pharmaceutical companies often use freeze-drying to increase the shelf life of products, such as vaccines and other injectables. By removing the water from the material and sealing the material in a vial, the material can be easily stored, shipped, and later reconstituted to its original form for injection. Another example from the pharmaceutical industry is the use of freeze-drying to produce tablets or wafers. The advantage of which is less excipient and a rapidly absorbed and easily administered dosage form.

Food Industry

Freeze-drying is used to preserve food and make it very lightweight. The process has been popularized in the forms of freeze-dried ice cream, an example of astronaut food. It is also popular and convenient for hikers because the reduced weight allows them to carry more food and reconstitute it with available water. Instant coffee is sometimes freeze-dried, despite the high costs of the freeze-driers used. The coffee is often dried by vaporization in a hot air flow, or by projection on hot metallic plates. Freeze-dried fruit is used in some breakfast cereal. Culinary herbs are also freeze-dried, although air-dried herbs are far more common and less expensive. However, the freeze-drying process is used more commonly in the pharmaceutical industry.

Technological Industry

In chemical synthesis, products are often freeze-dried to make them more stable, or easier to dissolve in water for subsequent use. In bioseparations, freeze-drying can be used also as a late-stage purification procedure, because it can effectively remove solvents. Furthermore, it is capable of concentrating substances with low molecular weights that are too small to be removed by a filtration membrane. Freeze-drying is a relatively expensive process. The equipment is about three times as expensive as the equipment used for other separation processes, and the high energy demands lead to high energy costs. Furthermore, freeze-drying also has a long process time, because the addition of too much heat to the material can cause melting or structural deformations. Therefore, freeze-drying is often reserved for materials that are heat-sensitive, such as proteins, enzymes, microorganisms, and blood plasma. The low operating temperature of the process leads to minimal damage of these heat- sensitive products.

Other Uses

Organizations such as the Document Conservation Laboratory at the United States National Archives and Records Administration have done studies on freeze-drying as a recovery method of water-damaged books and documents. While recovery is possible, restoration quality depends on the material of the documents. If a document is made of a variety of materials, which have different absorption properties, expansion will occur at a non- uniform rate, which could lead to deformations.

Water can also cause mold to grow or make inks bleed. In these cases, freeze-drying may not be an effective restoration method. In bacteriology freeze- drying is used to conserve special strains. In high-altitude environments, the low temperatures and pressures can sometimes produce natural mummies by a process of freeze-drying. Advanced ceramics processes sometimes use freeze- drying to create a formable powder from a sprayed slurry mist. Freeze-drying creates softer particles with a more homogenous chemical composition than traditional hot spray drying, but it is also more expensive. Freeze drying is also used for floral preservation. Wedding bouquet preservation has become very popular with brides who want to preserve their wedding day flowers

Freeze-Drying Equipment

Rotary freeze-driers are usually used with liquid products, such as pharmaceutical solutions and tissue extracts. Manifold freeze-driers are usually used when drying a large amount of small containers and the product will be used in a short period of time. A manifold drier will dry the product to less than 5 per cent moisture content. Without heat, only primary drying can be achieved. A heater must be added for secondary drying, which will remove the bound water and will produce a lower moisture content. Tray freeze-driers are more sophisticated and are used to dry a variety of materials. A tray freeze- drier is used to produce the driest product for long-term storage. A tray freeze- drier allows the product to be frozen in place and performs both primary and secondary freeze-drying, thus producing the driest possible end-product. Tray freeze-driers can dry products in bulk or in vials. When drying in vials, the freeze-drier is supplied with a stoppering mechanism that allows a stopper to be pressed into place, sealing the vial before it is exposed to the atmosphere. This is used for long-term storage, such as vaccines.

Improved freeze drying techniques are being developed to extend the range of products that can be freeze dried, to improve the quality of the product, and to produce the product faster with less labour. Ever since the 1930s, industrial freeze drying had been dependent on a single type of equipment: the tray freeze drier. In 2005 a quicker and less-labour intensive freeze drying method was developed for bulk materials. This freeze drying process proved to be able to produce free-flowing powder from a single vessel. Known as AFD technology, the new process used continuous motion to improve mass transfer and hence cutting processing time, while also eliminating the need to transfer to and from drying trays and downstream size reduction devices. There are essentially three categories of freeze-driers: the rotary evapourator freeze-drier, the manifold freeze-drier, and the tray freeze-drier.

FOOD IRRADIATION

Food irradiation is the process of exposing food to ionizing radiation to destroy microorganisms, bacteria, viruses, or insects that might be present in the food.

Further applications include sprout inhibition, delay of ripening, increase of juice yield, and improvement of re-hydration. Irradiated food does not become radioactive, but in some cases there may be subtle chemical changes.

Irradiation is a more general term of deliberate exposure of materials to radiation to achieve a technical goal. As such it is also used on non-food items, such as medical hardware, plastics, tubes for gas pipelines, hoses for floor heating, shrink-foils for food packaging, automobile parts, wires and cables, tires, and even gemstones. Food irradiation acts by damaging the target organism's DNA beyond its ability to repair. Microorganisms can no longer proliferate and continue their malignant or pathogenic activities. Spoilage- causing microorganisms cannot continue their activities. Insects do not survive, or become incapable of reproduction. Plants cannot continue their natural ripening processes. The energy density per atomic transition of ionizing radiation is very high; it can break apart molecules and induce ionization, which is not achieved by mere heating. This is the reason for both new effects and new concerns. The treatment of solid food by ionizing radiation can provide an effect similar to heat pasteurization of liquids, such as milk. However, the use of the term"cold pasteurization" to describe irradiated foods is controversial, since pasteurization and irradiation are fundamentally different processes. Food irradiation is currently permitted by over 40 countries, and the volume of food so treated is estimated to exceed 500,000 metric tons annually worldwide.

Processing of Food by Ionizing Radiation

By irradiating food, depending on the dose, some or all of the harmful bacteria and other pathogens present are killed. This prolongs the shelf-life of the food in cases where microbial spoilage is the limiting factor. Some foods, e.g., herbs and spices, are irradiated at sufficient doses to reduce the microbial counts by several orders of magnitude; such ingredients do not carry over spoilage or pathogen microorganisms into the final product.

It has also been shown that irradiation can delay the ripening of fruits or the sprouting of vegetables. Furthermore, insect pests can be sterilized using irradiation at relatively low doses. In consequence, the United States Department of Agriculture has approved the use of low-level irradiation as an alternative treatment to pesticides for fruits and vegetables that are considered hosts to a number of insect pests, including fruit flies and seed weevils; the US Food and Drug Administration has cleared among a number of other applications the treatment of hamburger patties to eliminate the residual risk of a contamination by a virulent *E. coli.*

The United Nations Food and Agricultural Organization has passed a motion to commit member states to implement irradiation technology for their national phytosanitary programmes; the General assembly of the International Atomic Energy Agency has urged to make wider use of the irradiation technology. Additionally, the USDA has made a number of bi-lateral agreements with developing countries to facilitate the imports of exotic fruits and to simplify the quarantine procedures creates softer particles with a more homogeneous chemical composition than radiation in specific directives since 1999; the relevant documents and reports are accessible online. The "implementing" directive contains a "positive list" permitting irradiation of only dried aromatic herbs, spices, and vegetable seasonings. However, any Member State is permitted to maintain previously granted clearances or to add new clearance as granted in other Member States, in the case the EC's Scientific Committee on Food has given a positive vote for the respective application.

Presently, six Member States have adopted such provisions. Because of the "Single Market" of the EC, any food—even if irradiated—must be allowed to be marketed in any other Member State even if a general ban of food irradiation prevails, under the condition that the food has been irradiated legally in the state of origin. Furthermore, imports into the EC are possible from third countries if the irradiation facility had been inspected and licensed by the EC and the treatment is legal within the EC or some Member State. The Scientific Committee on Food of the EC has given a positive vote on eight categories of food to be irradiated.

However, in a compromise between the European Parliament and the European Commission, only dried aromatic herbs, spices, and vegetable seasonings can be found in the positive list. The European Commission was due to provide a final draft for the positive list by the end of 2000; however, this failed because of a veto from Germany and a few other Member States. In 1992, and in 1998 the SCF voted "positive" on a number of irradiation applications that had been allowed in some Member States before the EC Directives came into force, to enable those Member States to maintain their national authorizations.

In 2003, when Codex Alimentarius was about to remove any upper dose limit for food irradiation, the SCF adopted a "revised opinion", which, in fact, was a re-confirmation and endorsement of the 1986 opinion. The opinion denied cancellation of the upper dose limit, and required that before the actual list of individual items or food classes can be expanded, new individual studies into the toxicology of each of such food and for each of the proposed dose ranges are requested.

The SCF has subsequently been replaced by the new European Food Safety Authority which has not yet ruled on the processing of food by ionizing radiation. Other countries, including New Zealand, Australia, Thailand, India, and Mexico, have permitted the irradiation of fresh fruits for fruit fly quarantine purposes, amongst others. Such countries as Pakistan and Brazil have adopted the Codex Alimentarius Standard on Irradiated Food without any reservation or restriction: i.e., any food may be irradiated to any dose.

Radiation Absorbed Dose

"Dose" is the physical quantity governing the radiation processing of food, relating to the beneficial effects to be achieved.

Unit of Measure for Irradiation Dose

The dose of radiation is measured in the SI unit known as Gray. One Gray dose of radiation is equal to 1 joule of energy absorbed per kg of food material. In radiation processing of foods, the doses are generally measured in kGy.

Dosimetry

The measurement of radiation dose is referred to as dosimetry, and involves exposing dosimetres jointly with the treated food item. Dosimetres are small components attached to the irradiated product made of materials that, when exposed to ionizing radiation, change specific, measurable physical attributes to a degree that can be correlated to the dose received.

Modern dosimetres are made of a range of materials, such as alanine pellets, perspex blocks, and radiochromic films, as well as special solutions and other materials. These dosimetres are used in combination with specialized read out devices. Standards that describe calibration and operation for radiation dosimetry, as well as procedures to relate the measured dose to the effects achieved and to report and document such results, are maintained by the American Society for Testing and Materials and are also available as ISO/ ASTM standards.

Applications

On the basis of the dose of radiation the application is generally divided into three main categories as detailed under:

Low Dose Applications (up to 1 kGy)

- Sprout inhibition in bulbs and tubers 0.03-0.15 kGy.
- Insect disinfestation including quarantine treatment and elimination of food borne parasites 0.07-1.00 kGy.

Medium Dose Applications (1 kGy to 10 kGy)

- Reduction of spoilage microbes to prolong shelf-life of meat, poultry and seafoods under refrigeration 1.50–3.00 kGy.
- Reduction of pathogenic microbes in fresh and frozen meat, poultry and seafoods 3.00–7.00 kGy.
- Reducing the number of microorganisms in spices to improve hygienic quality 10.00 kGy.

High Dose Applications (above 10 kGy)

- Sterilization of packaged meat, poultry, and their products that are shelf stable without refrigeration 25.00-70.00 kGy.
- Product improvement as increased juice yield or improved re-hydration.

It is important to note that these doses are above those currently permitted for these food items by the FDA and other regulators around the world. The Codex Alimentarius Standard on Irradiated Food does not specify any upper dose limit. NASA is authorized to sterilize frozen meat for astronauts at doses of 44 kGy as a notable exception. Irradiation treatments are also sometimes classified as radappertization, radicidation and radurization.

Technologies

Electron Irradiation: Electron irradiation uses electrons accelerated in an electric field to a velocity close to the speed of light. Electrons are particulate radiation and, hence, have cross section many times larger than photons, so that they do not penetrate the product beyond a few inches, depending on product density. Electron facilities rely on substantial concrete shields to protect workers and the environment from radiation exposure.

Gamma Irradiation

Gamma radiation is radiation of photons in the gamma part of the electromagnetic spectrum. The radiation is obtained through the use of radioisotopes, generally cobalt-60 or, in theory, caesium-137. Cobalt-60 is bred from cobalt-59 using neutron irradiation in specifically designed nuclear reactors. Caesium-137 is recovered during the processing of spent nuclear fuel. Because this technology—except for military applications—is not commercially available, insufficient quantities of it are available on the global isotope markets for use in large scale, commercial irradiators. Presently, caesium-137 is used only in small hospital units to treat blood before transfusion to prevent Graft- versus-host disease.

Food irradiation using Cobalt-60 is the preferred method by most processors, because the deeper penetration enables administering treatment to entire industrial pallets or totes, reducing the need for material handling. A pallet or tote is typically exposed for several minutes to hours depending on dose. Radioactive material must be monitored and carefully stored to shield workers and the environment from its gamma rays. During operation this is achieved by substantial concrete shields.

With most designs the radioisotope can be lowered into a water-filled source storage pool to allow maintenance personnel to enter the radiation shield. In this mode the water in the pool absorbs the radiation. Other uncommonly used designs feature dry storage by providing movable shields that reduce radiation levels in areas of the irradiation chamber. One variant of gamma irradiators keeps the Cobalt-60 under water at all times and lowers the product to be irradiated under water in hermetic bells. No further shielding is required for such designs.

X-ray Irradiation

Similar to gamma radiation, X-rays are photon radiation of a wide energy spectrum and an alternative to isotope based irradiation systems. X-rays are generated by colliding accelerated electrons with a dense material such as tantalum or tungsten in a process known as bremsstrahlung-conversion. X- ray irradiators are scalable and have deep penetration comparable to Co-60, with the added effect of using an electronic source that stops radiating when switched off. They also permit dose uniformity. However, these systems generally have low energetic efficiency during the conversion of electron energy to photon radiation requiring much more electrical energy than other systems.

Like most other types of facilities, X-ray systems rely on concrete shields to protect the environment and workers from radiation. Nominal X-ray energy is usually limited to 5 MeV; however, USA has provisions for up to 7.5 MeV, which increases conversion efficiency. Another development is the availability of electron accelerators with extremely high power output, up to 1,000 kW beam. At a conversion efficiency of up to 12 per cent, the X-ray power may reach 100 kW; This power would be equivalent to a gamma facility with Co-60 of about 6.5 MCi.

Irradiated Foods in the Market Place

Current US Market: Some U.S. supermarkets carry irradiated food products today ranging from fresh tropical fruit from Hawaii or Florida, dehydrated spices, spinach and ground meat products. Certain supermarkets like Whole Foods Market prefer not to carry irradiated products for reasons of consumer perception.

General Economic Aspects

Some foods, particularly fruits and vegetables, are not available for sale on the global market unless treated to prolong shelf life for transportation. This may include radiation processing. However, this application has not yet been exploited.

In contrast, irradiation to eliminate insect pests to fulfill quarantine requirements is gaining commercial significance. This is true for fruits Hawaii exports to the U.S. mainland, and increasingly for imports from subtropical countries to the US under bilateral agreements that allows those less-developed countries to earn income through food exports. As an example, Mexico has started to export irradiated guava to the US in 2008 and mango in 2009; and has received approval for citrus, star fruit and Manzano chili. Furthermore, a number of Asian countries hold bilateral agreements to irradiate exotic fruits for quarantine purposes and export it to the USA. The actual cost of food irradiation is influenced by dose requirements, the food's tolerance of radiation, handling conditions, i.e., packaging and stacking requirements, construction costs, financing arrangements, and other variables particular to the situation. Irradiation is a capital-intensive technology requiring a substantial initial investment, ranging from $1 million to $5 million.

In the case of large research or contract irradiation facilities, major capital costs include a radiation source, hardware, land, radiation shield, and warehouse. Operating costs include salaries, utilities, maintenance, taxes/ insurance, cobalt-60 replenishment, general utilities, and miscellaneous operating costs. Treatment costs vary as a function of dose and facility usage. Low dose applications such as disinfestation of fruit range between US $0.01/ lbs and US $0.08/lbs while higher dose applications can cost as much as US $0.20/lbs.

Consumer Protection

Irradiation has not been widely adopted due to an asserted negative public perception, the concerns expressed by some consumer groups and the reluctance of many food producers. Consumer organizations, environmentalist groups, and opponents to food irradiation refer to some studies suggesting that a large part of the public questions the safety of irradiated foods, and will not buy foods that have been irradiated.

On the other hand, other studies indicate the number of consumers concerned about the safety of irradiated food has decreased in the last 10 years and continues to be less than the number of those concerned about pesticide residues, microbiological contamination, and other food related concerns. The number of people reporting no concerns about irradiated food is among the lowest for food issues, comparable to that of people with no concern about food additives and preservatives. Consumers, given a choice and access to the real irradiated product, appear ready to buy it in considerably large numbers.

Globalized Food Supply

Opponents of food irradiation sometimes state that large-scale irradiation would increase processing, transportation, and handling times for fruits and vegetables thus contributing to a negative ecological balance compared to locally grown foods.

Labelling and Terminology Issues

Labeling laws differ from country to country. While Codex Alimentarius represents the global standard in particular under the WTO-agreement, member states are free to convert those standards into national regulations. With regard to labelling of irradiated food, detailed rules are published at CODEX-STAN—1 labelling of prepacked food. The provisions are that any "first generation" product must be labeled "irradiated" as any product derived directly from an irradiated raw material; for ingredients the provision is that even the last molecule of an irradiated ingredient must be listed with the ingredients even in cases where the unirradiated ingredient does not appear on the label.

The RADURA-logo is optional; several countries use a graphical version that differs from the Codex-version. In the US, as in many other countries, irradiated food must be labelled as "Treated with irradiation" or "Treated by radiation" and require the usage of the Radura symbol at the point of sale. However, the meaning of the label is not consistent. The amount of irradiation used can vary and since there are no published standards, the amount of pathogens affected by irradiation can be variable as well. In addition, there are no regulations regarding the levels of pathogen reduction that must be achieved.

Food that is processed as an ingredient by a restaurant or food processor is exempt from the labeling requirement in the US; other countries follow the Codex Alimentarius provision to label irradiated ingredients down to the last molecule. FDA is currently proposing a rule that in some cases would allow certain irradiated foods to be marketed without any labeling at all.

Under the new rules, only those irradiated foods in which the irradiation causes a material change in the food, or a material change in the consequences that may result from the use of the food, would bear the Radura symbol and the term "irradiated", or a derivative thereof, in conjunction with explicit language describing the change in the food or its conditions of use.

In the same rule FDA is proposing to permit a firm to use the terms "electronically pasteurized" or "cold pasteurized" in lieu of "irradiated", provided it notifies the agency that the irradiation process being used meets the criteria specified for use of the term "pasteurized". Food irradiation is sometimes referred to as "cold pasteurization" or "electronic pasteurization" because ionizing the food does not heat the food to high temperatures during the process, as in heat-pasteurization. The treatment of solid food by ionizing radiation can provide an effect similar to heat pasteurization of liquids, such as milk.

However, the use of the term, cold pasteurization, to describe irradiated foods is controversial, because pasteurization and irradiation are fundamentally different processes, although the intended end results can in some cases be similar. Consumer perception of foods treated with irradiation is more negative than those processed by other means. "People think the product is radioactive," said Harlan Clemmons, president of Sadex, a food irradiation company based in Sioux City, Iowa.

Enforcement of Labelling

There are analytical methods available to detect the usage of irradiation on food items in the marketplace. This may be understood as a tool for government authorities to enforce existing labelling standards and to bolster consumer confidence. The European Union is particularly strict in enforcing irradiation labelling requiring its member countries to perform tests on a cross section of food items in the market-place and to report to the European Commission; the results are published annually in the OJ of the European Communities.

United States Regulators of Food Irradiation

Food irradiation in the United States is primarily regulated by the FDA since it is considered a food additive.

Other federal agencies that regulate aspects of food irradiation include:

- United States Department of Agriculture: Meat and poultry products, fresh fruit.
- Nuclear Regulatory Commission: Safety of the processing facility.
- United States Department of Transportation: Safe transport of the radioactive sources.

Each new food is approved separately with a guideline specifying a maximum dosage; in case of quarantine applications the minimum dose is regulated. Packaging materials containing the food processed by irradiation must also undergo approval. Note: The Radura logo as regulated by FDA is slightly different from the international version as proposed in Codex Alimentarius.

Safety Aspects

Safety, Security and Wholesomeness Aspects: Hundreds of animal feeding studies of irradiated food, including multigenerational studies, have been performed since 1950. Endpoints investigated have included subchronic and chronic changes in metabolism, histopathology, and function of most systems; reproductive effects; growth; teratogenicity; and mutagenicity.

A large number of studies have been performed; meta-studies have supported the safety of irradiated food. Consumer advocacy groups such as Public Citizen or Food and Water Watch maintain that the safety of irradiated food is not proven, in particular long-term studies are still lacking, and strongly oppose the use of the technology. A report of fatal incidences with pet food in Australia led to some rumours and speculations about the safety of irradiated food and a nationwide recall. In the Australian case, sixteen cats were reported to have been euthanized after severe paralysis subsequent to being fed a certain cat food. The company issuing a recall stated that the problem only occurred with Australian pet-food. The company speculated this was due to irradiating the pet-food. The Australian Quarantine Inspection Services required the irradiation to a minimum dose of 50 kGy or heating of imported dry food. After the incident, the pet food manufacturer created a compassion fund for pet owners. The cause of the cat illness is not yet clearly understood and is still under investigation and verification.

Vitamin A depletion was not confirmed in the affected cats. Researchers from Wisconsin University announcing their conference presentation said in the published abstract: "Here, we show that cats fed an irradiated diet during gestation developed a severe neurologic disease resulting from extensive myelin vacuolation and subsequent demyelination." There are several Youtube videos claiming to show cats suffering from irradiated food and a video including excerpts from an interview with Dr. Georgina Childs, the veterinarian from SASH involved in the initial cat cases. There has been news that radiation processing of imported cat food has now been banned in Australia.

It had been a mandatory requirement for imports including dry and semi- moist food to be irradiated at a minimum dose of 50 kGy or to be heated to a temperature of 100°C for a minimum of 30 minutes. Actually, the AQIS— having jurisdiction on quarantine issues—has announced with date of 06-06-2009 that the alternative of radiation processing for cat food is no longer acceptable and that irradiated dog food needs to be labeled by "Must not be fed to cats." AQIS in its announcement refers to recently published scientific studies and reminds importers of their responsibility to regularly check whether new scientific results could have any implication for their products. This is to say a "ban" of food irradiation does not exist; and the theory about the causes of ataxia with cats food irradiated products has not been proven. Meanwhile, Dr. G. Child has published a report of the clinical signs and outcomes of those cats. The authors point to epidemiological and to toxicological studies that are still underway. It is not yet clear which mechanism and what changes in irradiated pet food cause damages in the white matter of spinal cord and brain.

Criticism and Concerns about Food Irradiation

Concerns have been expressed by public interest groups and public health experts that irradiation, as a non-preventive measure, might disguise or otherwise divert attention away from poor working conditions, sanitation, and poor food-handling procedures that lead to contamination in the first place. A complaint list may contain concerns and objections, not all of which are discussed in this substance.

Food irradiation might do any of the following:

- Mask spoiled food.
- Discourage strict adherence to good manufacturing practices.
- Preferentially kill "good" bacteria and encourage growth of "bad" bacteria.
- Devitalize and denature irradiated food.
- Impair flavour.
- Not destroy bacterial toxins already present.
- Cause chemical changes that are harmful to the consumer.
- Be unnecessary anyway, in today's food system.

"Food irradiation is a pseudo-fix", said Bill Freese, a science policy analyst with the Centre for Food Safety in Washington, DC. "It's a way to try to come in and clean up problems that are created in the middle of the food production chain. I think it's clearly a disincentive to clean up the problems at the source."

Processors of irradiated food are subject to all existing regulations, inspections, and potential penalties regarding plant safety and sanitation; including fines, recalls, and criminal prosecutions. But critics of the practice claim that a lack of regulatory oversight necessitates irradiation. "[Irradiation] is a total cop-out," said Patty Lovera, assistant director of Food and Water

Watch. "They don't have the resources, the authority or the political will to protect consumers from unsafe food." While food irradiation can in some cases maintain the quality of certain perishable food for a longer period of time, it cannot undo spoilage that occurred prior to irradiation. Irradiation cannot be successfully used to mask quality issues other than pathogens. However, as with heat pasteurization, processing by ionizing radiation can contribute to eliminate pathogen risks from solid food.

Milk heat pasteurization is not considered to be a method "to cover up poor food quality"; consequently, food irradiation should not be accused to serve such criminal purposes. Under a HACCP-concept radiation processing can serve and contribute as an ultimate critical control point before the food reaches the consumer. Opponents to food irradiation and consumer activists frequently state that the final proof is missing that irradiated food is "safe". Moreover, the lack of long-term studies should be a further reason not to permit food irradiation. Such questions, by the principle, cannot be answered by the scientific method: one cannot prove the absence of a negative.

For such reasons the basic question needs to be rephrased: What is the probability that consuming irradiated food in some way produces unhealthful effects? The scientific consensus is "very slim". A few quick answers to possible questions:

- Do irradiated foods cause cancer or genetic damage? It has never happened.
- Does irradiation change the chemical composition of whatever is irradiated? Of course it does. That's why it works.

Long-term studies have already been carried on huge numbers of laboratory animals, many species and multiple generations. No negative effects have been observed that could be causally correlated to irradiation treatment. However, the absence of a noxious effect does not prove the principle, even in long-term studies. A further complaint is that animal studies cannot be transferred to humans. There are many more concerns of such kind and the answers have to be found by validating the scientific evidence. During the now more than 60 years of research into food irradiation and its possible harmful effects a number of publications have reported the following:

- Polyploidy in malnourished Indian children.
- Increase of aflatoxin production by irradiated microorganisms.
- Vitamin deficiencies at extremely high doses to the complete diet.
- Non-vitamin effects at higher doses.
- Change in chronaxie in rats.

However, those experiments could be either not verified in later experiments, could not be clearly attributed to the radiation effect, could be attributed to an inappropriate design of the experiment, etc.

In more recent experiments a number of new issues have been raised:

- Possible tumor promoting effect of 2ACBs in extremely high concentrations.
- Ataxia caused in Australian cats by high-dose irradiated imported feed.
- Multiple sclerosis caused intentionally in cats by high-dose irradiated feed.
- Specific effects caused only in pregnant cats by high-dose irradiated feed.

In particular, for those very specific situations of those experiments it would be indispensable to determine whether those animal models have any relevance for human nutrition. Typically, food as intended for human consumption is never irradiated at such extremely high dose levels; on the other hand, feed sterilization by ionizing irradiation is widely accepted standard in rearing of laboratory animals and in producing gnotobiotic animals for agricultural production.

Worker Safety and Impact on the Environment

The safety of irradiation facilities is regulated by the United Nations International Atomic Energy Agency and monitored by the different national Nuclear Regulatory Commissions. The incidents that have occurred in the past are documented by the agency and thoroughly analyzed to determine root cause and improvement potential. Such improvements are then mandated to retrofit existing facilities and future design. Care must be taken not to expose the operators and the environment to radiation or radioactive contamination. Interlocks and safeguards are mandated to minimize this risk. Nevertheless there have been radiation related deaths and injury amongst workers of such facilities, many of them caused by the operators themselves overriding the interlocks. It should be noted that "ordinary" occupational safety regulations also apply to radiation processing facilities; the radiation aspect are typically excluded and supervised by special authorities.

An incident in Decatur, Georgia where water soluble Caesium-137 leaked into the source storage pool requiring NRC intervention has led to near elimination of this radioisotope; it has been replaced by the more costly, non- water soluble Cobalt-60. National and international regulations on the levels and types of energy used to irradiate food generally set standards that prevent the possibility of inducing radioactivity in treated foods, and, hence, excluding the risk to workers and the environment.

Alternatives

Other methods to reduce several pathogens in food include heat-pasteurization, ultra-high temperature processing, UV radiation, ozone or fumigation with ethylene oxide. For quarantine purposes, insect pests can also be eliminated by fumigation with methyl bromide or aluminum phosphine, vapour heat, forced hot air, hot water dipping, or cold treatment. Other methods to extend shelf life of food items include modified atmosphere packaging, carbon monoxide, dehydration, vacuum packaging, freezing and flash freezing as well as chemical additives. Opponents to food irradiation and consumer activists maintain that the best alternative to food irradiation to reduce pathogens is in good agricultural practices. For example, farmers and processing plants should improve sanitation practices, water used for irrigation and processing should be regularly tested for E. coli, and production plants should be routinely inspected. Concentrated animal feeding operations near farmland where produce is grown should be regulated. Proponents of food irradiation have said that practices of organic farming can only reduce the extent of the microorganism load. They assert that residual flora including pathogen germs always persist, and that processing by ionizing radiation could be the ultimate measure to practically eliminate such risks.

FRUIT PRESERVES

Fruit preserves are fruits, or vegetables, that have been prepared and canned or sealed air-tight for long term storage. The preparation of fruit preserves traditionally involves the use of pectin as a gelling agent, although sugar or honey may be used as well. The ingredients used and how they are prepared will determine the type of preserves; jams, jellies and marmalades are all examples of different styles of fruit preserves that vary based upon the ingredients used. There are various varieties of fruit preserves made globally, and they can be made from sweet or savory ingredients. In North America, the plural form preserves is used, while the singular preserve is used in British and Commonwealth English. Additionally, the name of the type of fruit preserves will also vary depending on the regional variant of English being used.

Variations

Chutney: A chutney is a pungent relish of Indian origin made of fruit, spices and herbs. Although originally intended to be eaten soon after production, modern chutneys are often made to be sold and so require a preservatives—often sugar and vinegar—to ensure it has a suitable shelf life. Mango chutney, for example, is mangoes reduced with sugar.

Confit: Confit, which is the past participle form of the French verb "confire" or "to preserve", is most often applied to preservation of meats, especially poultry and pork, by cooking them in their own fat or oils and allowing the fats to set. However, the term can also refer to fruit or vegetables which have been seasoned and cooked with honey or sugar until it has reached a jam-like consistency. Savory confits, such as ones made with garlic or tomatoes, may call for a savory oil such as virgin olive oil as the preserving agent.

Conserves

A conserve is a jam made of fruit stewed in sugar. Often the making of conserves can be trickier than making a standard jam, because the balance between cooking, or sometimes steeping in the hot sugar mixture for just enough time to allow the flavour to be extracted from the fruit, and sugar to penetrate the fruit, and cooking too long that fruit will break down and liquefy.

This process can also be achieved by spreading the dry sugar over raw fruit in layers, and leaving for several hours to steep into the fruit then just heating the resulting mixture only to bring to the setting point. As a result of this minimal cooking, some fruits are not particularly suitable for making into conserves, because they require cooking for longer periods to avoid issues such as tough skins.

Currants and gooseberries, and a number of plums are among these fruits. Due to this shorter cooking period, not as much pectin will be released from the fruit, and as such, conserves will sometimes be slightly softer set than some jams. An alternate definition holds that conserves are preserves made from a mixture of fruits and/or vegetables. Conserves may also include dried fruit or nuts.

Fruit Butter

Fruit butter, in this context, refers to a process where the whole fruit is forced through a sieve or blended after the heating process:

- "Fruit butters are generally made from larger fruits, such as apples, plums, peaches or grapes. Cook until softened and run through a sieve to give a smooth consistency. After sieving, cook the pulp... add sugar and cook as rapidly as possible with constant stirring.... The finished product should mound up when dropped from a spoon, but should not cut like jelly. Neither should there be any free liquid."

Fruit Curd

Fruit curd is a dessert topping and spread usually made with lemon, lime, orange, or raspberry. The basic ingredients are beaten egg yolks, sugar, fruit juice and zest which are gently cooked together until thick and then allowed to cool, forming a soft, smooth, intensely flavoured spread. Some recipes also include egg whites and/or butter.

Fruit Spread

Fruit spread refers to a jam or preserve with no added sugar.

Jam

Jam contains both fruit juice and pieces of the fruit's flesh, however, some cookbooks define jam as cooked and gelled fruit purees. Properly, the term jam refers to a product made with whole fruit, cut into pieces or crushed. The fruit is heated with water and sugar to activate the pectin in the fruit. The mixture is then put into containers. The following extract from a US cookbook describes the process:

- "Jams are usually made from pulp and juice of one fruit, rather than a combination of several fruits. Berries and other small fruits are most frequently used, though larger fruits such as apricots, peaches, or plums cut into small pieces or crushed are also used for jams. Good jam has a soft even consistency without distinct pieces of fruit, a bright colour, a good fruit flavour and a semi-jellied texture that is easy to spread but has no free liquid."

Jelly

Jelly is a clear or translucent fruit spread made from sweetened fruit juice and set using naturally occurring pectin. Additional pectin may be added where the original fruit does not supply enough, for example with grapes. Jelly can be made from sweet, savory or hot ingredients. It is made by a process similar to that used for making jam, with the additional step of filtering out the fruit pulp after the initial heating. A muslin or stockinette "jelly bag" is traditionally used as a filter, suspended by string over a bowl to allow the straining to occur gently under gravity. It is important not to attempt to force the straining process, for example by squeezing the mass of fruit in the muslin, or the clarity of the resulting jelly will be compromised.

- "Good jelly is clear and sparkling and has a fresh flavour of the fruit from which it is made. It is tender enough to quiver when moved, but holds angles when cut.
- Extracting Juice: Pectin is best extracted from the fruit by heat, therefore cook the fruit until soft before straining to obtain the juice.... Pour cooked fruit into a jelly bag which has been wrung out of cold water. Hang up and let drain. When dripping has ceased the bag may be squeezed to remove remaining juice, but this may cause cloudy jelly."

Marmalade

British-style marmalade is a sweet preserve with a bitter tang made from fruit, sugar, water, and a gelling agent. American-style marmalade is sweet, not bitter. In English-speaking usage, "marmalade" almost always refers to a preserve derived from a citrus fruit, most commonly oranges, although onion marmalade is also used as an accompaniment to savoury dishes. The recipe includes sliced or chopped fruit peel, which is simmered in fruit juice and water until soft; indeed marmalade is sometimes described as jam with fruit peel. Such marmalade is most often consumed on toasted bread for breakfast.

The favoured citrus fruit for marmalade production in the UK is the "Seville orange", Citrus aurantium var. aurantium, thus called because it was originally imported from Seville in Spain; it is higher in pectin than sweet oranges, and therefore gives a good set. Marmalade can also be made from lemons, limes, grapefruit, strawberries or a combination.

Regional Terminology

The term preserves is usually interchangeable with jam. Some cookbooks define preserves as cooked and gelled whole fruit which includes a significant portion of the fruit. The terms jam and jelly are used in different parts of the English-speaking world in different ways. In the United States, both jam and jelly are sometimes popularly referred to as "jelly", whereas in the United Kingdom, Canada, India and Australia, the two terms are more strictly differentiated. In Australia and South Africa, the term jam is more popularly used as a generic term for both jam and jelly. To further confuse the issue, the term jelly is also used in the UK, South Africa, Australia, India and New Zealand to refer to a gelatin dessert, known in North America as jello, derived from the brand name Jell-O.

Production

In general, jam is produced by taking mashed or chopped fruit or vegetable pulp and boiling it with sugar and water. The proportion of sugar and fruit varies just as to the type of fruit and its ripeness, but a rough starting point is equal weights of each. When the mixture reaches a temperature of 104°C, the acid and the pectin in the fruit react with the sugar, and the jam will set on cooling. However, most cooks work by trial and error, bringing the mixture to a "fast rolling boil", watching to see if the seething mass changes texture, and dropping small samples on a plate to see if they run or set. Commercially produced jams are usually produced using one of two methods. The first is the open pan method, which is essentially a larger scale version of the method a home jam maker would use. This gives a traditional flavour, with some caramelization of the sugars.

The second commercial process involves the use of a vacuum vessel, where the jam is placed under a vacuum, which has the effect of reducing its boiling temperature to anywhere between 65-80°C depending on the recipe and the end result desired. The lower boiling temperature enables the water to be driven off as it would be when using the traditional open pan method, but with the added benefit of retaining more of the volatile flavour compounds from the fruit, preventing caramelization of the sugars, and of course reducing the overall energy required to make the product. However, once the desired amount of water has been driven off, the jam still needs to be heated briefly to 95-100 °C to kill off any micro-organisms that may be present; the vacuum pan method does not kill them all.

During the commercial filling of the jam into jars, it is common to use a flame to sterilize the rim of the jar and the lid to destroy any yeasts and molds which may cause spoilage during storage. It is also common practice to inject steam into the head space at the top of the jar immediately prior to the fitting of the lid, in order to create a vacuum. Not only does this vacuum help prevent the growth of spoilage organisms, it also pulls down the tamper evident safety button when lids of this type are employed. How easily a jam sets depends on the pectin content of the fruit.

Some fruits, such as gooseberries, redcurrants, blackcurrants, most citrus fruits, apples, and raspberries, set very well; others, such as strawberries and ripe blackberries, often need to have pectin added. There are commercial pectin products on the market, and most industrially-produced jams use them. Home jam-makers sometimes rely on adding a pectin-rich fruit to a poor setter, for example apple to blackberries. Other tricks include extracting juice from apples or just the cores and skins; once cooled, this "stock" can then be frozen for later use. Making jam at home is a popular handicraft activity, and many take part in this. Homemade jam may be made for personal consumption, or as part of a cottage industry.

ASPIC

Aspic is a dish in which ingredients are set into a gelatin made from a meat stock or consommé. Similar dishes, made with commercial gelatin mixes instead of stock or consommé, are usually called gelatin salads. When cooled, stock that is made from meat congeals because of the natural gelatin found in the meat. The stock can be clarified with egg whites, and then filled and flavoured just before the aspic sets. Almost any type of food can be set into aspics.

Most common are meat pieces, fruits, or vegetables. Aspics are usually served on cold plates so that the gel will not melt before being eaten. A meat jelly that includes cream is called a chaud-froid. Nearly any type of meat can be used to make the gelatin: pork, beef, veal, chicken, turkey, or fish. Gelatin is also found in cartilage. The aspic may need additional gelatin in order to set properly. Veal stock provides a great deal of gelatin; in making stock, veal is often included with other meat for that reason. Fish consommés usually have too little natural gelatin, so the fish stock may be double-cooked or supplemented. Since fish gelatin melts at a lower temperature than gelatins of other meats, fish aspic is more delicate and melts more readily in the mouth. Vegetables and fish stocks need gelatin to create a mould.

Historically, meat jellies were made before fruit and vegetable jellies. By the Middle Ages at the latest, cooks had discovered that a thickened meat broth could be made into a jelly. A detailed recipe for aspic is found in Le Viandier, written in around 1375. In the 18th century, Marie-Antoine Carême created chaud froid in France. Chaud froid means "hot cold" in French, referring to foods that were prepared hot and served cold. Aspic was used an chaud froid sauce in many cold fish and poultry meals. The sauce added moisture and flavour to the food. Marie-Antoine Carême also invented various types of aspic and ways of preparing aspic.

Aspic didn't come into prominence until the early 20th century. Aspic was used to hold meats and prevented them from becoming spoiled. The gelatin prevented air and bacteria from ruining cooked meat. It wasn't eaten until the 1950s, when it became popular dish. In the 1950s, aspic was a popular dinner staple throughout the United States. Jello was popular in the 1950s and the demands for meat were abundant. One of the most popular dishes were the tomato aspic. Cooks used to show off aesthetic skills by creating inventive aspics.

Uses

Aspic can also be referred as a aspic gelèe or aspic jelly. Aspic jelly may be colourless or contain various shades of amber. Aspic can be used to protect food from the air, give food more flavour, or as a decoration. There are three types of aspic textures: delicate, sliceable, and inedible. The delicate aspic is soft. The sliceable aspic must be made in a terrine or in a aspic mould. It is more firmer than the delicate aspic. The inedible aspic is never for consumption. It is usually for decoration. Aspic is often used to glaze food pieces in food competitions to make the food glisten and making it more appealing to the eye. Foods dipped in aspic can have a lacquered finish for a fancy presentation. Aspic can be cut into various shapes and be used as a garnish for deli meats or pâtés.

JUGGING

In cooking, jugging is the process of stewing meat for a long time in a tightly covered container, such as a casserole or an earthenware jug. Sometimes the cooking liquid includes some of the animal's blood. In French, such a stew of a game animal, thickened with the animal's blood, is known as a civet. One common traditional dish that involves jugging is Jugged Hare which is a whole hare, cut into pieces, marinated and cooked with red wine and juniper berries in a tall jug that stands in a pan of water. It is traditionally served with the hare's blood and Port wine. The recipe goes on to describe cooking the pieces of hare in water in a jug that is set within a bath of boiling water to cook for three hours. Beginning in the nineteenth century, Glasse has been widely credited with having started the recipe with the words "First, catch your hare". This attribution is apocryphal. However, having a freshly caught, or shot, hare enables one to obtain its blood.

A freshly killed hare is prepared for jugging by removing its entrails and then hanging it in a larder by its hind legs, which causes the blood to accumulate in the chest cavity. One method of preserving the blood after draining it from the hare is to mix it with red wine vinegar in order to prevent it coagulating, and then to store it in a freezer. Many other British cookbooks from before the middle of the 20th century have recipes for Jugged Hare. Merle and Reitch have this to say about Jugged Hare, for example:

- The best part of the hare, when roasted, is the loin and the thick part of the hind leg; the other parts are only fit for stewing, hashing, or jugging. It is usual to roast a hare first, and to stew or jug the portion which is not eaten the first day. To Jug a Hare: This mode of cooking a hare is very desirable when there is any doubt as to its age, as an old hare, which would be otherwise uneatable, may be made into an agreeable dish. In 2006, a survey of 2021 people for the television channel UKTV Food found that only 1.6 per cent of the people aged lemons, redcurrants or gooseberries, or making a pectin stock with whole stated that they would refuse to eat Jugged Hare if it were served at the house of a friend or a relative. Jugged Rabbit is an alternative to Jugged Hare. It is considered a speciality of the cuisine of Martinique. Another jugged dish, also traditional in the United Kingdom, is Jugged Kippers, which is kippers in a covered jug, cooked in boiling water.

MODIFIED ATMOSPHERE

Modified atmosphere is an uncommon technical definition that describes the practice of modifying the composition of the internal atmosphere of a package in order to improve the shelf life. The modification process often tries to lower the amount of oxygen, moving it from 20 per cent to 0 per cent, In order to slow down the growth of aerobic organisms and the speed of oxidation reactions. The removed oxygen can be replaced with nitrogen, commonly acknowledged as an inert gas, or carbon dioxide, which can lower the pH or inhibit the growth of bacteria. Carbon monoxide can be used for keeping the red colour of meat. Re-balancing of gases inside the packaging can be achieved using active techniques such as gas flushing and compensated vacuum or passively by designing "breathable" films known as equilibrium modified atmosphere packaging.

Scientific Terms

- MAP = Modified atmosphere packaging
- MA/MH = Modified atmosphere/modified humidity packaging.

Products

Under MA products like red meat, seafood, minimally processed fruits and vegetables, pasta, cheese, bakery goods, poultry, cooked and cured meats, ready meals and dried foods are packaged. The three major commodity types are fruits and vegetables, meat and meat products and seafood. It has been estimated that 25-40 per cent of all fresh produce harvested will not reach the consumers table, due to spoilage and mishandling that occurs during distribution.

Modified Atmosphere Packaging

Modified Atmosphere Packaging is a technique used for prolonging the shelf-life period of fresh or minimally processed foods. In this preservation technique the air surrounding the food in the package is changed to another composition. This way the initial fresh state of the product may be prolonged. It is the shelf-life of perishable products like meat, fish, fruits and vegetables that will be prolonged with MAP since it slows the natural deterioration of the product. MAP is used with various types of products, where the mixture of gases In the package depends on the type of product, packaging materials and storage temperature.

Meat and fish need very low gas permeability films so for non-respiring products high barrier films are used. The initial flushed gas-mixture will be maintained inside the MA package. But fruits and vegetables are respiring products where the interaction of the packaging material with the product is important. If the permeability of the packaging film is adapted to the products respiration, an equilibrium modified atmosphere will establish in the package and the shelf-life of the product will increase.

Equilibrium Modified Atmosphere Packaging

Among fresh-cut produce Equilibrium Modified Atmosphere Packaging is the most commonly used packaging technology. When packaging vegetables and fruits the gas atmosphere of package is not air but consists usually of a lowered level of O2 and a heightened level of CO2. This kind of package slows down the normal respiration of the product and so to prolong the shelf-life of the product. Of course there are other factors like the size of the product, severity of preparation, maturity of the product and type of tissue that have an effect to the shelf-life of an EMA packaged produce.

Technology

There are two techniques used in the industry to pack vegetables namely gas-flushing and compensated vacuum. For its cheapness the gas-flushing is more widely used.

In gas-flushing the package is flushed with a desired gas mixture, as in compensated vacuum the air is removed totally and the desired gas mixture then inserted. The label "packaged in a protective atmosphere" can refer to either of these; an example of a gas mixture used for non-vegetable packaged food is 99.9 per cent nitrogen gas, which is inert at the temperatures and pressures the packaging is subjected to.

Gases

The atmosphere in an MA package consists of N2, O2, CO2. It is the altered ratio of these gases that makes a difference in the prolongation of shelf life. By reducing the O2-level and increasing the CO2-level, ripening of fruits and vegetables can be delayed, respiration and ethylene production rates can be reduced, softening can be retarded and various compositional changes associated with ripening can be slowed down. Oxygen is essential when packaging fresh fruits and vegetables as they continue to respire after harvesting.

The absence of O2 can lead to anaerobic respiration in the package which accelerates senescence and spoilage. Too high levels of O2 do not retard respiration significantly and it is around 12 per cent of O2 where the respiration rate starts to decrease. So oxygen is used in low levels for positive effect. When packaging meat and fish, the high CO2-levels are effective bacterial and fungal growth inhibitors.

In the case of vegetables and fruits, CO2 is not a major factor since CO2- levels above 10 per cent are needed to suppress fungal growth significantly. Unfortunately higher levels than 10 per cent of CO2 are working phytotoxic for fresh produce. Nitrogen is used as a filler gas since it neither encourages or discourages bacterial growth.

Packaging Films

When selecting packaging films for EMAP of fruits and vegetables the main characteristics to consider are gas permeability, water vapour transmission rate, mechanical properties, transparency, type of package and sealing reliability. Traditionally used packaging films like LDPE, PVC, EVA and OPP are not permeable enough for highly respiring products like fresh- cut produces, mushrooms and broccoli. As fruits and vegetables are respiring products, there is a need to transmit gases from and to the package. Films designed with these properties are called permeable films. Other films, called barrier films, are designed to prevent the exchange of gases and are mainly used with non-respiring products like meat and fish. EMAP films developed to control the humidity level as well as the gas composition in the sealed package are beneficial for the prolonged storage of fresh fruits, vegetables and herbs that are sensitive to moisture.

Quality Assurance of Map Packages

Although Modified Atmosphere Packaging is a well-established process, it is a good practice to maintain tight quality assurance through package testing. Incorrect oxygen levels, empty gas cylinders and bad sealing bars can cause imprecise gas blends and poor package seals that can result in product spoilage. Routine package testing with headspace gas analysers, on-line gas analysers and leak detectors assures package quality, hence helps ensuring the shelf life.

PICKLING

Pickling, also known as brining or corning is the process of preserving food by anaerobic fermentation in brine to produce lactic acid, or marinating and storing it in an acid solution, usually vinegar. The resulting food is called a pickle. This procedure gives the food a salty or sour taste. In South Asia, edible oils are used as the pickling medium with vinegar. Another distinguishing characteristic is a pH less than 4.6, which is sufficient to kill most bacteria. Pickling can preserve perishable foods for months. Antimicrobial herbs and spices, such as mustard seed, garlic, cinnamon or cloves, are often added.

If the food contains sufficient moisture, a pickling brine may be produced simply by adding dry salt. For example, sauerkraut and Korean kimchi are produced by salting the vegetables to draw out excess water. Natural fermentation at room temperature, by lactic acid bacteria, produces the required acidity. Other pickles are made by placing vegetables in vinegar. Unlike the canning process, pickling does not require that the food be completely sterile before it is sealed. The acidity or salinity of the solution, the temperature of fermentation, and the exclusion of oxygen determine which microorganisms dominate, and determine the flavour of the end product. When both salt concentration and temperature are low, Leuconostoc mesenteroides dominates, producing a mix of acids, alcohol, and aroma compounds. At higher temperatures Lactobacillus plantarum dominates, which produces primarily lactic acid. Many pickles start with Leuconostoc, and change to Lactobacillus with higher acidity.

Pickle Etymology and Humour

The term pickle is derived from the Dutch word pekel, meaning brine. In the US and Canada, the word pickle alone almost always refers to a pickled cucumber, except when it is used figuratively. Pickle is considered an inherently funny word. In Neil Simon's play The Sunshine Boys, a character explains, "Words with a k in it are funny. Alka-Seltzer is funny. Chicken is funny. Pickle is funny...." For example, the US Central Intelligence Agency is nicknamed "the pickle factory", When plans for the Chicago Picasso sculpture were first unveiled, to public derision, a waggish publicist erected a giant dill pickle statue on the proposed site.

The Pickling Process

The jar and lid are first boiled in order to sterilize them. The fruits or vegetables to be pickled are then added to the jar along with brine and/or vinegar and are then allowed to ferment until the desired taste is obtained.

POTTED MEAT FOOD PRODUCT

A potted meat food product or potted meat is a food made using a method of food preservation—canning, consisting of cooked meat product, seasoned, often creamed, minced, or ground, which is filled into cans, sealed and heat processed in a retort to commercial sterility. Various meats such as beef, pork, chicken, turkey and variety meats are used. It is produced internationally as a source of affordable meat. Its long shelf life and precooking makes it suitable for emergency food supplies, and for military and camping uses, although the high content of fat, protein, and/or preservatives may make it unsuitable for frequent consumption. The final product typically has a spreadable consistency, and typically contains high amounts of salt, as a preservative.

Reputation

Canned meats have a mixed reputation on account of the taste, texture, ingredients, preparation and nutrition. The canning process produces a product with a generally homogeneous texture and flavour. The low-cost ingredients used also affect the quality.

For example, mechanically separated chicken or turkey is a paste-like product made by forcing crushed bone and tissue through a sieve to separate bone from tissue. In the United States, mechanically separated poultry has been used in poultry products since 1969, after the National Academy of Sciences found it safe for use.

On November 3, 1995, the Food Safety and Inspection Service of the US Department of Agriculture published a final rule in the Federal Register on mechanically separated poultry, stating that it was safe to use without restrictions. However, it must be labelled as "mechanically separated chicken or turkey" in the ingredient statement. The final rule became effective on November 4, 1996.

Ingredients

- Armour Star: Mechanically separated chicken, beef tripe, partially defatted cooked beef fatty tissue, beef hearts, water, partially defatted cooked pork fatty tissue, salt, and less than 2 per cent: mustard, natural flavourings, dried garlic, dextrose, sodium erythorbate, and sodium nitrite.
- Hormel: Beef tripe, mechanically separated chicken, beef hearts, partially defatted cooked beef fatty tissue, meat broth, vinegar, salt, flavouring, sugar, and sodium nitrite.
- Libby's: Mechanically separated chicken, pork skin, partially defatted cooked pork fatty tissue, partially defatted cooked beef fatty tissue, vinegar, less than 2 per cent of: salt, spices, sugar, flavourings, sodium erythorbate and sodium nitrite.

PASCALIZATION

Pascalization, or high pressure processing is a method of preserving and sterilizing food, in which a product is processed under very high pressure, leading to the inactivation of certain microorganisms and enzymes in the food. The technique was named after Blaise Pascal, a French scientist of the 17th century whose work included detailing the effects of pressure on fluids distinguishing characteristic is a pH less than 4.6, which is sufficient to kill applied for around fifteen minutes, leading to the inactivation of yeast, mould, and bacteria.

Uses

Pascalization stops chemical activity caused by microorganisms that play a role in the deterioration of foods. The treatment occurs at low temperatures and does not include the use of food additives. From 1990, some juices, jellies, and jams have been preserved using pascalization in Japan. The technique is now used there to preserve fish and meats, salad dressing, rice cakes, and yogurts.

An early use of pascalization in the United States was to treat guacamole. It did not change the guacamole's taste, texture, or colour, but the shelf life of the product increased to thirty days, from three days without the treatment. However, some treated foods still require cold storage because pascalization does not stop all enzyme activity caused by proteins, some of which affects shelf life.

Process

In pascalization, food products are sealed and placed into a steel compartment containing a liquid, often water, and pumps are used to create pressure. The pumps may apply pressure constantly or intermittently. The application of high hydrostatic pressures on a food product will kill many microorganisms, but the spores of some bacteria may need to be separately treated with acid to prevent their reproduction. Pascalization works especially well on acidic foods, such as yogurts and fruits, because pressure-tolerant spores are not able to live in environments with low pH levels.

The treatment works equally well for both solid and liquid products. During pascalization, the food's proteins are denatured, hydrogen bonds are fortified, and non-covalent bonds in the food are disrupted, while the product's main structure remains intact. Because pascalization is not heat-based, covalent bonds are not affected, causing no change in the food's taste.

Because hydrostatic pressure is able to act quickly and evenly on food, neither the size of a product's container nor its thickness play a role in the effectiveness of pascalization. There are several side effects of the process, including a slight increase in a product's sweetness, but pascalization does not greatly affect the nutritional value, taste, texture, and appearance. As a result, high pressure treatment of foods is regarded as a "natural" preservation method, as it does not use chemical preservatives.

SALTING

Salting is the preservation of food with dry edible salt. It is related to pickling. It is one of the oldest methods of preserving food, and two historically significant such foods are dried and salted cod and salt-cured meat. Salting is used because most bacteria, fungi and other potentially pathogenic organisms cannot survive in a highly salty environment, due to the hypertonic nature of salt. Any living cell in such an environment will become dehydrated through osmosis and die or become temporarily inactivated. Jewish and Muslim dietary laws require the removal of blood from freshly slaughtered meat. Salt and brine are used for the purpose in both traditions, but salting is more common in Kosher Shechita than in Halal Dhabiha.

SMOKING (COOKING)

Smoking is the process of flavouring, cooking, or preserving food by exposing it to the smoke from burning or smoldering plant materials, most often wood. Meats and fish are the most common smoked foods, though cheeses, vegetables, and ingredients used to make beverages such as whisky, Rauchbier and lapsang souchong tea are also smoked. In Europe, alder is the traditional smoking wood, but oak is more often used now, and beech to a lesser extent.

In North America, hickory, mesquite, oak, pecan, alder, maple, and fruit-tree woods such as apple, cherry and plum are commonly used for smoking. Other fuels besides wood can also be employed, sometimes with the addition of flavouring ingredients. Chinese tea-smoking uses a mixture of uncooked rice, sugar, and tea, heated at the base of a wok. Some North American ham and bacon makers smoke their products over burning corncobs.

Peat is burned to dry and smoke the barley malt used to make whisky and some beers. In New Zealand, sawdust from the native manuka is commonly used for hot smoking fish. In Iceland dried sheep dung is used to cold smoke fish, lamb, mutton and whale, resulting in a unique and rather strongly smoked flavour. Historically, farms in the western world included a small building termed the smokehouse where meats could be smoked and stored. This was generally well-separated from other buildings both because of the fire danger and because of the smoke emanations.

Types

- "Hot smoking" exposes the foods to smoke and heat in a controlled environment. Although foods that have been hot smoked are often reheated or cooked, they are typically safe to eat without further cooking. Hams and ham hocks are fully cooked once they are properly smoked. Hot smoking occurs within the range of 165°F to 185°F. Within this temperature range, foods are fully cooked, moist, and flavourful. If the smoker is allowed to get hotter than 185°F, the foods will shrink excessively, buckle, or even split. Smoking at "cooked" away.
- "Smoke-roasting" or "Smoke-baking" refers to any process that has the attributes of smoking with either roasting or baking. This smoking method is sometimes referred to as "barbecuing", "pit- roasting", or "pit-baking". It may be done in a smoke-roaster, closed wood-fired masonry oven or barbecue pit, any smoker that can reach above 250°F or in a conventional oven by placing a pan filled with hardwood chips on the floor of the oven so the chips smolder and produce a smokebath. However, this

should only be done in a well-ventilated area to prevent carbon monoxide poisoning.

- "Cold smoking" can be used as a flavour enhancer for items such as pork chops, beef steaks, chicken breasts, salmon and scallops. The item can be cold-smoked for a short period, just long enough to give a touch of flavour. Such foods are ready to be finished to order by such cooking methods as grilling, sautéing, baking, and roasting, or they may be hot smoked to the appropriate doneness for an even deeper smoked flavour. Smokehouse temperatures for cold smoking should be maintained below 100 °F. In this temperature range, foods take on a rich, smokey flavour, develop a deep mahogany colour, and tend to retain a relatively moist texture. They are not cooked as a result of the smoking process, however.

Wood Smoke

Hardwoods are made up mostly of three materials: cellulose, hemicellulose, and lignin. Cellulose and hemicellulose are the basic structural material of the wood cells; lignin acts as a kind of cell-bonding glue. Some softwoods—especially pines and firs—hold significant quantities of resin, which produces a harsh-tasting soot when burned. Because of this, these woods are generally not used for smoking. Cellulose and hemicellulose are aggregate sugar molecules; when burnt, they effectively caramelize, producing carbonyls, which provide most of the colour components and sweet, flowery, and fruity aromas.

Lignin, a highly complex arrangement of interlocked phenolic molecules, also produces a number of distinctive aromatic elements when burnt, including smoky, spicy, and pungent compounds such as guaiacol, phenol, and syringol, and sweeter scents such as the vanilla-scented vanillin and clove-like isoeugenol.

Guaiacol is the phenolic compound most responsible for the "smokey" taste, while syringol is the primary contributor to smokey aroma. Wood also contains small quantities of proteins, which contribute roasted flavours. Many of the odour compounds in wood smoke, especially the phenolic compounds, are unstable, dissipating after a few weeks or months.

A number of wood smoke compounds act as preservatives. Phenol and other phenolic compounds in wood smoke are both antioxidants, which slow rancidification of animal fats, and antimicrobials, which slow bacterial growth. Other antimicrobials in wood smoke include formaldehyde, acetic acid, and other organic acids, which give wood smoke a low pH-about 2.5.

Some of these compounds are toxic to people as well, and may have health effects in the quantities found in cooking applications. Since different species of tree have different ratios of components, various types of wood do impart a different flavour to food. Another important factor is the temperature at which the wood burns. High-temperature fires see the flavour molecules broken down further into unpleasant or flavourless compounds. The optimal conditions for smoke flavour are low, smoldering temperatures between 570 and 750°F. This is the temperature of the burning wood itself, not of the smoking environment, which sees much lower temperatures. Woods that are high in lignin content tend to burn hot; to keep them smoldering requires restricted oxygen supplies or a high moisture content.

When smoking using wood chips or chunks, the combustion temperature is often raised by soaking the pieces in water before placing them on a fire.

Preservation

Smoke is an antimicrobial and antioxidant, but smoke alone is insufficient for preserving food in practice. The main problem is that the smoke compounds adhere only to the outer surfaces of the food; smoke does not actually penetrate far into meat or fish. In modern times, almost all smoking is carried out for its flavour.

This flavouring can be purchased as a liquid in most supermarkets to mimic the flavour of smoking—not its preservative qualities-without the actual cooking process. In the past, smoking was a useful preservation tool, in combination with other techniques, most commonly salt-curing or drying. For some long-smoked foods, the smoking time also served to dry the food. Drying, curing, or other techniques can render the interior of foods inhospitable to bacterial life, while the smoking gives the vulnerable exterior surfaces an extra layer of protection.

For oily fish, smoking is especially useful, as its antioxidant properties delay surface fat rancidification. Some heavily salted, long-smoked fish can keep without refrigeration for weeks or months. Such heavily-preserved foods usually require a treatment such as boiling in fresh water to make them palatable before eating.

Types of smokers

There are a few basic types of smoker designs, each with their own advantages and disadvantages.

Charcoal Smokers: Traditional American BBQ is cooked in one of two different types of smoker; the offset charcoal smoker or the Upright Drum Smoker.

The Uds

The Ugly Drum Smoker is exactly what its name suggests; an upright steel drum that has been modified for the purpose of pseudo-indirect hot smoking. There are many ways to accomplish this, but the basics include the use of a complete steel drum, a basket to hold charcoal near the bottom, and cooking rack near the top; all covered by a vented lid of some sort. They have been built using many different sizes of steel drums but the most popular size is the common 55 gallon drum.

This design is similar to smoking with indirect heat due to the distance from the coals and the racks. The temperatures used for smoking are controlled by limiting the amount of air intake at the bottom of the drum, and allowing a similar amount of exhaust out of vents in the lid. UDS's are very efficient with fuel consumption and flexible in their abilities to produce proper smoking conditions, with or without the use of a water pan or drip pan. Most UDS builders/users would say that a water pan defeats the true pit BBQ nature of the Ugly Drum Smoker, as the drippings from the smoked meat should land on the coals, burning up, and imparting a unique flavour that you cannot get with a water pan.

Vertical Water Smoker

A vertical water smoker is a variation of the upright drum smoker. It uses charcoal or wood to generate smoke and heat, and contains a water bowl between the fire and the cooking grates. The water bowl serves to hold the temperature down and also to add humidity to the smoke chamber. In addition the bowl catches any drippings from the meat that may cause a flare up. Vertical water smokers are extremely temperature stable and require very little adjustment once the deisired temperature has been reached. Because of their relatively low cost and stable temperature they are sometimes used in barbecue competitions where propane and electric smokers are not allowed

Propane Smoker

A propane smoker is a newer method that is designed to allow the smoking of meat in a somewhat more controlled environment. The primary differences are the source of heat and cause of the smoke. In a propane smoker, the heat is generated by lighting a gas burner. This lies directly under a steel or iron box that contains the wood or charcoal that is used to provide the smoke. The steel box has few vent holes which are on the top of the box only. By starving the heated wood of oxygen, it will smoke instead of burn. Any type of wood, charcoal or mix could be used. This method uses less wood and may be more convenient for some people.

Smoke Box Method

This is a more traditional method that uses a two box system: The fire box and the food box. The fire box is typically adjacent or under the cooking box, and can be controlled to a finer degree. The heat and smoke from the fire box exhausts into the food box, where it is used to cook and cure the meat. These may be as simple as a electric heating element with a pan of wood chips placed on it, although more advanced models have finer temperature controls.

Commercial Smoke House

Commercial smokehouses, mostly made from stainless steel, have independent systems for smoke generation and cooking. Smoke generators use friction, an electric coil or a small flame to ignite sawdust on demand. Heat from steam coils or gas flames is balanced with live steam or water sprays to control the temperature and humidity. Elaborate air handling systems reduce hot or cold spots, to reduce variation in the finished product. Racks on wheels or rails are used to hold the product and facilitate movement.

SUGARING

Sugaring is a food preservation method similar to pickling. Sugaring is the process of desiccating a food by first dehydrating it, then packing it with pure sugar. This sugar can be crystalline in the form of table or raw sugar, or it can be a high sugar density liquid such as honey, syrup or molasses. The purpose of sugaring is to create an environment hostile to microbial life and prevent food spoilage. Sugaring is commonly used to preserve fruits as well as vegetables such as ginger. From time to time sugaring has also been used for non-food preservations. For example, honey was used as part of the mummification process in some ancient Egyptian rites. A risk in sugaring is that sugar itself attracts moisture.

Once a sufficient moisture level is reached, native yeast in the environment will come out of dormancy and begin to ferment the sugars into alcohol and carbon dioxide. This leads to the process of fermentation. Although fermentation can be used as a food preservation method, it must be intentionally controlled, or the results will tend to be unpleasant.

VACUUM PACKING

Vacuum packing is a method of storing food and presenting it for sale. Appropriate types of food are stored in an airless environment, usually in an air-tight pack or bottle to prevent the growth of microorganisms. The vacuum environment removes atmospheric oxygen, protecting the food from spoiling by limiting the growth of aerobic bacteria or fungi, and preventing the evapouration of volatile components. Vacuum packing is commonly used for long-term storage of dry foods such as cereals, nuts, cured meats, cheese, smoked fish, coffee, and potato chips.

It is also for storage of fresh foods such as vegetables, meats, and liquids such as soups in a shorter term because vacuum condition cannot stop bacteria from getting water which can promote their growth. Vacuum packaging food can extend its life by up to 3-5 times. Vacuum packing is also used to reduce greatly the bulk of non-food items. For example, clothing and bedding can be stored in bags evacuated with a domestic vacuum cleaner or a dedicated vacuum sealer.

This technique is sometimes used to compact household waste, for example where a charge is made for each full bag collected. Vacuum packing can be used to reduce bulk of inflatable items as well. Vacuum packaging products using plastic bags, canisters, bottles, or mason jars are available for home use. Vacuum packaging delicate food items can be done by using an inert gas kit, typically available on chamber vacuum sealers. After air has been removed, an inert gas is added to maintain the preservation of packaged food while preventing damage.

An example of inert gas for packaging delicate foods is potato chips. External vacuum sealers involve a bag being attached to the vacuum-sealing machine externally. The machine will remove the air and seal the bag, which is all done outside the machine. Chamber sealers require the entire product to be placed within the machine. Like external sealers, a plastic bag is typically used for packaging. Once the product is placed in the machine, the lid is closed and air is removed. Once the air is removed, the bag is sealed and the atmosphere within the chamber is returned back to normal. The lid is then opened and the product removed. Chamber sealers are typically used for higher-volume packaging. Manufacturers of chamber type vacuum packing machines include: Cryovac, Multivac, Sammic, VC999, Sevana and several others. When foods are frozen without preparation, freezer burn can occur. It happens when the surface of the food is dehydrated, and this leads to a dried and leathery appearance.

Freezer burn also ruins the flavour and texture of foods. Vacuum packing prevents freezer burn by preventing the food from exposure to the cold, dry air.Vacuum packaging also allows for a special cooking method, Sous-vide. Sous-vide, meaning "under vacuum" in French, involves poaching food that is vacuum sealed in a plastic bag. Due to an oxygen-poor environment, anaerobic microorganism can proliferate, so vacuum packing is often used in combination with other treatment.

DRYING

Drying is a method of food preservation that works by removing water from the food, which inhibits the growth of microorganisms and hinders quality decay. Drying food using sun and wind to prevent spoilage has been practised since ancient times. Water is usually removed by evapouration but, in the case of freeze-drying, food is first frozen and then the water is removed by sublimation. Bacteria yeasts and moulds need the water in the food to grow. Drying effectively prevents them from surviving in the food.

Food Types

Many different foods are prepared by dehydration. Good examples are meat such as prosciutto, bresaola, and beef jerky. Dried and salted reindeer meat is a traditional Sami food. First, the meat is soaked/ pickled in saltwater for a couple of days to guarantee the conservation of the meat. Then the meat is dried in the sun in spring when the air temperature is below zero.

The dried meat can be further processed to make soup. Fruits change character completely when dried: the plum becomes a prune, the grape a raisin; figs and dates are also transformed in new, different products, that can be eaten as they are or else after rehydration. Home drying of vegetables, fruit and even meat may be carried out by a do-it-yourself practice, employing electrical dehydrators. If the user does not like to use additives as potassium metabisulphite, or BHA, BHT for meats, dried products may be hermetically shelf stored if it is to be consumed soon, or else in the refrigerator or even freezer if a long storage is to be expected.

Freeze dried vegetables are often found in backpackers food, hunters, military, etc. The exception to this rule are bulbs, such as garlic and onion, which are often dried. Also chilis are frequently dried. Edible and psilocybin mushrooms, as well as other fungi, are also sometimes dried for preservation purposes, to affect the potency of chemical components, or so they can be used as seasonings. For centuries, much of the European diet depended on dried cod, known as salt cod or bacalhau or stockfish. It formed the main protein source for the slaves on the West Indian plantations, and was a major economic force within the triangular trade. Dried shark meat, known as Hákarl, is a delicacy in Iceland.

Grain Drying

Hundreds of millions of tonnes of wheat, corn, soybean, rice and other grains as sorghum, sunflower seeds, rapeseed/canola, barley, oats, etc., are dried in grain dryers. In the main agricultural countries, drying comprises the reduction of moisture from about 17-30 per cent w/w to values between 8 and 15 per cent w/w, depending on the grain. The final moisture content for drying must be adequate for storage. The more oil the grain has, the lower its storage moisture content will be. Cereals are often dried to 14 per cent w/w, while oilseeds, to 12.5 per cent (soybeans), 8 per cent (sunflower) and 9 per cent (peanuts). Drying is carried out as a requisite for safet storage, in order to inhibit microbial growth. However, low temperatures in storage are also highly recommended to avoid degradative reactions and, especially, the growth of insects and mites.

A good maximum storage temperature is about 18°C. The largest dryers are normally used "Off-farm", in elevators, and are of the continuous type: Mixed-flow dryers are preferred in Europe, while Cross-flow dryers in the USA. In Argentina, both types are usually found. Continuous flow dryers may produce up to 100 metric tonnes of dried grain per hour.

The depth of grain the air must traverse in continuous dryers range from some 0.15 m in Mixed flow dryers to some 0.30 m in Cross-Flow. Batch dryers are mainly used "On-Farm", particularly in the USA and Europe. They normally consist of a bin, with heated air flowing horizontally from an internal cylinder through an inner perforated metal sheet, then through a annular grain bed, some 0.50 m thick in radial direction, and finally across the outer perforated metal sheet, before being discharged to the atmosphere.

The usual drying times range from 1 h to 4 h depending on how much water must be removed, type of grain, air temperature and the grain depth. In the USA, continuous counterflow dryers may be found on-farm, adapting a bin to slowly drying grain fed at the top and removed at the bottom of the bin by a sweeping auger. Grain drying is an active area of manufacturing and research. Now it is possible to simulate the performance of a dryer with computer programmes based on equations that represent the phenomena involved in drying: physics, physical chemistry, thermodynamics and heat and mass transfer.

Most recently the evolution of quality indices is beginning to be predicted with some confidence, in order to add an essential performance parametre with which to establish a compromise of reasonably fast drying rate, limited energy consumption, and satisfactory grain quality. A typical quality parametre in wheat drying is the breadmaking quality and germination percentage whose reductions in drying are somewhat related.

Methods

There are many different methods for drying, each with their own advantages for particular applications; these include:

- Bed dryers.
- Drum drying.
- Fluidized bed dryers.
- Freeze Drying.
- Shelf dryers.
- Spray drying.
- Sunlight.
- Commercial food dehydrators.
- Household oven.

□

3

Nutritive Value of Foods

INTRODUCTION

The nutritional value of food that we eat greatly governs our health and therefore most of the activities that we do in our life. Our food is the only source of energy, minerals and vitamin for our body and is responsible for the efficient metabolism of the same. In order to get different types of nutrients in the right quantities, we should eat all types of food including fruits such as apricot, banana, apple, orange, mango, pomegranate, grapes, grapefruit, pear, plum, cherry, dates, pineapple, blueberry, kiwi, lemon, strawberry, avocado, watermelon, etc.; edible nuts such as almond, walnut, cashew, peanuts, peanut butter, pecans, etc.; vegetables such as potato, tomato, mushroom, cucumber, beet, cabbage, radish, carrot, onion, broccoli, spinach, pumpkin, seaweed, chestnut, eggplant, turnip, sweet potato, lettuce, cauliflower, etc.; cereals such as corn or maize, wheat, rice, barley, oats, sorghums, millets, rye, etc.; animal products such as milk, cheese, butter, chicken, egg, egg whites, meat, beef, pork, fish, honey, shrimp, lobster, octopus, crab, etc.; spices such as celery, chilies, turmeric, clove, pepper, cinnamon, cardamom, ginger, garlic, etc.; oils such as mustard, flax seed, soybean, sunflower seed, coconut, olive, beverages such as wine, coffee, tea, alcohol, vodka, beer, etc.

It has become mandatory in many countries to print the nutritional value of the food item on the label. This gives consumers an idea of what they are eating, which is very necessary due to the increasing intake of fast food items such as pizza, burger, chips, etc., in our diet.

ALMOND

Almond and almond oil is used extensively in ancient medical techniques like Ayurveda and Unani medicines. Despite being a seed, it boasts of being counted in the premium health food category consisting whole foods such as other nuts.

Presence of high amounts of nutrients produces energy:

- **Nutrition Facts and Information about an Almond:** Almond is incredibly rich in minerals like Mangnese, Magnesium, Copper, Phosphorus, Iron, Zinc and Potassium. However, Selenium is also present in good amount.
- **Vitamin Content of an Almond:** These small nuts are a powerhouse of Vitamin E, Riboflavin, Thiamin, Niacin and Folate. Good amounts of Vitamin B6 and Pantothenic Acid are also present.
- **Calorie Content of an Almond:** Almonds have a large calorie content, being 575.0 per 100 gm.
- **Health Benefits of an Almond:** The small sized almond comes packed with sizeable amount of health benefits. It lowers the risk of gallstones, weight gain, high blood pressure, cardiovascular disease and diabetes. It reduces blood sugar level, weight and LDL (bad) cholestrol, including almonds in your diet keeps heart and blood healthy.

AVOCADO

Avocado is a fat-rich fruit having a fat content of about 23 per cent. It contains dietary fibres. It is rich in minerals such as copper, magnesium, manganese, and contains some amounts of iron, calcium, iodine, selenium, zinc and phosphorus.

- **Vitamin Content:** Avocado is well known for its high vitamin K and Vitamin A content. It also contains small amounts of Vitamin B, Vitamin C, Vitamin E, Thiamin, Riboflavin, Niacin, Vitamin B6, Biotin, and Folate.
- **Calorific Content of Avocado:** Fruits are normally not rich in calories and are eaten for their ability to provide vitamins, minerals and digestive fibrous content. However, avocado owing to its high fat content provides good quantity of calories. A 100 gm of edible portion of the fruit provides about 215 calories.
- **Health Benefits of Avocado:** The nutritional value of avocado makes it good for indigestion, hair care, heart health, skin care, psoriasis, and bad breath.

APPLE

An apple a day keeps the doctor away. The health benefits of apple are enormous making it one of the most valuable and savored fruits throughout the world.

- **Nutrition Facts and Information about Apple:** Apple contains minerals such as magnesium, copper, manganese, copper, calcium, iron, potassium and phosphorus in small quantities. Apple also contains dietary fibre, which help in reducing the bad cholesterol levels.
- **Vitamin Content:** Apple is rich in Vitamin A and Vitamin C. Vitamin A concentration is higher in the outer skin than the flesh. Like potatoes, Vitamin C concentration is higher just below the skin in apples also. Hence the skin of the apple should not be discarded. Other vitamins present in apple include Vitamin K, Thiamin, Riboflavin, and Vitamin B6.
- **Calorie Content of Apple:** Apple does not have calories as high as avocado or olives, yet, it is an excellent source of energy. The calorie content varies as per the type of apple. Further, apple contains sugars which are easily absorbed by the body. Hence, the weak and ill are often advised to eat apples for gaining weight and fast recovery.
- **Health Benefits of Apple:** The nutritional value of apple makes it useful for digestion, stomach disorders, anaemia, wekness, dental care, dysentry, heart disease, rheumatism, eye disorders, cancer, gout, and skin care.
- **How to Choose an Apple:** When you buy an apple make sure that the apple skin is shiny. Further, the apple should be firm and free of wrinkles. Apricot and Watermelon

APROCPT AMD WATERMELON

Apricot

Apricots can be related to the Peach family, and usually they are found first at the arrival of summers. This fleshy fruit with less juice is a rich source of Beta-Carotene and Lycopene. Apricots have a velvet like skin, it's kernels resemble and tastes like almonds and are used well as their substitute. Interestingly, not only the fruit but its kernel too has cancer fighting nutrient, in kernels it is Amygladin and the fruit contains Lycopene.

An Apricot can be consumed raw, in the fruit salad or even canned, interestingly canned ones are relatively high on Beta-Carotene as compared to raw.

- **Nutrition Facts and Information about an Apricot:** An Apricot is a rich source of potassium, manganese and copper. Iron, magnesium and phosphorus are present in small amounts. Traces of calcium and zinc are also found in it.
- **Vitamin Content of an Apricot:** An Apricot can be said to be loaded with Vitamin A and Vitamin C. It is enriched with Vitamin E, Vitamin K, Niacin and Vitamin B6. Whereas Thiamin, Riboflavin, Folate and Pantothenic Acid are present in small quantities.
- **Calorie Content of an Apricot:** Apricots are rich in many nutrients and fibre but has a calorie count of just 48.0 per 100 gm.
- **Health Benefits of an Apricot:** An Apricot's high content of Vitamin A protects eye sight. Its large Beta-Carotene and Lycopene content provides immunity to heart related disease. The carotenoid Lycopene has been found useful in the prevention of Prostate cancer in men. Presence of good amount of fibre makes an Apricot a must to eat fruit to avoid digestive problems.

Watermelon

This king sized fruit certainly is loaded with the power of quenching your thirst and meeting your physiological needs for nutrients. Just in case you are only thinking of savoring the fruit content, may we let you know that in China even the rind left is either pickled or stir fried to make it a delicious serving. Its seed which is high in fat and protein is also found useful as a snack or else as an oilseed. Altogether, it is a real treat to savor in extreme summers.

- **Nutrition Facts and Information about Watermelon:** It is not largely enriched with minerals but has considerable amounts of potassium, manganese, magnesium and copper. While calcium, iron, phosphorus, zinc and selenium are found in minute quantity.
- **Vitamin Content of Watermelon:** A Watermelon largely constitutes Vitamin A and Vitamin C. However, small amounts of Thiamine, Vitamin B6 and Pantothenic Acid are also present. Consists of Riboflavin, Niacin and Folate in small traces.
- **Calorie Content of Watermelon:** It counts 30.0 per 100 gm on the calorie metre.
- **Health Benefits of Watermelon:** This large sized fruit comes packed with large health benefits which ranges from prevention against cardio-vascular diseases to improving insulin sensitivity. The presence of antioxidants and lycopene scavenge free radicals, maintains a good eye vision, prevents from colon cancer, prostate cancer, breast cancer and endometrial cancer. It is a vital source of energy.

BANANA

- **Nutrition Facts and Information about Banana:** Banana is rich in potassium. It also contains other minerals such as calcium, iron, magnesium and phosphorus in large quantities. It is also rich in fibres making it a useful laxative and good for easing constipation.
- **Vitamin Content of Banana:** Banana is rich in Vitamin C. It also contains other vitamins such Vitamin A, and Vitamin B, especially folate.
- **Calorie Content of Banana:** Banana contains about 90 to 93 calories per 100 gm. This energy is easily absorbed by the body and hence eating 3-4 bananas daily, especially with milk, is often recommended to gain weight. At the same time, banana is useful for loosing weight. Since it has only 90 calories per 100 gm., banana reduces your calorie intake and thus helps in weight loss. Overweight people, should of course, stop eating banana chips to lose weight.
- **Health Benefits of Banana:** The nutritional value of banana makes it useful for weight gain as well as weight loss, constipation, bowel problems, anaemia, blood pressure, heart problems, ulcers, brain stimulation, depression, nervous disorders, stress, morning sickness, menstruation, etc.

KIWI FRUIT

- **Nutrition Facts and Information about Kiwi:** Kiwi or chinese gooseberries is rich in copper and potassium. Other minerals present in the fruit include calcium, manganese, magnesium, phosphorus, iron, and zinc. Like Apple, it also provides dietary fibre. This fibre makes it good for controlling blood sugar, colon and cardiovascular problems.
- **Vitamin Content of Kiwi:** Kiwi fruit is known for its high Vitamin C content. About 70gm of the fruit will be sufficient for your daily Vitamin C intake. It is also rich in Vitamin K. Kiwi fruits also contains some amount of Vitamin A, Vitamin E, Vitamin B.
- **Calorie Content of Kiwi Fruit:** Most of fruit is made up of water. Hence, 100 gm of Chinese Gooseberries contain about 61 calories only. However, as seen in many fruits, it is easy for the body to absord these calories.
- **Health Benefits of Kiwi:** The nutritional value of kiwi fruit makes it useful for high blood sugar, asthma, cardiovascular health, heart disorders, diabetes, infant growth, increasing immunity, cancer, colon disorders, cataract, macular degeneration, etc.

WHEAT AND BARLEY

Wheat

Wheat grains are used to make flour, which is transformed into doughs and then breads, which is a staple food in every country and culture. Eating whole grains are advisable to women for staying slim and healthy. It is rich in protein and provides daily requirement of energy.

Works as a good laxative. It has wide culinary uses, from the making of breads, pasta and cakes to fermentation of alcoholic beverages.

- **Nutrition Facts and Information about Wheat:** It contains manganese, phosphorus, magnesium and selenium in very large quantities. Rich in zinc, copper, iron and potassium. However, calcium is also present in small amounts.
- **Vitamin Content of Wheat:** It is rich in Vitamin B6, Niacin, Thiamin, Folate, Riboflavin and Pantothenic Acid. Vitamin E and Vitamin K are also present in small but considerable amounts.
- **Calorie Content of Wheat:** Wheat has a calorific value of 339.0 per 100 gm. Being a grain, it is very appropriate in calories and hence, filling as a food.
- **Health Benefits of Wheat:** Consumption of whole wheat is necessary for a healthy metabolism, as it prevents Breast Cancer, Gallstones, childhood Asthma and heart risks. Definitely an essential food to intake for women for gastro-intestinal health, also reduces risk of high blood pressure, Diabetes and high cholestrol. To add up to it all, it has phytonutrients which promotes better health through maintaining high blood levels.

Barley

It is a staple cereal grain, popular for breakfast meals and savored for its rich flavour which reminds you of nuts. It is loaded with dietary fibre and proteins for an energetic and healthy metabolism.

- **Nutrition Facts and Information about Barley:** Barley is rich in manganese, selenium, phosphorus, copper, magnesium, iron, zinc and potassium. While calcium is found in a small quantity.
- **Vitamin Content of Barley:** Barley is rich in Vitamin B6, Thiamin, Niacin, Riboflavin and Folate. Whereas, Vitamin K and Pantothenic Acid are present in small quantities.
- **Health Benefits of Barley:** Including Barley in your diet surely helps in prevention from high cholestrol, intestinal dysfunctions, Atherosclerosis, Heart ailments, Diabetes, Gallstones, Childhood Asthma and Cancer diseases. With presence of Phosphorus formation of ATP is enhanced and repair of tissue system is supported.

BEEF

The use of lean and clean beef is advisable to include in diet, it could be as an ingredient in stews or traditional recipes. Beef is a popular meat rich in protein, being a red meat had always made it a bad food when it comes to studies and researches. However, it has been established that a lean beef adds to health benefits related to heart and prevention of cancer. As a matter of fact, no one can deny that beef is an important source of protein.

- **Nutrition Facts and Information about Beef:** Beef is found to be very rich in zinc, selenium, phosphorus, potassium and magnesium.

  Sodium and copper are found in good quantities. However, minute quantities of calcium and mangnese are also present.
- **Vitamin Content of Beef:** Beef is one of the best source for Vitamin B12, Vitamin B6 Niacin and Riboflavin. However, it is also rich in Thiamin and Pantothenic Acid. Small amounts of Vitamin E, Vitamin K and Folate are present.
- **Calorie Content of Beef:** The calorie count of Beef per 100 gm is 155.0, it is meat which is higher in protein and moderate in fat.
- **Health Benefits of Beef:** Beef is good for bones and teeth. It enhances immunity against infections of ear, etc., and prevents blood vessel walls from damaging. Moderate consumption of lean beef is altogether good for cardiovascular health and to prevent cancer risks.

PORK

Pork makes to the position of most widely consumed meat till today, with being bred almost in all major parts of the world. It is a rich source of proteins and fats. This meat being used to make sausages, ham and bacon is an essential part of people's daily nutrients requirement in many countries.

No doubt, Pork has always been an energy packed food:

- **Nutrition Facts and Information about Pork:** Pork has a high mineral content of phosphorus, selenium, sodium, zinc, potassium and copper. The two minerals which are present in good quantities are iron and magnesium, while calcium and mangnese are found in traces only.
- **Vitamin Content of Pork:** Pork is highly enriched with Vitamin B6, Vitamin B12, Thiamin, Niacin, Riboflavin and Pantothenic Acid. However, Vitamin A and Vitamin E are found in very small amounts.

- **Calorie Content of Pork:** Calorific value of Pork is 458.0 per 100 gm. This is quite high when compared to other animal products like chicken.
- **Health Benefits of Pork:** Consumption of Pork in moderate quantities is helpful in gaining energy. It is good for skin, eyes, nervous system, bones and mental performance. Intake of Pork also ensures better immunity to body due to presence of essential antioxidants.

VODKA AND BEER

Vodka

Vodka is one of the most popular alcoholic beverages. It is made by fermentation of wheat mash, corn mash, potato mash or rye mash.

- **Calorie Content of Vodka:** Vodka is rich in calories. It contains about 228 calories every 100g serving. So if you are trying to lose weight, limit your intake of vodka.
- **Vitamin Content:** Vodka is devoid of vitamins. It contains only traces of Vitamin B.
- **Nutrient Facts and Information of Vodka:** So does vodka contain any minerals? Again, vodka is almost devoid of any minerals. It contains small quantities of phosphorus, potassium and sodium.
- **Health Benefits of Vodka:** It is believed that vodka helps in treating heart problems and certain cancers. There are indicative scientific studies proving this; however, these studies are preliminary and no conclusion can be drawn based on this. Remember—excessive drinking affects your liver and your health is best maintained when you abstain from excessive intake of alcohol.

Beer

Beer is another popular alcoholic beverage:

- **Calorie Content of Beer:** Beer is a good source of calories. It contains about 42 calories every 100gm serving. So if you drink one bottle of beer which contains about 750 ml, your calorie intake will be about 340 calories. Normally people who drink 2-3 bottles of beer a day find that their weight has increased drastically after few days. This is due to the large amount of calories present in beer.
- **Vitamin Content:** Like vodka, beer also contains traces of Vitamin B.

- **Nutrient Facts and Information Beer:** Beer is not rich in any mineral. It contains small amounts of calcium, magnesium, phosphorus and sodium.
- **Health Benefits of Beer:** It is claimed that beer is beneficial in reducing stress, heart diseases, facilitating urination and inducing sleep. Of course all this is applicable when one drinks beer in limited amount.

BEET AND RADISH

Beet

Beet has always been a vital source of energy enriched with nutrients and fibre. It is biennial and available almost throughout the year. Be it the modified root itself or Chard like edible green leaves both are incredibly contributing to a healthy metabolism. While Beta vulgaris is widely being relished in the form of salad with spicy and lemon like flavour and pickles, the edible green leaves too are loaded with rich vitamin and mineral content. It's subspecies are sources for highly nutritious garden beet juice, sugar production and animal fodder.

- **Nutrition Facts and Information about Beet:** Beet is a rich source of potassium, iron, magnesium, manganese, phosphorus and copper.

  Whereas calcium, sodium, zinc and selenium arc present in small amounts.
- **Vitamin Content:** Beet consists of Vitamin C, Folate and Betaine in large quantities. Vitamin A, Thiamin, Riboflavin, Niacin, Vitamin B6 and Pantothenic Acid are also present in small amounts. It also constitutes traces of Beta Carotene.
- **Calorie Content of Beet:** Beets are known for being rich in nutrients and low on calorie, having a calorific value of 43.0 per 100 gm. As a result it forms an important part of salads for people under controlled diet.
- **Health Benefits of Beet:** Beet has been found useful in the treatment of Colon Cancer and birth related defects. It is a natural cleanser which removes toxins from the body and nourishes the bloodstream. Beet is useful in the treatment of liver related dysfunctions like Jaundice, Cirrhosis, etc. Garden Beet juice is a good source of energy and is essential for human body. It is not advisable to feed beet to infants below six months but it is of good use to women under menstruation.

Radish

Radish is a root vegetable with a rich flavour. It is used in most of the world cuisines but is very popular in Japanese and Chinese cuisine.

- **Nutrition Facts and Information about Radish:** Radish has excellent levels of copper, manganese and potassium. It is also a good source of calcium, magnesium, iron, phosphorous, zinc and sodium.
- **Vitamin Content:** Radishes are a very good source of Vitamin C and Vitamin K. They also contain Riboflavin and Vitamin B6.
- **Calorie Content of Radish:** 100gm of radish contains 16 calories only. Radish is low in saturated fat and very low in cholesterol. They are also very good source of dietary fibre.
- **Health Benefits of Radish:** Radish has anti-bacterial as well as anti-fungal properties. It is beneficial for cough, respiratory problems, digestive disorders, asthma, bronchitis and liver and gallbladder troubles.

CABBAGE AND ICEBERG LETTUCE

Cabbage

Cabbage is a leafy vegetable, which is eaten raw as salads and used in many other recipes. The high nutrient content and numerous medicinal properties of cabbage make it popular throughout the world.

- **Nutrition Facts and Information about Cabbage:** Cabbage is an excellent source of manganese, calcium and potassium. It is a very good source of iron, phosphorous, magnesium. It is also a very good source of fibre, folate and omega-3 fatty acids. Further, sodium, zinc and copper are found in good amounts in cabbage.
- **Vitamin Content:** Cabbage is an excellent source of Vitamin C. Cabbage is also a good source of Thiamin, Riboflavin, Niacin, Vitamin B6. It contains good amounts of Vitamin K, Folate, Vitamin A and protein.
- **Calorie Content of Cabbage:** 100g of cabbage contains only 25 calories. This food is low in saturated fat, cholesterol and a good source of dietary fibre and folate. It largely contains carbohydrates.
- **Health Benefits of Cabbage:** Cabbage is low in calories and therefore it is good for weight loss. It also has anti-inflammatory properties. It is believed that cabbage juice helps in treating peptic ulcers. Since cabbage is abundant in Vitamin C, it is good for protection from free radicals.

Iceberg Lettuce

Iceberg lettuce is a main constituent in salads and is known for its crunchy texture. It has comparatively less nutrients than the other greens.

- **Nutrition Facts and Information about Iceberg Lettuce:** Iceberg lettuce is an excellent source of potassium and manganese and a very good source of iron, calcium, magnesium and phosphorous. It also contains traces of sodium, copper, zinc.
- **Vitamin Content:** Iceberg lettuce is an excellent source of Vitamin A, Vitamin K and Vitamin C. It is also a good source of Thiamin, Vitamin B6, Folate.
- **Calorie Content of Iceberg Lettuce:** Iceberg lettuce contains 14 calories/ 100 gm. It mainly has water and dietary fibre. This food is low in sodium and very low in saturated fat and cholesterol.
- **Health Benefits of Iceberg Lettuce:** Iceberg lettuce has high water content and is low in calories. Therefore, it is good in weight loss. However, it has relatively low amounts of nutrients. It is considered that, owing to folate content, iceberg lettuce helps in fighting heart diseases and strokes.

TOMATO AND CARROT

Tomato

- **Nutrition Facts and Information about Tomato:** Tomato is a good source of calcium and iron. It also contains some amounts of phosphorus, sulfur and potassium.
- **Vitamin Content:** Tomato is rich in Vitamin C and contains some Vitamin B and Vitamin A. The vitamin C content increases as the vegetable ripens.
- **Calorific Content of Tomato:** 100 gm of tomato contains only 20 calories. These calories are easy to absorb by the body. The low calorie content of tomato makes it a favourite of obese people. It is often recommended in weight loss programmes as it provides you some of the essential minerals and vitamins, fills your stomach and does not add calories to your body.
- **Health Benefits of Tomato:** The nutritional value of tomato makes it good for weight loss, obesity, eye disorders, night blindness, urinary tract infection, liver disorders, jaundice, indigestion, morning sickness, constipation, diarrhea, intestinal disorders, and diabetes. It also helps in cleansing the body of toxic compounds.

Carrot

- **Nutrition Facts and Information about Carrot:** Carrot is a good source of minerals such as potassium, and manganese. It also contains some amount of sodium, fluoride, phosphorus, iron, zinc, copper, selenium, and calcium.
- **Vitamin Content:** Carrot is an excellent source of beta carotene. It also contains large amount of Vitamin K. Further, carrot contains traces of Vitamin C, Vitamin E, and Vitamin B.
- **Calorific Content of Carrot:** 100gm of carrot contains about 43 to 48 calories.
- **Health Benefits of Carrot:** The nutritional value of carrot makes it good for eye disorders, cataract, tooth disorders, skin care, nervous disorders, indigestion, constipation, diarrhoea, arthritis, gout, and lung cancer.

CASHEW AND CHESTNUT

Cashew

Cashew, a kidney shaped seed, is a vital ingredient to include in your diet plan. It works as a health booster and is a good source of monosaturated fats and protein. It has originated from Brazil and is now being cultivated in many other countries.

- **Nutrition Facts and Information about Cashew:** Cahsews are said to be packed with huge amounts of minerals like copper, magnesium, manganese, phosphorus, zinc, iron, selenium and potassium. Calcium is present in good quantity. Further, sodium is found in traces only.
- **Vitamin Content of Cashew:** Huge amounts of Vitamin K, Thiamin, Vitamin B6 and Pantothenic Acid are present. Further, cashews are also rich in Vitamin E, Folate, Niacin and Riboflavin but consists of Vitamin C in traces only.
- **Calorie Content of Cashew:** Cashew has a calorific value of 553.0 per 100 gm.
- **Health Benefits of Cashew:** Like other nuts Cashew too has an obesity and gallstones fighting property. Presence of high amount of magnesium ensures healthy bones and teeth structure, while copper produces energy and increases capability of antioxidant defences. Effects in a healthy heart and bloodstream. Thus, the risk of heart related disease, diabetes and obesity is greatly reduced. Iron controls red-blood cell function and enzyme activity.

Chestnut

Chestnuts which crumble in the mouth to give a sweet flavour, unlike other nuts, are low in fat. Being low in fat, it is often compared to grains. It also has good amount of dietary fibre. It's cultivation is spread across the world and comes in many varieties.

- **Nutrition Facts and Information about Chestnut:** Chestnuts are enriched with large amounts of manganese, potassium, copper, phosphorus, magnesium and iron. Zinc and calcium are also present in small amounts.
- **Vitamin Content of Chestnut:** These nuts are a power house of Vitamin C. Vitamin B6, Thiamin, Folate and Riboflavin are the other nutrients which chestnuts are enriched with. Good amounts of Niacin and Pantothenic Acid are present. Traces of Vitamin A are also found.
- **Calorie Content of Chestnut:** Calorie count of Chestnuts is 213.0 per 100 gm.
- **Health Benefits of Chestnut:** Like all other nuts, chestnuts prevent heart risks, provides energy, are very low in cholestrol and mainly are good to include in diet as other grains. Preventing common cold and enhancing fertility in men are the health benefits which comes with the presence of Vitamin C.

CHERRY AND STRAWBERRY

Cherry

Cherry is a bright red coloured fruit, which can be eaten fresh. These fruits are found in yellow colour as well. Cherries are eaten raw and are also used for flavouring foods and preparation of wine.

- **NutritionFactsandInformationaboutCherry:**Cherryisanexcellent source of potassium and manganese. It is a very good source of magnesium and copper. Good amounts of iron and phosphorous are found in cherries. Other minerals present in cheries include calcium and potassium, which are present only in trace amounts.
- **Vitamin Content:** Cherry is an excellent source of Vitamin C, Vitamin K and is a very good source of thiamin, riboflavin, Vitamin B6 and pantothenic acid. It also contains traces of niacin, folate and Vitamin A.
- **Calorie Content:** 100g of cherries contain 63 calories. It is also a good source of dietary fibre. This food is primarily made up of water and carbohydrates ad is low in saturated fat, cholesterol and sodium.
- **Health Benefits of Cherry:** Cherry can reduce the pain of arthritis, gout and headaches. Cherry contains anthocyanin, a red pigment,

which acts as an antioxidant. The plant pigment along with Vitamin C strengthens collagen. Cherry juice contains melatonin, which is important for the function of the immune system.

Cherries are used as a sedative in nausea and vomiting. Wild cherry bark is an important cough remedy. Cherry is also beneficial in treating bronchitis, asthma and chronic diarrhoea. It has been found that cherries can reduce the risk of heart attack and the risk of cancer by fifty per cent.

Strawberry

Strawberry is a common fruit which can be consumed fresh, frozen or made into preserves. Strawberries are a popular addition to dairy products and are used as a natural acid/base indicator.

- **Nutrition Facts and Information about Strawberry:** Strawberry is an excellent source of potassium and magnesium. It contains very good amount of phosphorous, sodium, calcium, copper and manganese. Strawberry is a good source of iron.
- **Vitamin Content:** Strawberries are an excellent source of Vitamin C. Infact they have more Vitamin C than citrus fruit. Strawberry is also a good source of folate, thiamin, riboflavin, niacin, Vitamin B6, omega-3 fatty acids, Vitamin E, Vitamin A and Vitamin K.
- **Calorie Content of Strawberry:** Strawberries contain 32 calories/100 gm, which are mostly carbohydrates. They are a very good source of dietary fibre and iodine. Strawberries also contain an array of beneficial phytonutrients, including flavonoids, anthocyanidins and ellagic acid.
- **Health Benefits of Strawberry:** Strawberries have numberous medicinal properties includings its ability to lower the risk of cancers of the gastrointestinal tract due to presence of Vitamin C. Strawberry is an excellent anti-oxidant. It is also packed with flavonoids; these flavonoids help keep bad cholesterol from damaging artery walls. Strawberries can significantly decrease blood pressure, which may reduce the risk of heart disease. Strawberries are found to enhance memory function and reduce rheumatoid arthritis.

CORN AND RICE

Corn

Corn or maize is one of the most popular cereals in the world. Corn forms the staple food of numerous people in different countries including, US, India, etc.

- **Nutrition Facts and Information about Corn:** Corn is rich in phosphorus, magnesium, manganese, zinc, copper, iron and selenium. It also has small amounts of potassium.
- **Vitamin Content:** Corn has Vitamin B. It has traces of Vitamin A and Vitamin E.
- **Calorie Content of Corn:** Cereals are the prime source of calories for many people. The calorific value of most cereals lies between 330 to 350 calories per 100 gm, the calorific value of corn being 342 calories per 100 gm.
- **Health Benefits of Corn:** There are no particular health benefits of corn, except for the fact that it provides necessary calories for daily metabolism of the body. Corn is good for skin care, boosting nervous system, digestion, and maintaining low cholesterol levels.

Rice

- **Nutrition Facts and Information about Rice:** Rice is a good source of proteins, phosphorus and iron. It also contains some amounts of calcium. Most of the nutrients and minerals in rice are concentrated in the outer brown layers known as husk and germs. Hence brown rice, which is rice from which only husk has been removed, is the most nutritious type of rice. Unfortunately, many consumers prefer pseudo cosmetic preferences and demand white rice or polished rice, in which the germ and bran has been removed.
- **Vitamin Content:** Rice contains Vitamin B in small quantities.
- **Calorific Content of Rice:** There is no other food item that provides calories and energy to the world as provided by rice. It is not wrong to say that most of the people in the world as able to do their daily activities due to rice. Rice has about 345 calories per 100 gm. Further, it is very easy to digest rice and hence most of these calories are absorbed by the body. How many times has it happened with you that you have eaten stomach full of rice and have felt hungry just one hour later?
- **Health Benefits of Rice:** The nutritional value of rice makes it good for indigestion, diarrhoea, dysentery, nausea, skin disorders and high blood pressure.

EGG AND EGG WHITE

- **Nutritional Facts and Information of Eggs:** An egg is one of the most nutritious food items in our diet. It is rich in minerals, proteins, and vitamins, all of which are easily absorbed by the body.
- Eggs are a good source of essential minerals such as calcium, iron, phosphorus, zinc and iodine. When it comes to calories,

a medium sized egg has about 75-76 kcal. The most commonly eaten eggs are that of chicken. Eggs of other birds such as duck, quail and turkey are similar in their nutritional value to eggs of chicken, with the prominent different being that the eggs of these birds have higher mineral content as well as higher cholesterol content as compared to chicken eggs.

- **Vitamin Content of Eggs:** Eggs are rich in Vitamin B, especially Vitamin B12, Vitamin A, Vitamin D, Vitamin E and Vitamin K. It should be noted that very few food items that contain vitamin D, egg being one of them.
- **Protein Content of Eggs:** An egg is composed of about 11 per cent proteins. Further it contains all the amino acids necessary for body metabolism. This makes eggs an essential part of the diet of those who wish to increase weight and build muscles. Most of the proteins are concentrated in the white part of the egg, known as albumin or egg white.
- **Egg White and Egg Yolk:** There are two essential parts of an egg; the albumen or the white part and the yolk or the yellow part. The yolk is suspended in the albumin and contains about 80 per cent of the calories and almost all fats present in the egg. It contains vitamin A, D, E and K and minerals such as iron, calcium, and phosphorus. The egg albumen mostly contains water and proteins.
- **Health Benefits of Eggs:** The nutritional value of eggs makes it good for immunity, strong vision, treatment of macular degeneration, cataract treatment, skin care, nervous system, strong bones, and blood formation. Recent research has also shown that consuming eggs does not lead to increase in serum cholesterol levels.

FLAX SEED OIL AND SUNFLOWER SEED OIL

Flax Seed Oil

Flax seed is nutritious seed packed with all vital vitamins and minerals. It is abundant in omega 3 fatty acids. The seeds have high levels of fibre, which are useful for weight loss. Flax seed oil obtained from the seeds, also contains large amounts of omega 3 and hence has numerous health benefits.

- **Nutrition Facts and Information about Flax Seed:** Flax seed and its oil are excellent sources of manganese and magnesium. They are also a good source of copper, phosphorous, iron, zinc, selenium and calcium. They contain only traces of sodium.

- **Vitamin Content:** Thiamin is found in excellent levels in flax seed. It also has very good levels of Vitamin B6, niacin. Vitamin K is also found in good amounts in addition to riboflavin. Flax seed also contain traces of Vitamin C and Vitamin E.
- **Calorie Content of Flax seed:** As in the case of nuts and seeds, flax seed is also a high-calorie food. 534 calories are there in 100 gm of flax seed.
- **Health Benefits of Flax Seed:** Flax seed and its oil have anti-inflammatory benefits due to the abundance of omega-3 fatty acids. Flax seeds help prevent high blood pressure, heart disease, cancer, eye disorders and diabetes.

Sunflower Seed Oil

Sunflower seeds are often used in snacks and the production of sunflower oil. Sunflower oil is polyunsaturated in nature and hence often used as a healthy cooking oil.

- **NutritionFactsandInformationaboutSunflowerSeed:**Sunflower seeds are an excellent source of manganese, magnesium, copper, tryptophan, phosphorous and zinc. They also contain very good amounts of selenium, folate, iron, potassium and calcium.
- **Vitamin Content:** Sunflower seeds contain excellent levels of Vitamin E and thiamin. They are also very good source of Vitamin B1, niacin and riboflavin. Sunflower seeds also contain good levels of Vitamin B5 and Vitamin B6. Traces of Vitamin C and Vitamin A can also be found in sunflower seeds.
- **Health Benefits of Sunflower Seed:** Sunflower seeds helps in preventing hearth disorders, lower cholesterol levels, asthma, high blood presuure, migraine, headaches, indigestion and inflammations related to bones.

PINEAPPLE AND GRAPEFRUIT

Pineapple

Pineapple is a juicy sweet fruit, which is delicious, healthy and nutritious and can be eaten raw or used in cooking. The fruit is rich in a variety of minerals and vitamins and therefore has numerous health benefits.

- **Nutrition Facts and Information about Pineapple:** Pineapple is an excellent source of manganese and very good source of copper. Good amounts of magnesium, iron and potassium are also found in pineapple. It also contains small amounts of calcium, phosphorous, zinc and selenium.

- **Vitamin Content:** Pineapple is rich source of all vitamins and particularly Vitamin C is found in excellent levels. Pineapple also contains very good levels of Vitamin B1 and Vitamin B6. Good amounts of folate and Vitamin B3 are also found in pineapple in addition to traces of Vitamin K.
- **Calorie Content of Pineapple:** 100 gm of pineapple contains 86 calories. Pineapple has minimal fat and sodium with no-cholesterol. It is a good source of dietary fibre. This food is very low in saturated fat.
- **Health Benefits of Pineapple:** Since pineapples are rich in Vitamin C, they have antioxidant properties. It is also believed that pineapples are good for digestion proteins and food in general due to the presence of certain enzymes. Pineapples have diuretic, anti-cancer and anti-inflammatory properties. It is good for diarrhea, digestion, cancer, heart problems, detoxifying the body, intestinal infections, arthritis, wounds, sore throat, sinusitis and gout.

Grapefruit

Grapefruits, most popular weight loss diet, are found in white and red colour. Grapefruits are rich in vitamins and minerals and hence regular consumption of grapefruit juice during dieting helps in maintaining essential minerals and vitamins.

- **Nutrition Facts and Information about Grapefruit:** Grapefruit is an excellent source of potassium. Grapefruits are very good source of calcium, magnesium, copper and phosphorous. It also contains small amounts of manganese.
- **Vitamin Content:** Grapefruit is an excellent source of Vitamin C and Vitamin A. It is also a good source of folate, thiamin, riboflavin and Vitamin B6. It also contains small amounts of niacin and Vitamin E.
- **Calorie Content of Grapefruit:** 42 calories of energy can be found in 100g of grapefruit. This food is very low in saturated fat, cholesterol and sodium. It is also a good source of dietary fibre.
- **Health Benefits of Grapefruit:** Grapefruit helps in weight loss, boosting immune system, cold, breast cancer, lung cancer, colon cancer, reducing cholesterol levels, kidney stones and lowering insulin levels.

LEMON AND PEAR

Lemon

Lemons are small yellow fruits with acidic nature. Lemon juice is used throughout the world in various cuisines to add flavour and taste to foods.

- **Nutrition Facts and Information about Lemon:** Very good amounts of copper, magnesium, manganese, iron, phosphorous, potassium and calcium are found in lemons. Small amounts of zinc and sodium can also be seen in lemons.
- **Vitamin Content:** Lemon contains excellent levels of Vitamin C. It is also a good source of Thiamin, Vitamin C, Vitamin B6, Riboflavin and Pantothenic Acid. Lemon also contains traces of vitamin B2.
- **Calorie Content of Lemon:** One lemon of approximately 100 gm contains 22 calories of energy.
- **Health Benefits of Lemon:** Most of the health benefits of lemon can be attributed to the presence Vitamin C. Lemons are good for digestion, treating arthritis, boosting immune system, treating infections, dental care, hair care, skin care.

Pear

Pear is a juicy sweet fruit which comes in numerous varieties in various sizes, shapes and colours ranging from green, red, brown and yellow colours.

- **Nutrition Facts and Information about Pear:** Pear is an excellent source of copper, manganese and potassium. They are a good source of iron, magnesium and selenium. It also contains traces of calcium, phosphorous and zinc.
- **Vitamin Content:** Pear has abundant levels of Vitamin C and Vitamin K. It is an excellent source of Vitamin C and Vitamin K. Pears is a very good source of vitamin e, niacin (B3) and riboflavin (B2). It also contains small amounts of Vitamin B6.
- **Calorie Content:** Like many other fruit, pears are low in calories. 100 gm of pears consists of 42 calories of energy.
- **Health Benefits of Pear:** The health benefits of pear include it ability to lower cholesterol levels, promote cardiovascular health, weight gain, and prevent constipation. Like avocado, Pears are also used as baby food.

ORANGE AND MANGO

Orange

- **Nutrition Facts and Information about Orange:** Orange is a good source of minerals such as calcium, iron, sodium, copper, phosphorus, potassium, magnesium, and sulfur. It also contains traces of chlorine.
- **Vitamin Content:** Orange, like other citrus fruits, is known for Vitamin C content. Due to this high amount of Vitamin C, orange helps in absorbing calcium into the body and maintaining the health of teeth and bones. It also contains Vitamin A and Vitamin B.
- **Calorific Content of Orange:** 100 gm of orange contains about 60 calories. This energy is available in the form of sugar which can be absorbed by the body easily. Hence orange juice is often fed to people who have become weak due to some illness. Orange juice is also a good refresher after a long exhaustive day.
- **Health Benefits of Orange:** The nutritional value of orange makes it good for indigestion, constipation, bowel disorders, dyspepsia, dental care, pyorrhea, bone health, heart diseases, respiratory problems, cold, cough, influenza, skin care, pimples, acne, fever, measles, typhoid and tuberculosis (TB).

Mango

- **Nutrition Facts and Information about Mango:** Mango is a good source of minerals such as copper and potassium. It contains traces of magnesium, manganese, selenium, calcium, iron, and phosphorus.
- **Vitamin Content:** Mango is rich in Vitamin C and Vitamin A. Vitamin C content is more in raw mango as compared to that in ripe mango. It also has traces of Vitamin E, Vitamin B and Vitamin K.
- **Calorific Content of Mango:** 100 gm of mango contains about 75 calories. Raw mangoes contain starch, which is converted into sugar as the fruit ripens. These sugars are very useful in weight gain when consumed with milk, which is rich in proteins.
- **Health Benefits of Mango:** The nutritional value of mango makes it good for weight gain, eye disorders, hair loss, heat stroke, prickly heat, diabetes, bacterial infections, sinusitis, piles, indigestion, constipation, morning sickness, diarrhoea, dysentery, scurvy, spleen enlargement, liver disorders, menstrual disorders, leucorrhea, and vaginitis.

PEANUT AND PEANUT BUTTER

Peanut

Peanut is a legume used throughout the world for a variety of purposes including production of oil, butter, chocolates, cookies, etc. Peanuts are also eaten raw, roasted or added in various delicacies.

- **Nutrition Facts and Information about Peanut:** Peanuts are a rich source of protein. They are rich in almost all minerals. Peanuts contain excellent levels of manganese, copper and magnesium. It is also a very good source of iron, phosphorous, potassium, zinc, selenium and tryptophan. Peanuts contain traces of sodium.
- **Vitamin Content:** Peanut is a good source of Niacin and folate. Peanuts also contain thiamin, Vitamin E, pantothenic acid, Vitamin B6 and riboflavin.
- **Calorie Content of Peanut:** 100 gm of Peanuts contributes 567 calories of energy. They are a very good source of monounsaturated fats. Peanut is very low in cholesterol and sodium.
- **Health Benefits of Peanut:** Peanut contribute to brain health, brain circulation and blood flow. In addition to that, peanuts are also good antioxidants. Other health benefits of peanut include protection against colon cancer, prostate cancer, breast cancer, heart disease, and high cholesterol.

Peanut Butter

Peanut butter (also known as peanut paste) is made from ground roasted peanuts, with or without added oil. Peanut butter is rich in proteins and hence is a useful part of diet, especially for vegetarians.

- **Nutrition Facts and Information about Peanut Butter:** Peanut butter is an excellent source of potassium, phosphorous and magnesium. It also contains very good amounts of calcium and sodium. Peanut butter contains good amounts of iron, zinc, manganese and selenium.
- **Vitamin Content:** Peanut butter contains excellent levels of niacin and very good amounts of Vitamin B3 and vitamin E. It contains good amounts of vitamin k, thiamin, pantothenic acid and riboflavin.
- **Calorie Content of Peanut Butter:** Peanut butter is a high calorie food. The total calorie content in 100 gm of peanut butter is 589 calories. An excellent source of protein, peanuts also contains folate, dietary fibre and arginine.
- **Health Benefits of Peanut Butter:** The benefits of peanut butter include cardiovascular diseases, coronary heart diseases, high cholesterol levels, high blood sugar, cancer, and gallstones.

PLUM AND POMEGRANATE

Plum

Plum is one of those fruits which are rich in dietary fibre, effecting in a healthy digestive system. It is being cultivated over the world for jam manufacturing, it's dried version "prune", oil from prune kernels, drinks, pickles, and a popular alcoholic drink Slivovitz originated from Eatern Europe. Plums are often related to Apricots by researchers for the resemblance they noticed.

- **Nutrition Facts and Information about Plum:** It is enriched with minerals like potassium, magnesium, manganese, copper and phosphorus. While calcium, iron and zinc are present in minute quantities.
- **Vitamin Content of Plum:** Huge amounts of Vitamin C, Vitamin K and Vitamin A are present. Considerable amounts of thiamin, riboflavin and niacin are also contained. Whereas, Vitamin E, Vitamin B6, folate and pantothenic acid are present in traces.
- **Calorie Content of Plum:** Cashew has a calorific value of 46.0 per 100 gm.
- **Health Benefits of Plum:** A very important health benefit of eating Plum is that, it acts as a laxative and improves performance of the digestive system. Further, the presence of phenols and Vitamin C ensures good antioxidant protection. Prevents your eyesight from any deterioration and enhances immunity against cancer related diseases. Iron absorption in the body is increased by eating Plums and heart related risks are minimised.

Pomegranate

Pomegranate is a widely cultivated fruit and it's nectar is extracted for many commercial uses. An average sized Pomegranate contains approximately 600 edible seeds under it's thick red covering. Pomegranate juice, nectar and extracts are a major raw material of health industry. In some parts of the world like India, the edible seeds of this fruit is used as spice.

- **Nutrition Facts and Information about Pomegranate:** Pomegranate is enriched with minerals like potassium and copper. Iron is present in small quantity, while traces of magnesium, phosphorus, zinc and selenium are also there.
- **Vitamin Content of Pomegranate:** Pomegranate is a rich source of Vitamin C, Vitamin K, Vitamin B6 and Pantothenic Acid. It also consists of Vitamin A, Vitamin E, Thiamin and Riboflavin in small amounts. In addition to these, Niacin and Folate are present in traces.

- **Calorie Content of Pomegranate:** Pomegranate is rich in sugar, no wonder why the nectar is so exotic to savor. It has a calorific value of 68.0 per 100 gm.
- **Health Benefits of Pomegranate:** Pomegranate contains antioxidants like polyphenols, tannins and anthocyannins which effects in removal of free radicals from our body cells. It also helps in repair of cells and boosts the immune system. Pomegranate juice is known to be among the super healthy drinks of today. It is helpful in osteoarthritis and keeping the skin and heart healthy.

POTATO

The nutritional value of potato along with its taste and ease of cooking has made it the most popular vegetable in the entire world. Think of the day when you didn't eat even a single dish containing potatoes. Quite difficult, right? It is said that on an average, an individual consumes 62 kg of potatoes each year. We consume almost one spud of potato every day. No doubt, people consume so many potatoes because they are a good source of nutrition. Natural potato is a good source of calories. In fact many people in poor countries, who cannot afford high-calorie diet such as milk products, meat and pulses, use potatoes as their prime source of calories. In the seveenth century potato became famous across Europe as a crop that could save people during famines. But did you know that it is also a good source of nutrients? Some nutrient facts, information and nutritional value of potatoes:

- **Mineral Content:** If you eat potatoes regularly, you ensure a good supply of water and ions in your body. This is because, potato is rich in potassium. The concentration being higher in the skin and just beneath it. So, eating the potato with its skin is always beneficial. Potato also contains calcium, iron, and phosphorus.
- **Vitamin Content:** Natural potatoes are known for the large amounts of Vitamin C present in them. Typically, 100 gm of potato will contain about 17 mg of Vitamin C. In addition to this, natural potato also contains Vitamin A, B and P.
- **Water Content:** Potato looks very big in size, but water accounts for about 70-80 per cent of the weight of a potato. So the belief that you become fat by eating potatoes is a misconception. Of course if your potato servings contain large quantities of butter, or if you can't keep away from those high-in-fat-and-cholesterol French fries, you are bound to become overweight.
- **Starch Content:** Potato contains about 17 per cent starch and it is one of the best natural sources of starch. Potato sprouting leads to conversion of starch into sugar and hence you should avoid eating sprouted potatoes.

□

4

Oils, Fats and Dairy Products

AN OVERVIEW

Oils and fats are the most concentrated foods we have. Weight for weight, they contain more than twice as much fuel or energy value as any other food. Taken in moderation they are easily digested, but if taken in excess they become a burden to the system.

About 7 or 8 per cent of the weight of a normal body is fat, and this fat is formed chiefly from the fatty foods taken into the system, supplemented by the sugar and starch. When the body becomes very fat, it is a disease, called obesity. Fat people are never healthy. The fat usurps the place that should be occupied by normal tissues and organs. It crowds the heart and the lungs, and even replaces the muscle cells in the heart. The result is that the heart and lungs are overcrowded and overworked and the blood gets insufficient oxygen. Not only the lungs pant for breath after a little exercise, but the entire body. Much fat is as destructive of health as it is of beauty.

Those who find themselves growing corpulent should decrease their intake of concentrated foods and increase their physical activity. Our chief sources of fat supply are cream and butter, vegetable oils, nuts and the flesh of animals. Most meats, especially when mature, contain considerable fat. When the fat is mixed in with the meat, it is more difficult to digest than the lean flesh. Fresh fish, most of which contains very little fat, is digested very easily, while the fattest of all flesh, pork, is tedious of digestion.

There is an instinctive craving for fat with foods that contain little or none of it. That is why we use butter with cereals and lean fish, and oil dressings on vegetables. In moderation this is all right. Fats are not very rich in salts, which must be supplied by other foods. Because of their great fuel value, more fats are naturally consumed in cold than in hot climates. The Esquimeaux thrive when a large part of their rations is fat. Such a diet would soon nauseate people in milder climes. Fats and oils are used too much in cooking. Fried foods and those cooked in oil are made indigestible. Sometimes we read directions not to use animal fats, but to use olive oil or cotton seed oil for frying. It is poor cooking, no matter whether the grease is of animal or vegetable origin. So far as food value and digestibility are concerned, there is no difference between animal and vegetable fats. Fresh butter is very good, and so is olive oil. Some vegetable oils contain indigestible substances.

Cotton seed oil and peanut oil are much used. Sometimes they are sold in bottles under fancy lables as olive oil. The olive oils from California are fully as good as those imported from Spain, Italy and France and are more likely to be what is claimed for them than the foreign substances. In the past, much of our cotton seed oil has been bought by firms in southern Europe and sent back to us as fine olive oil! Such imposture is probably more difficult under our present laws than it was in the past.

Most oils become rancid easily and then are unfit for consumption. If taken in excess as food they have a splendid opportunity to spoil in the digestive tract, and then they help to poison the system. Taken in moderate quantities they are digested in the intestines and taken into the blood by way of the lymphatics. They may be stored in the body for a while, but finally they are burned, giving up much heat and energy. Taking oils between meals as medicine or for fattening purposes is folly. People get all they need to eat in their three daily meals. Lunching is to be condemned.

MILK AND OTHER DAIRY PRODUCTS

The dairy products vary greatly. Some cows give richer milk than others. Butter may be almost pure fat, or it may contain much water and salt. The cheeses are rich or poor in protein and fats according to method of making. Cottage cheese may be well drained or quite watery. Therefore, this table gives only approximate contents.

	Water	Protein	Fat	Carbohy-drates	Ash	Calories Per lb.
Whole milk	87.00	3.3	4.0	5.0	0.7	325
Cream	74.00	2.5	18.5	14.5	0.5	910
Buttermilk	91.00	3.0	0.5	4.8	0.7	165
Butter	...	..	82.4	..	..	3475
Cheese,	33.70	26.0	34.2	2.3	3.8	1965
whole milk "skimmed milk	45.70	31.5	16.4	2.2	4.2	1320

Milk is not a beverage. It is a food. A quart of milk contains as much food and fuel value as eight eggs or twelve ounces of lean beef. That is, a cupful is equal to two eggs or three ounces of lean beef. This shows that milk should not be taken to quench thirst, but to supply nourishment. Milk is one of our most satisfactory and economical albuminous foods, even at the present high prices. In many foods from 5 to 10 per cent of the protein goes to waste. In milk the waste does not ordinarily amount to more than about 1 per cent.

This fluid generally leaves the stomach within one or one and one-half hours after being ingested. In spite of its merits as a food some writers on dietetics advocate that adults stop using it, giving it only to the young. Milk is an excellent food when properly used. When abused it tends to cause discomfort, disease and death, and so does every other food known to man. Milk is given in fevers and in other diseases, when the digestive and assimilative processes are suspended. This is a serious mistake and has caused untold numbers of deaths. When the digestion has gone on a strike all feeding is destructive.

Milk and meat broths, which are generally given, are about the worst foods that could be selected under the circumstances, for they decay very easily, and are excellent food for the numerous bacteria that thrive in the digestive tract during disease. These foods must decay when they are not digested, for the internal temperature of the body during fevers is over one hundred degrees Fahrenheit. When bacteria are present in excess they give off considerable poison, which makes the patient worse. If circumstances are such that it is necessary to feed during acute disease, which is always injurious to the patient, let the food be the least harmful obtainable, such as fruit juices.

Even they do harm. In our country cow's milk is used almost exclusively. In other lands the milk of the mare, the ass, the sheep, the goat and of other animals is used. The objection voiced against cow's milk is that it is an unnatural food for man, only fit for the calf, which is equipped with several stomachs and is therefore able to digest the curds which are larger and tougher than the curds formed from human milk. It is said that the curds of cow's milk are so indigestible that the human stomach cannot prepare them for entry into the blood. This is probably true, but it is also true of other protein-bearing foods. The digestion and assimilation of proteins are begun in the stomach and completed in the intestines, and the protein in milk is one of the most completely utilized of all proteins.

To call a food unnatural means nothing, for we can call nearly all foods unnatural and defend our position. A natural food is presumably a nutritious and digestible aliment that is produced in the locality where it is consumed, one that can be utilized without preparation or preservation.

So we may say that a resident of New York should not use figs, dates, bananas and other products of tropical and semi-tropical climates, for they are not natural in the latitude of New York. We can take the position that it is unnatural for people to eat grains, which need much grinding, for the birds are the only living beings supplied with mills.

We can further say that it is unnatural to eat all cooked and baked foods. But such talk is not helpful. The more a person uses his brain the less power he has left for digestion and therefore it is necessary to prepare some of the foods so that they will be easy to digest. Man is such an adaptable creature that we are not sure what he subsisted on before he became civilized and are therefore unable to say what his natural food is. We know that in the tropics fruits play an important part in nourishing savages, while in the frozen north fat flesh is the chief food.

Perhaps there is no natural food for man. Some of those who advocate the disuse of milk have a substitute or imitation to take its place, nut milk made from finely ground nuts and water. Like all other imitations, it is inferior to the original. It is more difficult to digest than real milk and the flavour is quite different. The objection that milk is indigestible is not borne out by the experience of those who give it under proper conditions. It is true that milk disagrees with a few, but so do such excellent foods as eggs, strawberries and Concord grapes, and many other aliments which are not difficult to digest. This is a matter of individual peculiarity. Some can take boiled milk, but are unable to take it fresh, and vice versa. Outside of the few exceptions, milk digests in a reasonable time and quite completely. It is easier to digest than the legumes which are rich in protein.

It is also easier to digest than nuts, which contain much protein. The milk sugar causes no trouble and cream is one of the easiest forms of fat to digest, if taken in moderation. The protein in milk will cause no inconvenience if the milk is eaten slowly, in proper combinations and not to excess. The rennet in the stomach curdles the casein. The hydrochloric acid and the pepsin in the gastric juice then begin to break down and dissolve the clots, and the process of digestion is completed in the small intestines.

Those who overeat of milk in combination with other foods will derive benefit from omitting the milk. They will also be benefitted if they continue using milk and omit either the starch or the meat. When foods disagree, in nearly every instance it is due to the fact that too much has been eaten and too many varieties partaken of at a meal. Some may single out the milk or the meat as the offenders.

Others may point to the starches, and still others to the vegetables with their large amount of indigestible residue. They are all right and all wrong, for all the foods help to cause the trouble. However, such reasoning does not solve the problem.

If the meals cause discomfort and disease, reduce the amount eaten, take fewer varieties at a meal and simplify the cooking. Those who eat simple meals and are moderate are not troubled with indigestion. Those who eat such mushy foods as oatmeal and cream of wheat usually take milk or cream and sugar with them. This should not be done, for such dressing stimulates the appetite and leads to undermastication. Neither children nor adults chew these soft starchy foods enough. The result is that the breakfast ferments in the alimentary tract. After a few months or years of such breakfasts, some kind of disease is sure to develop. Mushy starches dressed with rich milk and sugar are responsible for a large per cent of the so-called diseases of children, which are primarily digestive disturbances. Colds, catarrhs and adenoids are, of course, due to improper eating extending over a long period of time.

Nothing should be eaten with mushy starches except a little butter and salt. After enough starch has been taken, a glass of milk may be eaten. If parents would only realise that they are jeopardizing the health and lives of their dear ones when they feed them habitually on these soft messes, which ferment easily, there would be a remarkable decrease in the diseases of childhood and in the disgraceful infant and childhood mortality, for several hundred thousand children perish annually in this country.

Milk is often referred to as a perfect food, and it is the perfect food for infants. The young thrive best on the healthy milk given by a female of their own species. Every baby should be fed at the breast. The milk contains the elements needed by the body. The ash is composed of the various salts necessary for health, containing potassium, chlorine, calcium, magnesium, iron, silicon and other elements. For the nourishment of the body we need water, protein, fat, carbohydrates and salts, so it will be seen that milk is really a complete food. However, as the body grows the nutritive requirements change and milk is therefore not a balanced food for adults.

It may be interesting to note that there is no starch in milk and that infants fed at the breast exclusively obtain no starchy food. Many babies get no starch for nine, ten or even twelve months, and this is well, for they do not need it. They grow and flourish best without it. Milk is an emulsion. It is made up of numerous tiny globules floating in serum. The size of the globules varies, but the average is said to be about 1/10,000 of an inch in diameter. These globules are fatty bodies. There are other small bodies, containing protein and fat, which have independent molecular movement. The milk is a living fluid. When it is tampered with it immediately deteriorates. Without doubt, nature intended that the milk should go directly from the mammary gland into the mouth of the consumer, but this is not practicable when we take it away from the calf. However, if we are to use sweet milk it is best to consume it as nearly like it is in its natural state as possible.

It is quite common to drink milk rapidly. This should not be done. Take a sip or a spoonful at a time and move it about in the mouth until it is mixed with saliva. It is not necessary to give it as much mouth preparation as is given to starchy food. If it is drunk rapidly like water large curds from in the stomach. If it is insalivated it coagulates in smaller curds and is more easily digested, for the digestive juices can tear down small soft curds more easily than the large tough ones. Milk should not form a part of any meal when other food rich in protein is eaten. Our protein needs are small, and it is easy to get too much. Whole wheat bread and milk contain all the nourishment needed. On such a diet we can thrive indefinitely. This is information, not a recommendation. The bread should be eaten either before or after partaking of the milk. Do not break the bread into the milk. If this is done, mastication will be slighted. Bread needs much mastication and insalivation. When liquid is taken with the bread, the saliva does not flow so freely as when it is eaten dry.

Fruit and milk make a good combination, but no starchy foods are to be taken in this meal. Take a glass of milk, either sweet or sour, and what fruit is desired, insalivating both the fruit and the milk thoroughly. If you have read that the combination of fruit and milk has proved fatal, rest assured that those who made such reports only looked at the surface, for other foods and other influences were having their effects on the system.

Many people die of food-poisoning and apoplexy. These bad results are due to wrong eating covering a long period and it is folly to blame the last meal. It would be queer if fruit and milk were not occasionally a part of the last meal. In winter, figs, dates or raisins with milk make an excellent lunch or breakfast. These fruits take the place of bread, for though they are not starchy, they contain an abundance of fruit sugar, which is more easily digested than the starch. Starch must be converted into sugar before the system can use it. On hot days milk and acid fruit make a satisfying meal. Many believe that milk and acid fruit should not be taken in the same meal, because the acid curdles the milk.

As we have already seen, the milk must be curdled before it can be digested. If this step in digestion is performed by the acid in the fruit no more harm is done than when it is performed by the lactic acid bacteria. Fruit juices and milk do not combine to form deadly poisons. If fruit and milk are eaten in moderation and no other food is taken at that meal the results are good. However, if fruit, milk, bread, meat, cake and pickles make up the meal, the results may be bad. Such eating is very common. But do not blame the fruit and the milk when the whole meal is wrong.

Likewise, if a hearty meal has been eaten and before this has had time to digest a lunch is made of fruit and milk, trouble may ensue. All the foods may be good, but a time must come when the body will object to being overfed. In summertime much less food is needed than during the cold months. Nevertheless, barring the Christmas holidays and Thanksgiving, people overeat more in summer than at any other time of the year. Picnics often degenerate into stuffing matches. We should expect many cases of serious illness to follow them, and such is the case.

Sometimes the milk is so carelessly handled that it becomes poisonous and at other times the fruit is tainted, but generally bad combinations and overeating are the factors that cause trouble when the fruit and milk combination is blamed. Buttermilk and clabbered milk are more easily digested by many than is the fresh milk. In Europe sour milk is a more common food than in this country. Here many do not know how excellent it is.

Two glasses of milk, or less, make a good warm-weather lunch. Those who have a tendency to be bilious should use cream very sparingly. Bilious people always overeat, otherwise their livers would not be in rebellion. The fat, in the form of cream, arouses decided protest on the part of overburdened livers.

A theory has found its way into dietetic literature, sometimes disguised as a truth, to the effect that boiled or hot milk is absorbed directly into the bloodstream without being digested. This is contrary to everything we know about digestion and assimilation, and although it is a fine enough theory it does not work out in practice. We have seen bad results when nothing but a small amount of the hot milk was fed to patients with weak digestive power. Perhaps others have had better results. When the system demands a rest from food, nothing but water should be given. Boiled or natural milk is then as bad as any other food, and worse than most, for in the absence of digestive power it soon becomes a foul mass, swarming with billions of bacteria. The system is compelled to absorb some of the poisons given off by the micro-organisms and the results are disastrous.

Every food we take must be modified by our bodies before entering the circulation, and milk is no exception. When milk is allowed to stand for a while the sugar ferments, through the action of the lactic acid bacteria. The sugar is turned into lactic acid, which combines with the casein and when this process has continued for a certain length of time the result is clabbered milk or sour milk. The length of time varies with the temperature and the care given the milk. If milk remains sweet for a long time during warm weather, discharge the milkman and patronize one whose product sours more quickly, for milk that remains sweet has been subjected to treatment.

All kinds of preservative treatment cause deterioration. If extraordinary care is taken with the milk and it is kept at a temperature of about forty-two degrees Fahrenheit, it may remain sweet five or six weeks, provided it is not exposed to the air, but such care is at present not practicable in commercial dairies. The milk contains unorganized ferments which spoil it in time without exposure to bacterial influences. These ferments cause digestion or decay of the milk.

Fresh butter is a palatable form of fat, which digests easily. Like all other milk products, it must be kept clean and cold, or it will soon spoil. Butter absorbs other flavours quickly and should therefore not be placed near odourous substances. It is best unsalted and in Europe it is very commonly served thus. When people learn to demand unsalted butter they will get good butter, for no one can palm off oleomargarine or other imitations under the guise of fresh unsalted butter. Unsalted butter must be fresh or it will be refused by the nose and the palate. Salt and other preservatives often conceal age and corruption of foods. Butter combines well with starches and vegetables, in fact, it can be used in moderation with any other food, when the body needs fat. Butter should not be used to cook starches or proteins in. Greasy cooking should be banished from our kitchens.

Milk is a complex food, highly organized, and therefore is easily injured or spoiled. The general rule is that the more complex a food is, the more easily it spoils. It is rather difficult at present to get wholesome milk enough to supply the people of our large cities. When it is boiled, the milk keeps longer, but boiled milk is spoiled milk. The fine flavour is lost, the casein, which is the principal protein of milk, is toughened, the milk, which is normally a living liquid, is killed, the chemical balance is lost, the organic salts being rendered partly inorganic. Milk that is unfit to eat without being boiled is not fit to eat afterwards, for the poisonous end products of bacterial life remain.

The milk is soured by the bacteria it contains. The lactic acid bacteria are harmless. When there is a lack of care and cleanliness, other bacteria get into the milk, and these are also harmless to people in good health, and most of them are not injurious to sick people. The bacteria do not cause disease, but when disease has been established, they offer their kindly offices as scavengers. Bacteria thrive in sick people, especially when they are fed when digestive power is lacking.

Boiling retards the souring of milk, but when fat and protein are boiled together the protein becomes hard to digest. Milk is rich in both fat and protein. Excessive heat turns the milk brown, the milk sugar being carameled. Babies do not thrive on boiled milk. They may look fat, but instead of having the desirable firmness of normal children, they are puffy. Children fed on denatured milk fall victims to diseases very easily, especially to diseases which are due to lack of organic salts, such as rickets and malnutrition.

Pasteurization of milk is very popular. This is objectionable for the same reasons that boiling is condemned, though not to the same extent.

Pasteurization is heating the milk to about 140 to 150 degrees Fahrenheit. This kills many of the bacteria, but many escape and when the milk is cooled off they begin to multiply and flourish again. It is estimated that pasteurized milk contains one-fourth as many bacteria as natural milk. So nothing is gained, and the milk is partly devitalized.

The advocates of pasteurization give statistics showing that milk so treated has been instrumental in decreasing infant mortality. But please bear in mind that previously a great deal of milk unfit for consumption was fed to the babies. Those who pasteurize milk generally are careful enough to see that they get a good product in the first place. If we can't get good milk we can do without it, for it is not a necessary food, but we can get good milk if we make the effort.

If the milk is filthy, boiling or pasteurizing does not remove the dirt. Gauthier says of pasteurization: "Sometimes it is heated up to 70 degrees with pressure of carbonic acid. But even in this case pasteurization does not destroy all germs, particularly those of tuberculosis, peptonizing bacteria of cowdung, and the dust of houses and streets, etc."

Even boiling does not kill the spores of bacteria unless it is continued until the milk is rendered entirely unfit for food. To kill these spores it is necessary to boil the milk several times. The spores are small round or oval bodies which form within the bacterial envelope when these micro-organisms are subjected to unfavourable conditions.

The spores resist heat and cold that would kill almost any other form of life. When conditions are favourable they develop into bacteria again. After heating, the cream does not rise so quickly nor does it separate so completely as it does in natural milk. This is due to the toughening of the casein in the milk. Heating partly disorganizes the delicately balanced salts contained in the milk.

The result is that they can not be utilized so easily and completely by the body, for the human organism demands its food in an organic state, that is, in the condition built up by vegetation or by animals.

We may consume iron filings and remain anemic, in fact, the effect the iron medication has is to ruin the teeth, digestive organs and other parts of the body as a consequence. But if we partake of such foods as apples, cabbage, lettuce and spinach, the necessary salt is taken into the blood. Heating milk also makes it constipating. True, normal people can take boiled milk without becoming constipated, but how many normal people are there? We are sorely enough afflicted in this way now. Let us have a supply of natural milk or go without it.

It is not my desire to convey the impression that it does any harm to scald or boil milk occasionally, but if done daily it does harm, especially to the young. Scalded milk has its proper place in dietetics. Occasionally we find a person who has persistent chronic diarrhaea. If he is in condition to eat anything, this annoying affliction is usually overcome in a reasonable time if the patient will take boiled or scalded milk in moderation three times a day, and nothing else except water. How are we to obtain good milk? We can do it by using common sense, care and cleanliness.

It is well to remember that there are bacteria in all ordinary milk, and that if the milk is from healthy cows and is kept clean and cold these bacteria are harmless. Most of them are the lactic acid bacteria, which change the milk sugar into acid. When the milk has attained a certain degree of acidity, the lactic acid bacteria are unable to thrive and the souring process is slowed up and finally stopped. Most of the other bacteria in milk perish when lactic acid is formed.

This is why stale sweet milk is often harmful, when the same kind of milk allowed to sour can be taken with impunity. If the milk is kept in a cold place the bacteria multiply slowly. If it is kept in a warm place they increase in numbers at a rate that is marvelous, and consequently the milk sours much sooner. Even if the milk is kept cold, bacterial growth will soon take place, but it will perhaps not be lactic acid bacteria. It may be a form that causes the milk to become ropy and slimy or one that gives it a bad odour.

Bacteria are like other forms of vegetation, such as grass, weeds, flowers and trees, in that some flourish best under one condition and others under dissimilar conditions, and they struggle one against the other for subsistence and existence. Like flowers there are thousands of different forms of bacteria and they vary according to their food and environment. Peculiar odours in milk generally come from certain kinds of food given to the cows, such as turnips; from bacterial action; or from flavours absorbed from other foods or from odours in the air. Milk should not be exposed to odourous substances, for it becomes tainted very quickly.

Sometimes yeast finds its way into milk and causes decomposition of the sugar with the formation of carbon dioxide and alcohol. A count of the bacteria in milk often serves a good purpose, for it shows whether it is good and has had proper care. The consumers have a right to demand milk low in bacteria, for if no preservatives have been used, that means clean milk. If we could live in our pristine state of beatific bliss, if such it was, we would not have to use milk after childhood is past, but our present condition demands the use of easily digested foods and to many milk is almost a necessity.

The milk in the udder of a healthy cow is almost surely free from bacteria, but the moment it is exposed to the air these little beings start to drop into the fluid. The bacterial standards given by various city health departments vary. Those who are mathematically inclined may find the following figures interesting: In some great cities they allow 500,000 bacteria to the cubic centimetre of milk.

A cubic centimetre contains about twenty-five drops. In other words, they allow 20,000 bacteria per drop. This may seem very lively milk, but these bacteria are so small that about 25,000 of them laid end to end measure only about an inch, and it would take 17,000,000,000,000 of them to weigh an ounce, according to estimates. These are the tiny vegetables we hear and read so much about, that we are warned against and fear so much.

Truly the pygmies are having their innings and making cowards of men. The bacteria multiply by the simple process of growing longer and splitting into two, fission, as it is called, and the process is so rapid that within an hour or two after being formed a bacterium may be raising a family of its own. Some of the milk brought to the cities contains as many as 15,000,000 bacteria per cubic centimeter, that is, about 600,000 per drop. This milk is either very filthy or it has been poorly cared for and should not be given to babies and young children. The filthiest milk may contain several billion bacteria to the cubic centimetre. By using care milk containing but 100, or even fewer, bacteria per drop can be produced.

From the standpoint of cleanliness this is excellent milk. Of course, the dairyman who takes pride enough in his work to produce such milk will sell nothing but what is first-class, and if he has business acumen he can always get more than the market price for his product.

The talk about germs has been overdone, but no one can deny that the study of bacteriology has made people more careful about foods. The filthy dairies that were the rule a few years ago are slowly being replaced by dairies that are comfortable, well lighted and clean. Do not allow the germs to scare you, for if ordinary precautions are taken no more of them will be present than are necessary, and they are necessary.

They thrive best in filth, and they are dangerous only to those who live so that they have no resistance. Wholesome milk can be produced only by healthy animals.

Bovine health can be secured by the same means as human health. The cows must be properly fed and housed. They must have both ventilation and light. They must not be unduly worried. If a nursing of an angry mother's milk is at times poisonous enough to kill a baby, you may be sure that the milk from an abused, irritated and angry cow is also injurious.

If the animals are kept comfortable and happy they will do the best producing, both in quality and quantity. It may sound far-fetched to some to advocate keeping animals happy in order to get them to produce much and give quality products, but it is good science and good sense. Happy cows give more and better milk than the mistreated ones. The singing hens are the best layers. Cows should have fresh green food all the year, and this can be obtained in winter time by using silage.

It is a mistake to give cows too much of concentrated foods, such as oil meals and grains. Cattle cannot long remain well on exclusive rations of too heating and stimulating foods. When fed improperly they soon fall prey to various diseases, such as rheumatism and tuberculosis. It is the same with other domestic animals.

The horse when overfed on grain develops stiff joints. The hogs that are compelled to live exclusively on concentrated, heating rations are liable to die of cholera.

Young turkeys that have nothing but corn and wheat to eat die in great numbers from the disease known as blackhead. It is the same law running all through nature, applying to the high and to the low, that improper nourishment brings disease and death. When cattle roam wild, the green grasses are their principal source of food. Man should be careful not to deviate too much, for forced feeding is as harmful to animals as it is to man.

The following excellent recommendations for the care of milk are given by Dr. Charles E. North of the New York City Milk Commission:

- "No coolers, aerators, straining cloths or strainers should be used.
- "The hot milk should be taken to the creamery as soon as possible.
- "The night's milk should be placed in spring or iced water higher than the milk on the inside of the can. It should not be stirred, and the top of the can should be open a little way to permit ventilation.
- "The milking pails and cans will be sterilized and dried at the creamery, and should be carefully protected until they are used.
- "Brush the udder and wipe with a clean cloth; wash with clean water and dry with a clean towel.
- "Whitewash the cow stable at least twice yearly.
- "Feed no dusty feed until after milking.
- "Remove all manure from cow stable twice daily.
- "Keep barnyard clean and have manure pile at least 100 feet from the stable.
- "Have all stable floors of cement, properly drained.
- "Have abundant windows in cowstables to permit sunlight to reach the floor.
- "Arrange a proper system of ventilation.
- "Do not use milk from any cows suspected of gargot or of any udder inflammation. Such milk contains enormous numbers of bacteria.
- "Brush and groom cows from head to foot as horses are groomed.
- "Use no dusty bedding; wood shavings or sawdust give least dust.
- "Use an abundance of ice in water tank for cooling milk."

Perhaps some will take issue with the doctor on the first paragraph of his recommendation. If straining cloths are used they should be well rinsed in tepid water, washed and then boiled. However, if his recommendations are carried out in letter and spirit no straining is necessary.

Herr Klingelhofer near Dusseldorf, Germany, runs a model dairy. The cows, stables, milkers, containers, in fact, all things connected with the dairy are scrupulously clean. The milkers do not even touch the milk stools, carrying them strapped to their backs. The milk is strained through sterilized cotton and cooled.

The cows are six and seven years old and are milked for ten or twelve months and they are not bred during this time. The first part of the milk drawn from each teat is not used, for that part is not clean, containing dirt and bacteria. This milk is practically free from bacteria, for without adding preservatives it will remain sweet, for as long as thirteen days.

It ordinary milk fails to sour in two or three days it shows that it has been treated. According to the Country Gentleman, it will cost from one cent and a quarter to one cent and three-quarters extra per quart to produce clean milk. Healthy adults can take milk teeming with bacteria without harm, but for babies it is best to have very few or none in the milk. At Dusseldorf the babies used to die as they do here when fed unclean milk.

Herr Klingelhofer says that when fed on his product "sterben keine". This is submitted to those who advocate pasteurizing the milk. Denatured milk makes sickly babies. Clean natural milk makes healthy babies. The extra cost of less than two cents a quart is not prohibitive. Most fathers, no matter how poor, waste more than that daily on tobacco and alcoholics.

The extra cost would be more than saved in lessened doctor bills, to say nothing of funeral expenses. The recompense that comes from the satisfaction of having thriving, sturdy, healthy children can not be figured in dollars and cents. Dr. Robert Mond, of London, after investigating for years, has come to the cease that sterilized milk predisposes to tuberculosis, instead of preventing it. He believes that milk so treated is so inferior that he would not personally use it. That sterilized milk predisposes to tuberculosis, as well as to other diseases which can attack the body only when it is run down, is natural.

Any food that has been rendered inferior can not build the robust health that comes to those who live on natural food. Adults who use sterilized milk should counteract its bad effects by partaking liberally of fresh fruits and vegetables. If the milk is clean, put into clean containers by careful milkers and is then kept cold until delivered, it will reach the consumers in good condition. Do not let the fact that when you consume a glass of milk you are also engulfing some millions of bacteria bother you, for bacteria are necessary to our existence. If all the bacteria on earth should perish, it would also mean the end of the human race.

Today the progressive farmer is coming to the fore. He is a man who is justly proud of his work, so it will probably not be long before all city people who desire clean milk can get it. The milk cure consists in feeding sick people on nothing but milk for varying periods. Generally the patient is told to either take great quantities three or four times a day, or to take smaller quantities perhaps every half hour. The milk cure has no special virtue, except that it is a monotonous diet.

The body soon rebels if forced to subsist on an excessive amount of but one kind of food. The individual loses his desire for food and even becomes nauseated. If the advocates of the milk cure would prescribe milk in moderation, instead of in excess, they would have better success. The benefit derived from the milk cure comes from the simplicity, not from the milk. A grape cure, an orange cure or a bread and milk cure would be as beneficial. The milk cure is ancient. It was employed twenty-five centuries ago.

"Clabbered Milk"

Clabbered milk or sour milk needs no special preparation. Put the milk into an earthen or china dish. Do not use metal dishes, for the lactic acid acts upon various metals. Cover the dish so as to keep particles of matter in the air away, but the covering is not to be airtight. Put the dish in a warm place, but not in the sun. Milk that sours in the sun or in an air-tight bottle is generally of poor flavour. Clabbered milk is a good food. It does not form big, tough curds in the stomach, it is easy to digest, and the lactic acid helps to keep the alimentary tract sweet. The various forms of milk may be used in similar combinations.

"Buttermilk"

The real buttermilk is what remains of the cream after the fat has been removed by churning. It is slightly acid and has a characteristic taste, to most people very agreeable. The flavour is different from that of artificially made buttermilk. In composition it is almost like whole milk, except that it contains very little fat. Many people make buttermilk by beating the clabbered milk thoroughly, until it becomes light. The buttermilk made from sweet milk and the various brands of bacterial ferments obtainable at the drug stores is all right.

These ferments have as their basis the lactic acid bacteria, and if the manufacturers wish to call their germs by other names, such as Bacillus Bulgaricus, no harm is done. It is unnecessary to add any of these ferments, for the milk clabbers about as quickly without them. Buttermilk is an excellent food. The casein can be seen in fine flakes in the real buttermilk. Adults usually digest buttermilk and clabbered milk more easily than the sweet milk. The lactic acid seems to be quite beneficial. Metchnikoff thought for a while that he had discovered how to ward off decay and old age by means of the lactic acid bacteria in milk. Milk can be clabbered quickly by adding lemon juice to sweet milk.

"Junket"

Add rennet to milk and let it stand until it thickens. The milk is not to be disturbed while coagulation takes place, for agitation will cause a separation of the whey. The rennet can be bought at the drug stores. "Whey" contains milk sugar, some salts, and a little albumin. It is easily digested, but not very nourishing. It is what is left of the milk after the fat and almost all of the protein are removed.

"Cottage Cheese"

This is sometimes called Dutch cheese or white cheese. It is a delicious and nutritious dairy product that is easy to digest. Put the clabbered milk in a muslin bag, hang tha bag up and allow th milk to lose its whey through drainage. In summer this bag must be kept in a cool place. After draining, beat the curds.

Then add enough clabbered milk to make the curds soft when well beaten. A small amount of cream may also be added. Cottage cheese made in this way is superior in flavour and digestibility to that which has been scalded. No seasoning is needed. A little salt is allowable, but sugar and pepper should not be used. Fruit and cottage cheese make a satisfying as well as nutritious meal. Delicious cottage cheese is also made by using the whole clabbered milk.

Hang it up to drain in a bag until it has lost a part of its whey. Then beat it until the curds are rather small, but not fine. No milk or cream is to be added to this, for it contains all the fat that is in the whole milk. Do not drain this cheese so long that it becomes dry.

"Other Cheeses"

The various cheeses on the market are made principally from ripened curds, with which more or less fat has been mixed. The ripening is a form of decay, and it is no exaggeration to say that some of the very ripe cheeses on the market are rotten. The flavours are due to ferments, moulds and bacteria, which split up the proteins and the fats.

The mild cheeses are generally good and may be eaten with fruits or vegetables or with bread. Two or three ounces are sufficient for the protein part of the meal, taking the place of flesh. Use less if less is desired. When cheese becomes very odourous and ripe, no one with normal nose and palate will eat it. People who partake of excessive amounts of meats or alcoholic beverages are often fond of these foul cheeses. One perversion leads to another.

Cheese of good quality, eaten in moderation, is a nutritious food, easily digested. Gauthier says of cheese: "Indeed, this casein, which has the composition of muscular tissue, scarcely produces during digestion either residue or toxins." Because good cheese is concentrated and of agreeable flavour, it is necessary to guard against overeating. An excess of rich cheese soon causes trouble with the liver or constipation or both.

Cheese should not be eaten in the same meal with fish, meat, eggs, nuts or legumes, for such combining makes the protein intake too great. There is nothing incompatible about such combinations, but it is safest not to make them. The course dinners, ending up with a savory cheese, crackers and coffee, are abominations. They are health-destroyers. They lead to overeating. As nearly everybody overeats, and because overeating is the greatest single factor in producing disease and premature death, it is advisable not to eat cheese and other foods rich in protein in the same meal. The greater the variety of food, the more surely the diner will overeat. The term,"full cream cheese" is misleading, for cheeses are not made of whole cream. The cream does not contain enough protein for the manufacture of cheese. Some cheeses are made of skimmed milk. Others are made of milk which contains part, or even all, of the cream. Some have cream added. The cheeses containing but a moderate amount of fat are the best.

The popular Roquefort cheese is made of a mixture of goat's milk and sheep's milk. The savor is due to bacterial action and fat saponification, which result in ammonia, glycerine, alcohol, fatty acids and other chemicals in very small quantities. The peculiar colourings which run in streaks through some cheeses that are well ripened are due to molds, bacteria and yeasts.

Gentlemen who would discharge the cook if a moldy piece of bread appeared on the table, eat decaying, moldy cheese with relish. The best cheese of all is cottage cheese. People of normal taste will soon weary of the frequent consumption of strong cheese, but they can take cottage cheese every other day with relish. Occasionally put a few caraway seeds in it if this flavour is agreeable.

Cottage cheese may be eaten plain or with bread, or with fruit or vegetables. It may be used as dressing both on fruit and vegetable salads. Cheese should play no part in the alimentation of the sick, with the exception of cottage cheese, which may be given to almost anyone who is in condition to eat anything. The other cheeses are too concentrated for sick people. In acute disease nothing is to be fed.

"Skimmed Milk"

It is about the same in composition as buttermilk. It is inferior in flavour, but a good food. It is used a great deal in cooking. Milk should not be used very much in cooking. When cooked it does not digest very readily and it has a tendency to make other foods indigestible."Sour cream" or clabbered cream is best when it is taken from clabbered milk. It may be used as dressing on fruits and salads. Sweet cream will clabber, but it is not as delicious as when it clabbers on the milk."Clotted cream" is made by putting the milk aside in pans in a cool place until the cream rises. Then, without disturbing the cream, scald the milk. Put the pan aside until the contents are cold and remove the cream, which has a rich, agreeable flavour.

This may be used as a dressing. Whipped cream and ice cream are so familiar that they hardly need comment. Cream is such a rich food that it must be eaten in moderation.

Otherwise it will cause discomfort and disease. Ice cream is made of milk and cream, in varying proportions, flavoured to taste and frozen. It is not necessary to add eggs and cornstarch. If eaten slowly it is a good food, but taken in too large quantities and too rapidly it may cause digestive troubles. It is not best to chill the stomach. Those with weak digestion should be very careful not to do so. Buttermilk is sometimes flavoured and frozen. This ice is easy to digest. Some doctors recommend this dish to their convalescents. It is an agreeable change, and can be eaten by many who are unable to take care of the rich ice cream.

DRINK

There is but one real beverage and that is water. The other so-called beverages are foods, stimulants or sedatives. Milk is a rich food, one glass having as much food value as two eggs. Coffee, tea, chocolate and cocoa are stimulants, with sedative after-effects. Their food value depends largely on the amount of milk, cream and sugar put into them. Chocolate and cocoa are both drugs and foods. Alcohol is a stimulant at first, afterwards a sedative, and at all times an anaesthetic. When we think of drinking for the sake of supplying the bodily need of fluid, we should think of water and nothing else. If other liquids are taken, they should be taken as foods or drugs. Water is the best solvent known.

The alchemists of old spent much time and energy trying to find the universal solvent, believing that thereafter it would be easy to discover a method of making base metals noble. But they never found anything better than water. Water is the compound that in its various forms does most to change the earth upon which we live, and it is more necessary for the continuation of life than anything else except air. Pure water does not exist in nature, that is, we have never found a compound of the composition H2O. Water always contains other matter.

The various salts are dissolved in it and it absorbs gases. The nearest we come to pure water is distilled. Pure water is an unsatisfied compound, and as soon as it is exposed it begins to absorb gases and take up salts and organic matter. Pure water differs from clean water. Clean or potable water is a compound which contains a moderate amount of salts, but very little of organic matter. Bacteria should be practically absent. Water that contains much of nitrogenous substances is unfit to use.

If the water is very hard, heavily loaded with salts, it should not be used extensively as a drink, for if too much of earthy and mineral matter is taken into the system, the body is unable to get rid of all of them. The result is a tendency for deposits to form in the body. In places where the water is excessively charged with lime it has been noticed that the bones harden too early, which prevents full development of the body.

If the bones of the skull are involved, it means that there will not be room enough for the brain. Such diseases are rare in this country, but in parts of Europe they are not uncommon. If the water is very hard, a good plan is to distill it and then add a little of the hard water to the distilled water. People who partake of an excessive amount of various salts can perhaps drink distilled water to advantage, but those who take but a normal amount of the salts in their foods should have natural water. Water forms three-fourths of the human body, more or less. It is needed in every process that goes on within the body. "To be dry is to die."

Water keeps the various vital fluids in solution so that they can perform their function. Without water there would be no sense of taste, no digestion, no absorption of food, no excretion of debris, and hence no life. The water is the vehicle through which the nutritive elements are distributed to the billions of cells of the body, and it is also the vehicle which carries the waste to the various excretory organs.

We can live several weeks without food, but only a few days without water. Hot water and ice-cold water are both irritants. Water may be taken either warm or cool. It is best to avoid the extremes. The amount of water needed each twenty-four hours varies according to circumstances. Two quarts is a favourite prescription. Those who eat freely of succulent fruits and vegetables do not need as much as those who live more on dry foods. Salt in excess calls for an abnormal amount of water, for salt is a diuretic, robbing the tissues of their fluids and consequently more water has to be taken to keep up the equilibrium.

Naturally, more water is required when the weather is hot than when it is cool. On hot days warm water is more satisfying and quenches thirst more quickly than ice water. Warm water also stimulates kidney action, which is often sluggish in summer. Ice water is the least satisfactory of all, for the more one drinks the more he wants. A normal body calls for what water it needs, and no more. An abnormal body is no guide for either the amount of food or drink necessary. Many people do not like the taste of water, especially in the morning.

This means that the body is diseased. To a normal person cool water is always agreeable when it is needed, and it is needed in the morning. People with natural taste do not care for ice water, but other water is relished. The common habit of drinking with meals is a mistake. Man is the only animal that does this, and he has to pay dearly for such errors. Taking a bite of food and washing it down with fluid lead to undermastication and overeating, and then the body suffers from autointoxication. A mouthful of food followed by a swallow of liquid forces the contents of the mouth into the stomach before the saliva has the opportunity to act.

The best way is to drink one or two glasses of water in the morning before breakfast. Partake of the breakfast, and all other meals, without taking any liquid. Sometimes there is a desire for a drink immediately after the meal is finished. If so, take some water slowly. If it is taken slowly a little will satisfy. If it is gulped down it may be necessary to take one or two glasses of water before being satisfied. Those who have a tendency to drink too much during warm weather will find very slow drinking helpful in correcting it. If there is any digestive weakness, the liquid taken immediately after a meal should be warm and should not exceed a cupful. Those with robust digestion may take cool water.

Cold water chills the stomach. Digestion will not take place until the stomach has reached the temperature of about one hundred degrees Fahrenheit again, and if the stomach contents are chilled repeatedly the tendency is strong for the food to ferment pathologically, instead of being properly digested. For this reason it is not well to drink while there is anything left in the stomach to digest.

As stomach digestion generally takes two or three hours at least, it is well to wait this long before taking water after finishing a meal, and then drink all that is desired until within thirty minutes of taking the next meal. If the thirst should become very insistent before two or three hours have elapsed since eating, take warm water. Those who eat food simply prepared and moderately seasoned are not troubled much with excessive thirst. Two quarts of water daily should be sufficient for the adults under ordinary conditions. Here, as in eating, no exact amount will fit everybody. Make a habit of drinking at least a glass of water before breakfast, cleaning the teeth and rinsing the mouth before swallowing any, and then take what water the body asks for during the rest of the day. Taking too much water is not as injurious as overeating, but waterlogging the body has a weakening effect.

To drink with the meals is customary, not because it is necessary, but because we have a number of drinks which appeal to many people. Water is the drink par excellence. A food-beverage that is used by many is cambric tea, which is made of hot water, one-third or one-fourth of milk and a little sweetening. Children generally like this on account of the sweetness. It may be taken with any meal, when fluid is needed, but the amount should be limited to a cupful. It is not well to dilute the digestive juices too much.

The water taken in the morning helps to start the body to cleanse itself. Water drinking is a great aid in overcoming constipation. Constipated people generally overeat. Less food and more water will prove helpful in overcoming the condition. Unfortunately for the race, we have accustomed ourselves to partake of beverages containing injurious, poisonous substances. Inasmuch as this is the place to discuss the drugs contained in coffee and tea, we shall take the liberty of dwelling upon other habit-forming substances.

They are all a part of the drug addictions of the race. For scientific discussion of these various substances we refer you to technical works. Coffee, tea and chocolate contain a poisonous alkaloid which is generally called caffeine. The theine in tea and the theobromine in cocoa are so similar to caffeine that chemists can not differentiate them. These drinks when first taken cause a gentle stimulation under which more work can be done than ordinarily, but this is followed by a reaction, and then the powers of body and mind wane so much that the average output of work is less than when the body is not stimulated. The temporary apparently beneficial effect is more than offset by the reaction and therefore partaking of these beverages makes people inefficient. Coffee is very hard on the nerves, causing irritation, which is always followed by premature physical degeneration. Experiments of late indicate that children who use coffee do not come up to the physical and mental standard of those who abstain. The effect on the adults is not so marked because adults are more stable than children.

Those who are not used to coffee will be unable to sleep for several hours after partaking of a cup. Some people drink so much of it that they become accustomed to it. Coffee is not generally looked upon as one of the habit-forming drugs, but it is. However, of all the drugs which create a craving in the system for a repetition of the dose, coffee makes the lightest fetters.

It is surprising how often health-seekers inform the adviser that they "can not get along without coffee". If they would take a cup a few times a year, it would do no harm, but the daily use is harmful to all, even if they feel no bad effects and make it "very weak," which is a favourite statement of the women. Smoking, drinking beer and drinking coffee have a tendency to overcome constipation in those who are not accustomed to these things, but their action can not be depended upon for any length of time and the cure is worse than the disease. Tea drinking has much the same effect as coffee drinking, except that it is decidedly constipating. Perhaps this is because there is considerable of the astringent tannin in the tea leaves.

Chocolate is a valuable food. Those who eat of other aliments in moderation may partake of chocolate without harm, but if chocolate is used in addition to an excess of other food, the results are bad. The chocolate is so rich that it soon overburdens some of the organs of digestion, especially the liver. The Swiss consume much of this food and it is valuable in cases where it is necessary to carry concentrated rations.

Alcohol in some form seems to have been consumed by even very primitive people as far back as history goes. The Bible records an early case of intoxication from wine, and beer was brewed by the ancient Egyptians.

So much has been consumed that some people have a subconscious craving for it. There are cases on record where the very first drink caused an uncontrollable demand for the drug. Fortunately these cases are very rare. Alcohol is really not a stimulant, though it gives a feeling of glow, warmth and well-being at first, but this is followed by a great lowering of physical power, which gives rise to disagreeable sensations. Then the drinker needs more alcohol to stimulate him again. Then there is another depression with renewed demand: There is no end to the craving for the drug once it has mastered the individual. The lungs, heart, digestive organs, muscles, in fact, every structure in the body loses working capacity. Alcohol seems to have a special affinity for nervous tissue. A glass of beer or wine taken daily is no more harmful than a cup of coffee per day, but the coffee drinker does not make of himself such a public nuisance and menace as the man often does who drinks alcohol to excess. Formerly, it was respectable to drink. Some of our most noted public men were drunkards. Now a drunkard could not maintain himself in a prominent public position very long. To drink like a gentleman was no disgrace. Now real gentlemen do not get drunk.

In backward Russia they are becoming alarmed about the inroads of vodka, and are trying to decrease its consumption. France is trying to teach total abstinence to its young men because it disqualifies so many of them from military service to drink. Scandinavia is temperance territory. The German Kaiser has recently given a warning against drinking. The United States discourages drinking in the army and navy. Field armies are not supplied with alcoholics. Drinking is becoming disreputable.

It is very difficult to prove the harm done by excessive drinking of tea and coffee, also by the use of much tobacco, even if we do know that it is so. Everyone knows something about the deleterious effect of alcohol upon the consumer. Solomon wrote: "Wine is a mocker, strong drink is raging, and whosoever is deceived thereby is not wise. Who hath wounds without cause? Who hath redness of eyes?" Alcohol permanently impairs both body and mind. Depending on how much is taken, it may cause various ills, ranging from inflammation of the stomach to insanity. It reduces the power of the mind to concentrate and it diminishes the ability of the muscles to work. It reduces the resistance of the body and shortens life. Its first effect is to lull the higher faculties to sleep.

Most drunkards do not recover from their disease, for drunkenness is a disease. The various drugs given to cure the afflictions are delusions. Strengthening the body, mind and the will and instilling higher ideals are the best methods of cure. Suggestive therapeutics, and the awakening of a strong resolve for a better life are powerful aids. Proper feeding should not be overlooked, for bad habits do not flourish in a healthy body.

Civilization necessitates self-control and considerable self-denial. Those who go in the line of least resistance are on the road to destruction. It is often necessary to overcome habits which produce temporary gratification of the senses. Warden Tynan of the Colorado Penitentiary, 96 per cent of the prisoners are brought there because they use alcohol. It is also well known that moral lapses are most common when the will is weakened through the use of liquor.

Those who have the welfare of the race at heart are therefore compelled to give considerable thought to this subject. Past experience, it will not help to try to legislate sobriety into the people. Education and industrialism are the factors which it seems to me will be most potent in solving the alcohol problem. Morality, which in the last analysis is a form of selfishness, will teach many that it is poor policy to reduce one's efficiency and thereby reduce the earning capacity and enjoyment of life.

More and more the employers of labour will realise that the use of alcohol decreases the reliability and worth of the worker. Many will take steps like the following: "In formal recognition of the fact, established beyond dispute by the tests of the new psychology, that industrial efficiency decreases with indulgence in alcohol and is increased by abstinence from it, the managers of a manufacturing establishment in Chester, Penn., have attacked the temperance problem from a new angle. "Unlike many railways and some other corporations, they do not forbid their employees to drink, but they offer 10 per cent advance in wages to all who will take and keep—the teetotaler's pledge. Incidentally, a breaking of the promise will mean a permanent severance of relations, but there is no emphasizing of that point, it being confidently expected that the advantage of perfect sobriety will be as well realised on one side as on the other."

Business has during the past two centuries been the great civilizer, the great moral teacher. It has found that honesty and righteousness pay and that injustice is folly. Business has led the way to the acceptance of a new ethics, and new morals. What has been said about alcohol applies to tobacco in a much smaller degree. The use of tobacco seems to lead to the use of alcohol. It retards the development of children. It is surely one of the causes of various diseases. Tobacco heart, sore throat and indigestion are well known to physicians. Tobacco contains one of the deadliest of poisons known. One- sixteenth of a grain of nicotine may prove fatal. The reason there are so few deaths from acute tobacco poisoning is that but very little of the nicotine is absorbed. Men who chew tobacco make themselves disagreeable to others. Smoking of cigarettes is to be condemned not only because it poisons the body, but causes inattention and inability to concentrate on the part of the smoker, as well.

Every little while he feels the desire to take a smoke, and if smoking is forbidden he devises means of getting away. He robs his employer of time for which he is paid and injures himself. The ability to work is decreased by indulgence in smoking. Recent experiments show that for a short time there is increased activity after a smoke, but the following depression is greater than the stimulation, so there is an actual loss.

A few years ago, according to Mr. Wilson, who was then Secretary of Agriculture, there were about 4,000,000 drug addicts or "dope fiends" in the United States. Without doubt this estimate was too high, for the proportion of addicts in the country is not as great as in the large cities. The drugs chiefly used are cocaine, opium, laudanum, morphine and heroin. These drugs are much more destructive than alcohol. Cocaine and heroin are the worst. It is very difficult to stop using any of them once the habit has been formed. Nearly every "fiend" dies directly or indirectly from the effect of his particular drug. Every one weakens the body so that there is not much resistance to offer to acute diseases. Every one destroys the will power so that a cure is exceedingly difficult.

It is well to bear in mind that all are not possessed of strong enough will power to resist their cravings and that some take to cocaine when they can not get liquor. Cocaine is far worse than alcohol.

People should be very careful about taking patent medicines. There is no excuse for taking them. The most popular ones have as their basis one of the habit-forming drugs. Most of the soothing syrups contain opium in some form. To give babies opiates is a grave error, to speak mildly. It weakens the child, may lay the foundation for a deadly habit later in life, and often an overdose kills outright. Well informed mothers avoid such drugs and keep their children reasonably quiet by means of proper care. Many of the remedies for nasal catarrh and hay fever contain much cocaine. Cocaine is an astringent and a painkiller and people mistake the temporary lessening of discharge from the nose and disappearance of pain for curative effects. But there is nothing curative about it. In a short time the mucous membrane relaxes again and then the discharge is re-established. The nerves which were put out of commission resume their function and then the pain reappears.

Opium or one of its derivatives is generally present in the patent medicines given for coughs. Opium is also an astringent and will suppress secretions, but this is not a cure. Excessive secretions are an indication that the body is surcharged with poison and food. Let them escape and then live so that there will be internal cleanliness and then there will be no more coughs and colds.

The unfortunate people who get into the habit of using these drugs degenerate physically, mentally and morally. They need more and more of their drug to produce the desired effect until they at last take enough daily to kill several normal men. Sometimes they are able to keep everybody in ignorance of what they are doing for years. They develop slyness and secretiveness.

They become very suspicious. They are nearly always untruthful, and those who deal with them are surprised and wonder why those who used to be open and above-board now are furtive and dishonest. They often lie when there is not the slightest excuse for it. The moral disintegration is often the first sign noticed. After habitually using any of these drugs for a while the body demands the continuation and if the victim is deprived of his accustomed portion there will be a collapse with intense suffering. Every tortured nerve in the body seems to call out for the drug. The victim will do anything to get his drug. He will lie, steal, and he may even attack those who are caring for him. For the time being he is insane. Many professional men use cocaine. It is a favourite with writers. It often shows in their work. Those who write under the inspiration of this drug often do some good work, but they are unable to keep to their subject. Their writings lack order. We have enough of such writings to have them classified as "cocaine literature". If there are 4,000,000, or even fewer, of these people in our land, it is a serious problem, for every one is a degenerate, to a certain degree. If the medical profession and the druggists would cooperate it would be easy enough to prevent the growth of a new crop of dope fiends. Of course, people would have to stop taking patent medicines, which often start the victims on the road to degeneration.

Then the physicians should stop prescribing habit-forming drugs, as well as all other drugs, and teach the people that physical, mental and moral salvation come through right living and right thinking. Unfortunately the medical profession is careless and is responsible for the existence of many of the drug addicts. A patient has a severe pain. What is the easiest way to satisfy him? To give a hypodermic injection of some opiate. The patient, not realizing the danger, demands a pain-killer every time he suffers. He soon learns what he is getting and then he goes to the drug store and outfits himself with a hypodermic outfit and drugs, and the first thing he knows he is a slave, in bondage for life.

This is no exaggeration. There are hundreds of thousands of victims to the drug habit who trace their downfall to the treatment received at the hands of reputable physicians, who do not look upon their practice with the horror it should inspire because it is so common. Doctors do not always bury their mistakes. Some of them walk about for years.

In spite of laws against the sale of various drugs, they can be obtained. There are doctors and druggists of easy conscience who are very accommodating, for a price. There is no legitimate need for the use of one- hundredth of the amount of these drugs that is now consumed. A local injection of cocaine for a minor operation is justifiable, but none of the habit-forming drugs should be used in ordinary practice to kill pain, for the proper application of water in conjunction with right living will do it better and there are no evil after effects. Massage is often sufficient.

To show a little more clearly how some people become addicted to drugs, let us consider one of the latest, heroin: A few years ago this drug, which is an opium derivative, was practically unknown. It is much stronger than morphine and consequently the effect can be obtained more quickly by means of a smaller dose. Physicians thought at first that it was not a habit-forming drug, for they could use it over a longer period of time than they could employ morphine, without establishing the craving and the habit.

So they began to prescribe heroin instead of morphine, and many a morphine addict was advised to substitute heroin. All went well for a short while, until the victims found that they were enslaved by a drug that was even worse than morphine. Now, thanks chiefly to the medical profession, it is estimated that we have in our land several hundred thousand heroin addicts. Sallow of face, gaunt of figure, looking upon the world through pin-point pupils, with all of life's beauty, hope and joy gone, they are marching to premature death.

The medical profession furnishes more than its proportion of drug addicts. They know the danger of the drugs, but familiarity breeds contempt. If the public but knew how many of their medical advisers, who should always be clear-minded, are befuddled by drugs, there would be a great awakening. One eminent physician who has now been in practice about forty-five years and has had much experience with drug addicts, has said that according to his observations, about one physician in four contracts the drug habit. I believe this is exaggerated, but I am acquainted with a number of physicians who are addicts. Physicians who smoke do not condemn the practice. Those who drink are likely to prescribe beer and wine for their patients. Those who are addicted to drugs use them too liberally in their practice. Those who have watched the effects of the various drugs, from coffee to heroin, must condemn their use. It is true that an occasional cup of coffee or tea, a glass of wine or beer does no harm. A cigarette a week would not hurt a boy, nor would on occasional cigar harm a man.

But how many people are willing to indulge occasionally? The rule is that they indulge not only daily, but several times a day, and the results are bad. One bad habit leads to another, and the time always comes when it is a choice between disease and early death on one hand, and the giving up of the bad habits on the other, and when this time comes the bonds of habits are often so strong that the victim is unable to break them. We realise that knowledge will not always keep people out of temptation and that some individuals will take the broad way that leads to destruction in spite of anything that may be said. Youth is impatient of restraint and ever anxious for new experiences.

Regarding this serious matter of destructive drug use, much could be done by teaching people their place in society: That is, what they owe to themselves, their families and the public in general. In other words, teach the young people the higher selfishness, part of which consists of considerable self-control, self-denial and self-respect. Drugs are too easy to obtain today. Some day people will be so enlightened that they will not allow themselves to be medicated. This is the trend of the times. Until such a time comes, society should protect itself by making it very difficult to get any of the habit-forming drugs. If necessary, the free hand of the physician should be stayed. Much of the confidence blindly given him is misplaced.

SLEEP

A young baby should sleep almost all the time, and it will if intelligently cared for. Overfeeding is the bane of the baby's life and is the cause of most of its restlessness. The first few months the baby should be awake enough to take its food, and then go to sleep again. As it grows older it sleeps less and less. There is no fixed time for an adult to sleep. The amount varies with different individuals. The idea is quite prevalent that eight hours nightly are necessary.

This may be true for some. Many do very well on seven hours' sleep, and even less. The great inventor, Thomas Edison, is said to have had but very little sleep for many years, and it is reported that when interested in some problem he would miss a night or two. Yet he has lived longer than the average individual and is now in good health. Very few have done as much constructive work as he. Many other prominent people have been light sleepers.

As people grow older they require less sleep than they did in youth. It is not uncommon for septuagenarians to sleep but five hours nightly. Although we can not say how much sleep any individual may require, each person can find out for himself, and this is much better than to try to live by rules, which are often erroneous. Those who live as they should otherwise and select a definite hour for retiring and adhere to it, except on special occasions, get all the sleep that is necessary. They awake in the morning refreshed, ready to do a good day's work. During sound sleep all conscious endeavors cease. The vital organs do only enough work to keep the body alive. The breathing is lighter, the circulation is slower and in sound sleep there is no thinking.

This letting up in the great activity of body and mind gives an opportunity for the millions of cells, of which the body is composed, to take from the blood what is needed to restore them to normal. During the day many of these cells become worn and weary. At night they recuperate. Hence undisturbed sleep is very important. Many believe that "early to bed and early to rise" is the proper way, that the hours of sleep before midnight are more refreshing and invigourating than those after. This is merely a belief, perhaps a good one. Early retiring leads to regularity, which is very desirable.

Late retiring often means loose mental and physical habits. Those who are regular about their time of retiring and live well otherwise feel refreshed whether they go to bed early or late. Children should always retire early, otherwise they do not get enough sleep. The night is the natural sleeping time for most creatures, as well as for man. This is a heritage of ages. There was no artificial illumination during the stone age. Man could do nothing during the darkness, so he rested. However, those who must work at night find no trouble in sleeping during the day. The tendency among men is the same as among animals, to sleep more in winter than in summer, not that more sleep is required, but because the winter nights are longer.

Children should go to bed early. They require more sleep than adults because of the greater cell activity. Also, children who stay up late generally become irritable and nervous. It is not well to eat immediately before retiring. The sleep following a late meal is generally interrupted, and there is not that feeling of brightness and clearness of mind, with which one should awake, next morning. Lunching before going to bed is a bad habit. Some believe they must have an apple, or perhaps a glass of milk, before retiring, for they think that this will bring sleep. The body should not be burdened with extra food to digest during the sleeping hours. This time should be dedicated to the restoring of the body, and the blood contains ample material. Dreaming is largely a bad habit. A normal individual rarely dreams, and then generally following some imprudence. Dreams begin in childhood and are then due principally to excessive food intake.

As a producer of nightmares overfeeding has no equal. During adult life dreaming is caused by bad physical and mental conduct, plus the habit which was formed in childhood. Fear, anger, worry, stimulants, too much food, impure air and too warm clothes are some of the causes that produce dreams. Like other bad habits, dreaming is difficult to overcome once it is firmly established. The cure consists in righting one's other bad habits and in not thinking about the dreams.

A sleep that is disturbed by dreams is not as sound as it should be and consequently not as refreshing as normal sleep. The conscious mind is not completely at rest and, the subconscious mind is running riot. Normal sleep is complete unconsciousness. This is the sleep of the just and must be earned. Before retiring all the clothes worn during the day should be removed. The night apparel should be light—cotton, linen or silk. The bed should be comfortable, but not too soft. There should be enough covering to keep the sleeper comfortably warm, but not hot.

Those who cover themselves with so many quilts or blankets that they perspire during the night are not properly refreshed. It prevents sound sleep and makes the skin too sensitive. It reduces a person's resistance to climatic changes. The feet should be kept warm, even if necessary to put artificial heat in the foot of the bed. During cold weather the feet and the legs should have more covering than the rest of the body.

From the waist up the covering should be rather light. Sound sleep is dependent on relaxation of mind and body. Those who live the day over after going to bed do not go to sleep quickly or easily. This habit should be overcome. Do business at the business place, during business hours, if you would have the mind fresh.

There are days so full of cares that the night does not bring mental relaxation, but those who have begun early in life to practice self-control find these days growing fewer as the years roll by. When they learn their true relationship to the rest of humanity, to the universe and to eternity, they are generally willing and able to let the earth rotate and revolve for a few hours without their personal attention. They realise that worry and anxiety waste time and energy. Many complain that they can not sleep. This they repeat to themselves and to others many times a day. At night they ask themselves why they can not sleep. They do it so often that it becomes a powerful negative suggestion frequently strong enough to prevent their going to sleep. It is an obsession. Real insomnia exists only in the mind of the sufferer. Every physician, sooner or later, has experience with people who say that they can not sleep.

The doctors who give such patients sleeping powders or potions make a grave mistake. These drugs are taken at the expense of some of the physical structures, and the day of settlement always comes. Perhaps it will find the patient with bankrupted nerves or a failing heart. To be effective, the size of the dose must be increased from time to time. At last the result will be some disease, either physical or mental.

Those who insist that they "do not sleep at all", or that they sleep "but a few minutes" each night, sleep a few hours, but they make themselves believe that they do not sleep. We are compelled to sleep, and even those who "do not sleep at all" cannot remain awake indefinitely. Those who are troubled with the no-sleep obsession will soon realise that they sleep as well as others if they cease thinking and talking so much about the subject.

We have seen people suffering from this bad habit recover in one week. Those who have been taking drugs to induce sleep generally have a few bad nights when they give them up, after which the nervous storm subsides and sleep becomes normal. All drugs should be discarded. The physician who understands more about the working of nature than about the giving of drugs will have the best success in these cases. Soothing sleep always comes to people possessed of a controlled mind in a healthy body. If the day has been exhausting and the nerves are so alive and wrought up that sleep will not come, do not allow the mind to delve into worry about it.

Do not say to yourself: "I wish I could sleep. Why can't I sleep?" Such fretful thinking produces mental tension, which drives sleep away. Instead, say to yourself: "I am very comfortable. I am having a refreshing rest. It does not matter whether I sleep or not." By all means relax the body. Choose a comfortable position and remain quiet, having the muscles relaxed.

It is remarkable how soon a relaxed body brings tranquility to a disturbed mind. Let a man in pugnacious mood relax his face and his fists and in a very short time his anger vanishes. It makes no difference whether a person sleeps eight hours on a certain night. If he is fairly regular about going to bed he will get enough sleep. Those who realise this truth do not complain of insomnia.

Most people who think much have an occasional night when an idea takes such strong possession of the brain and demands so forcibly to be put into proper shape, that they can not sleep. Under such circumstances it is as well to to get up and work out the idea. Three or four nights like that in the course of a year will do no harm. People rarely sleep well when lying on the back. If the theory of evolution is correct, we were not intended to lie on our backs during sleep. A good position is to lie on the right side, the right leg being anterior to the left, both being flexed. Another position that is restful to many is to lie on the abdomen, the arms extended away from the body.

The breathing should be entirely nasal. It will not be nasal if there is obstruction in the nose. A healthy person who breathes through his mouth at night must use autosuggestion to overcome the habit. He should suggest to himself, "I will breathe through the nose; I will keep my lips together." If he persists in this, closes the mouth when he goes to sleep, in time the mouth- breathing will cease, and with it the disagreeable habit of snoring. At all times the bedroom should be well ventilated. Some people are in the habit of sleeping in unventilated bedrooms, but upon rising in the morning they throw the windows open and give the room a good airing. The ventilation does not do much good except when there is someone in the room. During the day the bedroom could be closed with very little harm ensuing, though it is best to have it sunned and aired as much as possible.

The sleeping porch is excellent. Outdoor sleeping is all right and it is not a modern fad. Where Benjamin Franklin got his information we do not know, but he has this to say about outdoor sleeping: "It is recorded that Methusaleh, who, being the longest liver, may be supposed to have best preserved his health, that he slept always in the open air; for when he had lived five hundred years an angel said to him: 'Arise, Methusaleh, and build thee an house, for thou shalt live five hundred years longer.' But Methusaleh answered, and said: 'If I am to live but five hundred years longer, it is not worth while to build me an house; I will sleep in the air as I have been used to do.'" This may partly account for some of his many years. His alleged conversation with the angel indicates that he was a man of equanimity.

Under ordinary circumstances those who sleep indoors should have one sash of window fully open for each person in the chamber, or more. It is well to have plenty of fresh air, but it is not best to sleep in a draught. When the wind is blowing through the windows it is not necessary to have them wide open, for an aperture of four inches will then give as much fresh air as a sash opening in calmer weather.

It is best to get up promptly upon awakening in the morning. Remaining in bed half asleep is productive of slothfulness. Too much sleeping and dozing make one dull. Those who overeat require more sleep than moderate people. The sluggishness and sleepiness following a too heavy meal are familiar to all.

Animals that do not get food regularly, but are dependent on the vicissitudes of preying for their nourishment, often gorge themselves so that they can not stay awake, but fall into a stupor, which may last for days. Man, who is generally assured of three meals a day, has no excuse for this form of self-abuse, but unfortunately he practices it too often. It is a gross habit, one in which people of refinement will not continue to indulge.

Young children should take a nap each day. They are so active that they need this rest. Adults can with profit take a short nap, not to exceed thirty minutes, after lunch. Those who are nervous owe it to themselves to take a nap. Those who use the brain a great deal will find the midday nap a great restorer. If sleep will not come, they should at least close their eyes and remain relaxed for a short time. A long nap makes one feel stupid.

Those unfortunate people who are addicted to various enslaving drugs, such as cocaine and morphine, often are very light sleepers. They are deteriorating physically, mentally and morally. Such people are ill and are no guides to the needs of healthy people.

Coffee drinking is a destroyer of sound sleep. At first the coffee seems to soothe the nerves, but in a few hours it has the opposite effect. The habitual use of coffee helps to bring on premature nervous instability and physical degeneration. Sleep is self-regulating. If we are normal otherwise we need give the subject no thought except to select a regular time to go to bed and get up promptly in the morning upon awaking. It is easy to drive away sleep. Those who wish to enjoy this sweet restorer at its best must be regular.

□

5

Food and Nutrition Guidelines for Healthy Adults

INTRODUCTION

This chapter presents recommendations for high-priority measures to promote proper nutrition in the years ahead. The National Council for Nutrition, an independent council appointed by the Ministry of Health and Care Services in 2003, has formulated overall health and diet objectives. These are based on nutrition-related challenges and the vision of a healthy diet for lifelong good health.

The nutrition policy is rooted in health policy and builds on the following three documents: recommendations for nutrition and physical activity 2005, which presents updated scientific information on which intake of nutrients is best. Prescriptions for a healthier, which sets outs strategies for nutrition and public health work in a 10-year perspective; and the Global strategy on diet, physical activity and health adopted by the World Health Organization in May 2004. Social disparities in health are a major challenge for nutrition policy.

Eating habits and levels of physical activity vary greatly throughout the population according to education and income. Segments of the population with low income and little education eat more energy-dense foods and fewer vegetables than high-income, highly-educated segments of the population. Reducing social disparities in health is a primary goal in nutrition work. The efforts to encourage a healthy diet are linked to the goal of preventing health problems and promoting good health. Eliminating or reducing the scope of diet-related health problems is of utmost importance.

At the same time, the role of nutrition in treatment merits more attention. The efforts to promote good health through a healthy diet must have a global perspective. Sustainable food production is an aim in food and nutrition policy.

A sustainable diet is both healthy, and takes environmental issues like production, processing and transport into account. Promoting a healthy diet requires efforts in a number of sectors. Food and food culture form an important frame-work for day-to-day life. It is vital to ensure that dietary recommendations are based on reliable, up-to-date information.

The National Council for Nutrition attaches great importance to issuing recommendations to the population and the health authorities that are based on solid scientific documentation. Knowledge about the relation between diet and health is comprehensive and growing, but much remains to be learned and new questions continue to emerge. Public health services and social services at all levels must be provided by competent personnel, whether dealing with the prevention or the treatment of diet-related health problems. Schools and day-care centres are key arenas for promoting a healthy diet for children and adolescents.

There are huge economic interests at stake in the food and beverage industry, and reconciling commercial interests and the interests of nutrition can be challenging. The authorities should promote cooperation with industrial players in order to promote healthy diet through the production, and supply of foods. As voluntary organizations also play an important role in nutrition work, the National Council for Nutrition aspires to promote strong alliances for good health.

The National Council for Nutrition's main concern is nutrition as it relates to diet. The Food Safety Authority is responsible for inspecting food production and sales to ensure that food is safe and healthy and complies with regulations. Determining what is necessary for food to be healthy and safe requires knowledge in a broad range of fields. Both the National Council for Nutrition and the Food Safety Authority's Scientific Committee for Food Safety play important roles in this process. Among other tasks, the Scientific Committee carries out risk assessments on foods and food components.

NUTRITION AND HEALTH

Continuing to reduce cardiovascular disease and the prevention of cancer and health problems associated with overweight and obesity are currently the most important challenges facing nutrition policy. Prescriptions for a healthier, and in the WHO global strategy on diet, physical activity and health. A healthy diet and regular physical activity can reduce the incidence of cardiovascular disease and cancer and prevent increases in overweight, obesity and type 2 diabetes.

The nutritional needs and health problems change throughout the life cycle. The risk of developing chronic diseases can be influenced at all ages. Health-promoting and preventive nutrition work must take a comprehensive approach to the human life cycle and to different needs at the various stages of life. The foundation for health and disease is laid already in utero. The mother's nutrition during pregnancy has consequences not only for the child's health as a newborn, but also for its health later in life. In other words, the eating habits and nutrition of pregnant women and women of childbearing age have consequences not only for themselves but for the next generation as well. It is important to ensure that women in this stage of life have proper nutrition, and that their intake of folic acid and iron meets recommended levels.

Breastmilk is of great importance to infants' nutrition, immune systems and development. The greatest possible number of infants should be breastfed in accordance with recommendations. Infants and toddlers are in a biologically vulnerable stage of life, and it is essential that baby and toddler food is healthy and safe, and contains the nutrients required to meet their nutritional needs.

Commissioned by the Ministry of Health and Care Services and completed in the spring of 2005, the action plan for infant and toddler nutrition identifies measures designed to achieve these objectives. Eating habits established during childhood and adolescence, have an impact on the risk of disease later in life. Food and drinks are important indicators of social and cultural identity for everyone, and perhaps particularly for adolescents. The physiological need for nutrients is greater during adolescence than during childhood, and high-quality diet is important. Given society's obsession with perfect bodies, many young people feel pressured to lose weight, and eating disorders are a problem. Children and adolescents are an important target group for health-promoting nutrition work. People who have developed diet-related diseases may benefit greatly from dietary measures to improve their condition. Most chronic diseases have their onset during adulthood. The need for certain nutrients increases with age. Many elderly people experience a loss of appetite and some eat too little, becoming undernourished and frailer than need be.

Settling in a new country that has a different culture and language can lead to changes in diet, physical activity and health. Dietary changes, including a higher intake of fats and sugar and a lower intake of vegetables, fruits, lentils and beans, have been documented. Immigrants from non-Western countries differ in many ways, and there are substantial differences in health among the various groups. Some nutritional problems, such as overweight and obesity, type 2 diabetes, and iron and vitamin D deficiency, occur more often in certain immigrant groups.

Cardiovascular Disease

Cardiovascular disease is the most common cause of death and has a great impact on morbidity. For people under the age of 70, deaths from cardiovascular disease have been reduced by more than half in the past 30 years. A large part of this decline is due to improvements in diet. In particular, decreased consumption of solid fats has improved the blood cholesterol level

in the population. There is great potential for prevention of these diseases through reduced dietary intake of solid fats and salt and increased intake of fruits and vegetables. A combination of a healthy diet, regular physical activity and no smoking plays an important part in preventing and treating cardiovascular disease.

Cancer

Cancer is the second most common cause of death and the overall incidence is on the rise. Obesity and physical inactivity are important risk factors for cancer. Diet plays an important role in preventing and treating cancer. A healthy diet with a high intake of fibre-rich foods, fruits and vegetables combined with a low salt intake can help prevent the development of a number of types of cancer. Cancer treatment not only exacts toil on the body mentally and physically, it may also alter or disrupt eating habits. As a consequence, proper nutrition is crucial when undergoing treatment.

Overweight and Obesity

Overweight and obesity have become increasingly prevalent in population in recent decades, as in other Western countries. All segments of the population are experiencing weight gain, regardless of age, gender or education level. Nevertheless, overweight and obesity are most common in the lower socio-economic strata. Weight gain is the result of an imbalance between energy intake and energy expenditure. Overweight readily occurs when a reduced level of physical activity is combined with easy access to energy-dense foods.

There is a need for viable treatment options for those who become seriously overweight or obese. Obesity is a risk factor for developing type 2 diabetes, cardiovascular disease, certain types of cancer and osteoarthritis of the hips and knees. Overweight and obesity represent a growing pro-blem for individuals and society-at-large, meaning prevention is of tremendous importance.

Diabetes Mellitus

Diabetes mellitus is the most common metabolic disorder in Norway. Diabetes is a result of a combination of genetic disposition and environmental factors. Overweight, obesity and physical inactivity increase people's risk of developing type 2 diabetes. These days, people are developing diabetes at an increasingly younger age. Diabetes is a contributing factor to cardiovascular disease, stroke, kidney failure, blindness, foot ulcers and amputation.

It is estimated that many people may have undiagnosed diabetes. Among immigrants from the Middle East and the Indian sub-continent, particularly among females, there is a substantial over-representation of type 2 diabetes.

Dietary changes, increased physical activity, smoking cessation, controlling high blood pressure and weight loss play important roles in the treatment of type 2 diabetes. The single most important nutrition-related risk-factor of bone fractures is underweight. It is important to prevent underweight among the elderly. It is also important to ensure an adequate intake of vitamin D and calcium.

VISION

A healthy diet meets the recommendations for the composition of nutrients, is varied, tasty and in harmony with cultural values. It is the sum of what is consumed, how much and how often, that is decisive in the long run. From a health-promoting and preventive perspective, health is more than the absence of disease. In addition to physical health, it encompasses contentment and well-being.

STRATEGIC GOALS

Work in the nutrition sector should contribute to:

- Reducing the incidence of cardiovascular disease;
- Reducing the incidence of diet-related cancer;
- Halting the increase in overweight and obesity;
- Preventing type 2 diabetes;
- Preventing underweight and malnourishment;
- Strengthening the role of nutrition in treating the sick.

High-priority initiatives include:

- Increased consumption of vegetables, fruits, berries and whole-grain products;
- Decreased intake of solid fats;
- Decreased intake of energy-dense, nutrient- poor foods.

Facilitating healthy choices and increasing the health literacy of the population should be given priority in an attempt to achieve these strategic goals.

Increased Consumption of Fruits, Vegetables, Berries and Whole-Grain Products

Fruits, berries, vegetables, potatoes and whole-grain products are good sources of fibre, vitamins, minerals and a number of other nutrients. There is substantial documentation to show that a diet rich in fruits, vegetables, and whole-grain products reduces the risk of cardiovascular disease and certain types of cancer. Such a diet is not energy-dense and can reduce the risk of obesity. Consumer surveys, the consump-tion of vegetables increased from 80 gm./day in the 1970s to 110 gm./day in 2002, and there was a corresponding increase in the consumption of fruits and juice from 120 gm./day to 170 gm./day. Altogether, consumption has risen from 200 gm./day to 280 gm./day during this period.

The consumption of potatoes has declined by half during the same period. Only about 10 per cent of the population has an intake of vegetables and fruits. There are clear social disparities in the consumption of these foods. The intake of grain products has remained relatively stable, but the consumption of whole- grain flour accounts for less than 20 per cent of total consumption. The goal is to increase the consumption of vegetables and fruits throughout the population to an average total intake of fruits and vegetables of at least 400 gm./day by 2009 to meet WHO recommendations.

Meanwhile, another goal is to increase the consumption of whole-grain products and potatoes at the expense of fat-rich potato products.

Reduced Intake of Solid Fats (Saturated Fats and Trans Fats)

Saturated fatty acids, and particularly trans fatty acids, in the diet have a negative effect on blood lipid profiles and increase the risk of coronary heart disease. It is estimated that a reduction in the intake of solid fats can substantially reduce the risk of coronary heart disease. In the 1970s, saturated fats accounted for 17 per cent, while the percentage has fallen to 14 per cent today, according to consumer surveys. The diet's content of trans fatty acids has been reduced from 4 per cent to less than 1 per cent of the diet's total energy content in the past 30 years.

The most important sources of saturated fats and trans fats in the diet are milk, dairy products, meat and meat products. Bread products, biscuits and cakes can also contain trans fats. The intake of solid fats should be limited to 10 per cent of total energy intake. By promoting the consumption of foods that are low in fat and foods that contain unsaturated fats, the intake of solid fats as well as the total fat intake can be reduced. The goal is to further reduce the consumption of solid fats to 12 per cent.

Reduced Intake of Energy-Dense, Nutrient-Poor Foods

A diet rich in energy-dense, nutrient-poor foods is linked to an increased risk of overweight and obesity, type 2 diabetes and caries. This type of diet can also result in a low intake of vitamins and minerals. A consumer surveys, over the past 30 years, total sugar consumption has risen slightly to 15 per cent of energy intake.

Sugar consumption patterns have changed, and the consumption of soft drinks and sweets has increased in particular. The sugar intake of children and adolescents has climbed sharply and is considerably higher than desired levels. Dietary studies among 13-year-olds reveal that sugar accounted for 13 per cent of their energy intake in 1993 and 18 per cent in 2000.

On average, they drank 4–5 dl of sugared soft drinks and fruit drinks a day, and ate 40–45 g of sweets a day. Sugared fruit drinks, soft drinks, and sweets accounted for 65 per cent of 13-year-olds' total sugar intake. Added sugar comprises sucrose, fructose, starch hydrolysate and other isolated sugars, which are used either in their pure form, as components of other food products or in cooking. Added sugar should not exceed 10 per cent of total energy intake. Another goal is to reduce the consumption of sugared soft drinks from some 85 litres per person per year to 60 litres per person annually, corresponding to the level of con-sumption in 1990. An additional goal is to reduce the consumption of sweets, sugared, nutrient-poor beverages, snack foods and fat-rich potato products.

DIET FOR WOMEN

With the way they are conditioned, women end up doing more or less work equivalent to men. However, the kind of recognition they get is pretty less compared to what men get. Many women feel bad when they even put on one pound of weight. They go on crash diet and try and reduce their weight to make it to normal. But fact is many women don't even realise that they are too skinny to go on diets that make them thinner. Iron deficiency in women is definitely a big cause of worry for many women. We do not teach you special kinds of diets, instead as suggested, be discussing about what foods are advised for women, and what are not.

What Foods to Avoid, gives a detail of what type of foods should be avoided, and why. Actually, avoiding bad foods is half the job done to stay healthy. And when you know what foods you avoid, you should also be worried about what gives you a healthy structure and figure. Most of the body weight is constituted by bone weight.

Hence it is important that take foods that give loads of calcium to your body. Nutrition for Healthy Bones, will help you understand how to build up healthy bones, and a healthy life.

Pregnancy Diet

Though not always, many a woman is always in two minds whenever she is confronted with a new situation. The same is the case when a woman gets pregnant. Unfortunately one cannot say that all pregnant women know how to take care of their health during this important time.

Nutrition During Pregnancy

A stable diet is a critical component of good health always in an individual's life. All though pregnancy, diet is still more significant. The foods that one consumes are the chief suppliers of the nutrients for one's baby. As the baby develops, one will require more of the majority of nutrients.

Prior to becoming pregnant is the most excellent time to commence eating a beneficial diet. Eating correctly prior to becoming pregnant can assist an individual in ensuring that both she and her baby start off with the nutrients that both require.

Supplement

Folic acid is a kind of vitamin that is crucial to the development of the baby, particularly all through the initial months of pregnancy. Not receiving sufficient folic acid in one's diet prior to one becoming pregnant and initially in pregnancy augments the threat of birth flaws, for example neural tube imperfection. Receiving good health care ahead of one becoming pregnant will assist an individual all through one's pregnancy.

Pregnant women are occasionally worried about gaining surplus weight. However, it should be borne in mind that one's diet is the foremost source of energy for the baby. That signifies one has to consume more while pregnant. When an individual is pregnant, she requires approximately 300 calories additionally everyday day than she generally consumes. The amount of weight a woman puts on during pregnancy is dependent on her weight prior to pregnancy.

A beneficial gain for the majority of women is between 25 and 35 pounds. If a woman is obese, she should put on less, but certain weight gain is usual. If a woman is underweight, she should put on additional weight. The initial move in the direction of healthy eating is to take into account the foods in one's everyday diet.

Additional Nutrients:

- Pregnant women may require additional nutrients and these may consist of iron, folic acid and calcium.
- They can be made available as single pills or as an amalgamated pill.
- Occasionally a prenatal vitamin has all that one requires.

- In order to avert neural tube flaws, a woman ought to receive 0.4 mg. of folic acid every day ahead of and all through pregnancy.
- It should be taken for one month ahead of pregnancy and throughout the initial three months of pregnancy.

Women who have had a child with a spine or skull blemish are more liable to have one more child with this trouble. These women require greater amounts of folic acid-4 mg. every day. Milk and additional dairy products are the most excellent sources of calcium in one's diet. However, several women have indications, for example bloating, diarrhoea, gas and indigestion subsequent to drinking milk or consuming dairy products. This is referred to as lactose intolerance. If a pregnant woman is lactose intolerant, she should ensure that she is receiving adequate calcium.

Diet for Healthy Weight Gain During Pregnancy

Acquiring the correct quantity of weight all through pregnancy by consuming a nourishing, stable diet is an excellent sign that the baby is receiving all the nutrients he or she requires and is developing at a healthy rate. It is not essential to consume for two in pregnancy. It's a reality that pregnant women require additional calories from nutrient-rich foods to aid the growth of her baby, but a pregnant woman commonly should consume just 100 to 300 more calories than she did ahead of becoming pregnant to fulfil the requirements of the developing baby.

It is imperative for a pregnant woman to take the advice of the health care provider on the amount of weight she should put on for the period of pregnancy. A woman of standard weight ahead of pregnancy should put on 25 to 35 pounds for the period of pregnancy. Women who are underweight should put on 28-40 pounds for the period of pregnancy. Obese women may require putting on just 15-25 pounds during pregnancy.

Ideal weight gain:

- Generally, one should put on approximately 2 to 4 pounds all through the initial three months of pregnancy and 1 pound a week for the rest of the pregnancy period.
- If an individual is anticipating twins she should put on 35 to 45 pounds for the period of her pregnancy.
- This would be a typical of 1 ½ pounds for every week following the normal weight increase in the initial three months.

The Additional Weight is Distributed in the Following Manner

For the baby it is 8 pounds, for the placenta 2-3 pounds, for amniotic fluid 2-3 pounds, for breast tissue 2-3 pounds, blood supply 4 pounds, fat reserves for delivery and breastfeeding 5-9 pounds and for uterus increase 2-5 pounds. This makes for a total weight of 25 to 30 pounds.

It is by no means risk-free to shed weight for the period of pregnancy since both the mother and the baby require the appropriate nutrients so as to be healthy. In order to gain the required weight during pregnancy one should consume five to six minor, regular meals everyday. One should stock swift, trouble-free snacks on hand, for example nuts, raisins, cheese and crackers, dried fruit, in addition to ice cream or yogurt. It is imperative to apply peanut butter on toast, crackers, apples, bananas, or celery approximately 100 calories and 7gm. of protein. One should include non-fat powdered milk in foods for example mashed potatoes, scrambled eggs plus hot cereal.

It is crucial to include condiments in one's meal, for example, butter or margarine, cream cheese, gravy, sour cream as well as cheese. Certainly, patterns of weight increase all through pregnancy differ. It's usual to put on less if an individual is heavier at the time of pregnancy and it is normal to put on extra weight if an individual is expecting twins or triplets or if an individual is underweight prior to becoming pregnant.

What Foods to Avoid

Eating proportionate meals is vital at all times, but it is especially crucial when one is pregnant. There are important nutrients, vitamins and minerals that a growing baby requires. The majority of foods are harmless; nonetheless, there are certain foods that one ought to stay away from during pregnancy. Raw seafood and exceptional or undercooked beef or poultry should be shunned due to the danger of infectivity with coliform bacteria, toxoplasmosis, and salmonella.

Deli meats have been acknowledged to be infected with Listeria, which can trigger miscarriage. Listeria has the capacity to traverse the placenta and may contaminate the baby resulting in contamination or blood poisoning, which can be critical. If a pregnant woman is contemplating to eat deli meats, she should ensure to reheat the meat until it is steaming.

Avoiding fish:

- Fish that has high quantities of mercury ought to be avoided.
- Mercury ingested during pregnancy has been associated with developmental hindrance and brain harm.
- Examples of these kinds of fish comprise: shark, swordfish, king mackerel and tilefish.
- Canned, chunk light tuna usually contain less quantities of mercury in comparison to other tuna, but still should only be consumed in restraint.
- Some kinds of fish employed in sushi should also be shunned because of high concentration of mercury.

Frozen, smoked seafood frequently described as lox, nova style, kippered, or jerky should be shunned since they could be infected with Listeria. Preserved or shelf-safe smoked seafood is considered safe for consumption.

Individuals who are pregnant should shun fish from polluted lakes and rivers that may be subjected to high quantities of polychlorinated biphyenyls. Most of seafood borne sickness is attributable to undercooked shellfish, which homocysteine plays a part in heart-disease threat and probably of infection, but it does not thwart the algae-related illness that is linked to red tides. Uncooked shellfish create apprehension for everyone and they should be shunned in general all through pregnancy.

Uncooked eggs or any foods that has uncooked eggs should be shunned due to the possible exposure to salmonella. Several home-produced Caesar dressings, mayonnaise, home-produced ice cream or custards, and Hollandaise sauces may be prepared with uncooked eggs. If the recipe is cooked at certain stage, this will reduce the contact with salmonella. Commercially produced ice cream, dressings and eggnog are prepared with pasteurized eggs and do not augment the threat of salmonella. Restaurants also are supposed to be utilizing pasteurized eggs in whichever recipe that is made with uncooked eggs, for example Hollandaise sauce or dressings.

Imported soft cheese may have bacteria recognized as Listeria, which can trigger miscarriage. Listeria has the capacity to traverse the placenta and can contaminate the baby resulting in infection or blood poisoning that can be life-intimidating. Pregnant women should keep away from soft cheese for example, brie, camembert, Roquefort, feta, gorgonzola and Mexican type cheeses that comprise queso blanco and queso fresco.

Iron Deficiency Anaemia in Women

Iron insufficiency anaemia—a shortage of iron in the blood affects a large number of women globally. Iron is a vital nutrient in pregnancy; hence it's imperative to be certain that pregnant women have an ample ingestion. There are three major causes that an adequate iron ingestion to thwart anaemia is vital.

First, iron is indispensable for the development of maternal and foetal hoemoglobin, the oxygen-transporting constituent of blood.

As a woman's blood volume swells by 25 to 40 per cent in pregnancy, and the baby is producing blood cells, as well, the requirement for iron rises putting the mother in danger of anaemia. Second, in the final trimester, the baby extracts from the mother a quantity of the iron reserves that it will require in the initial four to six months of life. Third, the augmented blood volume and iron stores aids the mother's body adjust, to certain extent, to the blood loss that takes place in childbirth.

Maternal iron deficiency anaemia:

- Maternal iron deficiency anaemia is linked to an augmented frequency of anaemia in the baby in the initial year of life, in addition to anaemia and reduced iron reserves in the mother.
- Pregnant women with iron deficiency anaemia, chiefly in the first and second trimesters, have an augmented danger for early delivery and for delivering a low-birth weight baby.

The majority of doctors suggest iron supplements for pregnant mothers. In general, an every day 60 mg. iron supplement is recommended to check anaemia, although the suggested quantity of iron in pregnancy is 30 mg. every day. It is for the reason that iron from supplements is not completely assimilated. Receiving 60 mg. of iron daily will make certain that a pregnant woman in reality assimilated the suggested daily quantity of iron. Iron supplements are appropriately assimilated if taken with foods enriched with vitamin C, for example orange, grapefruit, or tomato juice. Absorption is weakened if one takes them with antacids or foods containing calcium for example milk and cheese. Iron supplements occasionally trigger upset stomach, constipation, or nausea.

If such a condition arises one can obtain most of the iron an individual requires from iron-rich foods, for example organ meats like liver red meat, egg yolks, and legumes such as dried peas and beans. Iron deficiency anaemia in pregnant women and in babies in the aftermath of delivery is without difficulty avoidable by the consumption of a stable, wholesome, iron-rich diet and taking iron supplements as stipulated by one's doctor. Iron deficiency anemia is linked to psychomotor and cognitive defects in children. Iron deficiency anaemia in pregnancy has been connected with augmented danger for low birth weight, preterm delivery, and prenatal death. Recent studies entail that maternal iron deficiency anaemia may be related to postpartum melancholy and inferior performance on mental and psychomotor tests in children.

Anti Aging Nutrition

Although ageing is unavoidable, physical decay is not. More than a few of the external manifestations of growing old can be decelerated - and life can even be protracted - by sustaining a wise and meaningful approach to diet. As individuals grow old, their bodies' process nutrients less competently, leading to the requirement for individuals to enhance their nutrient ingestion. For instance, Vitamin D is a nutrient necessary for the deterrence of osteoporosis.

The human body produces vitamin D when the skin is subjected to sunlight, but when individuals are in their 70s their bodies manufacture merely 40 per cent of it. An ample quantity of vitamin D for people in their 20s is 200 IU; for individuals who are grown-up, 400 IU to 600 IU is required for performing the identical amount of work.

Requirement related to age:

- The requirement for B vitamins rises with age also.
- Three B vitamins—folic acid, vitamin B6 and vitamin B12—are crucial for maintaining levels of a compound described as homocysteine at a low level in the blood; if permitted to increase, memory loss, as indicated by studies in the relevant sphere.
- When individuals age it is imperative for them to augment their B6 amount from 2 mg to 5 mg; augment B12 in due course from 2 mcg to 10 mcg.
- Women ought to receive 400 mcg of folic acid every day; pregnant women ought to ingest 800 mcg everyday in order to thwart neural-tube flaws in the foetus.

Women, specifically, should be conscious that their calcium ingestion should augment as they age to avert osteoporosis. Individuals who eat diets rich in fresh fruits and vegetables have reduced ailment rates, additional energy and less danger for weight gain that can result in health troubles in comparison to those who omit these foods.

With the omission of avocados, olives and coconuts, fresh fruits and vegetables are devoid of fat, cholesterol or sodium. Fresh fruits and vegetables are furthermore rich in fibre. Eight servings of fruits and vegetables consumed everyday offers roughly 27 gm. of fibre, which is well inside the everyday requirement of 25 gm. to 35 gm.. Foods rich in fibre reduce an individual's threat for developing age-linked ailments for example heart disease, cancer, diabetes and hypertension. Foods rich in fibre are moreover reduced in calories, nonetheless satisfying; consequently they assist in filling up individuals without filling him or her.

Fresh fruits and vegetables are rich in nutrients, making available sufficient quantities of calcium, iron, magnesium, vitamin C, beta carotene and folic acid, and they are short in calories. Fruits and vegetables also contain longevity-boosting compounds referred to as antioxidants which comprise vitamins C and E in addition to beta carotene. Antioxidants resist free radicals, oxygen fragments that strike and harm cell membranes, life-supporting proteins and even genetic code of cells that trigger aging and ailments.

Diets high in antioxidants check ailment and untimely aging. Antioxidants, moreover, invigourate the immune system and defend the nervous system and brain from the oxidative harm connected with age-linked memory loss.

Diet During Menopause

Menopause is the expression employed to signify the cease of the period of probable sexual reproduction, as demonstrated by the termination of menstrual periods. This is completely usual and happens between 45 to 55 years. Menopause does not reduce women's physical capability, sexual energy and capacity to enjoy life. Menopause fetches specific freedoms to female life. Such as no longer they have to be anxious about the monthly bleeding and about birth control. Still then in this period a woman suffers a great deal of emotional strain. Ovaries discontinue making oestrogen and this result in oestrogen deficiency. This hormonal disparity may trigger short-term symptoms and long term health threat.

Adhering to a healthy diet:

- Sticking to a healthy diet can be beneficial for vitality in general and this in the process assists in providing a woman with better resistance against any troubles during menopause.
- Hot flushes can be diminished by acquiring vitamin E rich foods similar to wheat germ, nuts, eggs and olive oil.
- Vitamin A, D, calcium, phosphorous and magnesium can assist in checking osteoporosis.
- Fish, drumstick leaves, ragi and dairy products are outstanding suppliers of calcium. During menopause women should shun consuming uncooked bran, which hinders calcium absorption and should reduce the consumption of tea, coffee which advances the excretion of calcium.

Many women gain weight which augments the blood cholesterol level. To regulate body weight and blood cholesterol one should choose low fat dairy foods and reduce the consumption of saturated fats such as butter and cheese. Studies indicate that substances from plants identified as phytoestrogens can assist in diminishing the acuteness of hot flushes and additional indications of menopause.

Phytoestrogens, which imitate human oestrogen, are obtained chiefly from soybeans and alfalfa sprouts. Soya bean flour can be combined with wheat flour for making bread. Additional soya foods are soymilk, tofu, as well as soy sauce. Carrot in addition to beet root juice is considered to be extremely helpful in menopausal maladies. Oats, corn, barley, brown rice, whole wheat are as well outstanding sources of phytoestrogens.

Frequent exercise is necessary in this period. This stage is to be considered as a usual period in a women's life. Nonetheless the family members ought to understand that this stage in the life of a woman requires a great deal of thought, attention and sympathy to make the daily life stress free. A nourishing diet can not only diminish the indications of menopause, but also bring about an improved lifestyle and augmented energy levels, enabling one to do the types of activities that will support an improved body and an improved lifestyle in general. Foods rich in calcium and supplements are an excellent suggestion if one intends to lead a vigourous way of life during menopause. Calcium is mainly helpful when used with additional vitamins and minerals such as magnesium and vitamin D, which supports superior skeletal health.

Nutrition for Healthy Bones

Healthy bones provide the body with power and firmness to defend the internal organs from damage. Significant as the skeleton is, it accounts for living tissues and are continuously experiencing remodeling since old bone tissue gets worn-out and fresh bone is produced. A subtle equilibrium has to be kept between these two procedures. If that equilibrium is disrupted, problems can take place, including brittle bones and osteoporosis.

Ensuring healthy bones needs:

- Frequent physical exercise and a nourishing, stable diet are equally vital.
- Evading threat factors similar to smoking and strain also add to healthy bones.
- Every individual can do a bit to shape the health of their bones.
- By indulging in weight-bearing physical work out one can promote bone mineralization.
- By eating correctly one can make certain that the essential nutrients are obtainable for bone metabolism.
- These major nutrients are Calcium and Vitamin D.

Calcium is essential for strong teeth and bones and furthermore, plays a vital part in a variety of bodily systems, for example, the health and performance of nerves and muscle tissue. Superior sources of calcium comprise dairy foods and leafy green vegetables, even though calcium from milk and milk products is more effortlessly assimilated and present in larger quantities. Individuals at various life phases require dissimilar quantities of calcium. Adolescents, young children in addition to elderly women all have bigger than normal necessities. Calcium is one of the vital nutrients required for healthy growth of bone.

Ample calcium ingestion is crucial for the accom-plishment of peak bone mass in the late teen. This is the maximum stage of bone strength which takes place at cease of growth, and consequently results in tough healthy bones, which will prolong the consequences of ageing on the skeleton. It is vital to have a proportionate diet with sufficient quantities of dairy products, which are the principal sources of foods high in calcium.

Vitamin D is the broad name for a cluster of steroid-like substances with anti-rachitic action. Vitamin D is obtained only from animals and there are simply some foods which have vitamin D like oily fish, fish oils, butter and eggs. Different from other vitamins, individuals can in reality produce vitamin D in their bodies as an outcome of contact to sunlight, on condition that ingestion of ascorbic acid is sufficient.

The two major members of this vitamin cluster are ergocalciferol or vitamin D2 and cholecalciferol or vitamin D3. Vitamin D is necessary for the assimilation of calcium and phosphorus from the small intestine, their re- assimilation in the kidneys, and the mineralization procedure of the bones. It therefore promotes healthy bone development. It, furthermore performs a vital role in the appropriate working of muscles, nerves, blood clotting, cell growth and energy utilization.

Breast Cancer Diet

When an individual is coping with breast cancer, appropriate nutrition becomes especially vital. Nonetheless, a proportionate diet and breast cancer treatment may not be effective simultaneously. The side effects from breast cancer treatments, together with the emotional stress of being afflicted by the disease can make it tough for patients to eat. By pursuing recommen-dations to deal with the side effects when eating; selecting beneficial foods to eat; and drawing assistance and support from others, breast cancer patients can preserve a well-balanced diet during cure and recuperation. While taking into account the diet in breast cancer treatment, one should initiate a hunt for cancer- combating nutrients. Foods with such nutrients should assist in satisfying the palate of the breast cancer patient. One may start by looking for foods that are rich in selenium.

Selenium effective in fighting cancer:

- Selenium is equally an indispensable natural mineral and a helpful cancer-fighting antioxidant.
- Foods rich in selenium require being an ingredient of a diet for breast cancer treatment.
- Selenium aids to fortify the immune system, and helps in easing the action of the thyroid. It also assists in stimulating specific enzymes.
- One can acquire a required ingestion of selenium by consuming tuna, eggs, wheat grain, chicken, liver, garlic as well as Brazil nuts.

The benefits of selenium make it suitable for addition in the diet for breast cancer cure. Studies indicate a connection between the capacity of selenium to initiate the action of specific enzymes and the mineral's ability to defend against cancer threats.

An every day ingestion of no less than 70 microgm. of selenium should be the aim of every woman who is concerned with regard to her diet for breast cancer treatment. If an individual consumes a quantity far higher than 100 microgm. every day, then this surplus quantity of selenium can trigger nausea, awful breath, skin complaints, giddiness, feebleness and cold indications.

Ingestion of above 60 microgm. of selenium every day is unsuitable for pregnant women. An excessive ingestion of selenium seems connected with birth problems. However, certain women can include extra selenium to a diet in breast cancer treatment. One more nutrient that should be an ingredient of every diet in breast cancer treatment is indole-3-carbinol, a chemical that is as well described as 13C. This phytochemical, a crucial component of the chemical composition of broccoli and additional cruciferous vegetables has been revealed to be a natural means of averting specific cancers. The useful 13C utilizes three dissimilar means for supplying its beneficial effects. Initially, 13C disrupts the cancer cell phase; a broken up cycle checks cell division. Second, 13C checks the development of blood vessels in the tumor; with no blood vessels, the tumor cells can not obtain required nutrients. Third, 13C work in a way that is capable of preparing the phase for the death of the cancer cells. The maximum worth of 13C stems from the anticipated product formed when an individual has consumed a diet high in 13C.

HEALTH DIETS FOR PATIENTS

When taking care of various health issues, one has to be extremely careful about one's diet. Doctors advise medicines mentioning what kind of diet should be taken with it. If this diet isn't followed carefully, medicines do not do the complete job.

Diet for Cancer

A strict diet is advised for Cancer because some foods directly affect cancer maturity. Fat, especially saturated fats do more harm than any one can imagine. Hence diets for Cancer should increase as much as only 55gm. of Fat intake daily.

Diet for Gout

Gout is one type of arthritis and is called metabolic arthritis. It is one of the worst types of arthritis. Gout makes sodium urate crystals deposit on the particular cartilage of joints and tendon tissues. It might even cause stones in kidneys. Rich Carbohydrate diet is advised for people who suffer from Gout. Protein intake should be very limited as well.

Diet During Acid Reflux

When someone feels heartburn, or suddenly realises that he or she gets food back into their mouths, they should suspect Acid Reflux. Gastric juices that contain acids are pushed back from stomach to esophagus, and this condition is called acid reflux. Diet for acid reflux starts off with taking smaller meals, more than three times a day. And the diet is all given in the substance called diet during acid reflux.

Diet During Diarrhoea

Diarrhoea is one of the most irritating health problems. It could be cause by contaminated food or even climate change. And importantly one should not stop diarrhea because it is nature's way of eliminating virus.

Diet for Constipation

Constipation is the exact opposite situation of diarrhoea. While you struggle to control defecating in diarrhoea, Constipation doesn't allow easy defecating. Fibre is the most suggested diet for constipation. And make sure you find the correct sources of Fibre from the substance.

Diet for Obese

United States suffers with an ever increasing population of obese people. Though obesity doesn't kill right away, one needs to be specially aware of what it can do to ones body. Obesity isn't a disease but a condition which definitely leads to disease over a period of time. Fat is the mean reason behind obesity.

So, if you think and find that you are growing in weight regularly, you should first consult your doctor. One can be called obese when is unable to see their toes, when they stand straight. All you need to do is avoid food, and you lose weight. But why should any one take food for weight loss? All foods play an important role in the way we act and think daily. Hence if we do not have foods over a period of time, it is imperative that we are not as good as when we have enough food in our bellies. However, we need to understand that certain foods with too much of fat in them, make us fatter, and certain foods have lesser amounts of fat. Hence, taking food that has lesser amounts of fat helps.

Low Carb Diets

Food, in general, contains proteins, carbohydrates, fat, minerals, water and other nutrients. In all these we proteins are digested for various activities performed inside the body.

Carbohydrates provide energy required for the body to do various physical activities. Fat helps our body in many ways, and it acts as a substitute for carbs. So when carbs fall short, fat is burnt to provide energy. That's how low carb diets help.

Safe Sweeteners and Fat Burners

If you crave for that sweet taste and can't get adjusted to not having sugar in your tea and coffee, then sweeteners help you out. These small tablets contain sucralose or saccharin apart from various other ingredients. Importantly they add lesser amounts of calories to your body. Fat burners are dangerous if not taken under a doctor's advice. They simulate burning of excessive calories in your body, and their effect is felt immediately.

Healthy Eating

Healthy eating should be made a daily routine and cannot be taken easy. Healthy eating guildelines provide apart from few easy tips for weight loss, with an substance especially for new moms who want to shed weight.

LOW CARB DIETS—HOW THEY WORK?

Low carb diets are anchored in the principle that a diet extremely low in carbohydrate results in a decrease in the body's insulin production, leading to fat and protein stores being utilized as its major energy source.

Objective

- The objective of low carbohydrate diets is to compel the body to utilize fat as its chief energy source.
- When this takes place an individual produces "ketone bodies" to stimulate parts of the body that cannot utilize fat as an energy source—the brain, and red blood cells, specifically.
- When this occurs an individual is said to be in a condition of ketosis—typified by stinking breath and side effects for example sickness and exhaustion.

In essence an individual eliminates practically all carbohydrate from his or her diet and increases the protein and fat ingestion. Hence one reduces the consumption of pasta, bread, rice in addition to alcohol, and consumes unrestricted quantities of meat, cheese in addition to butter.

In the short term, the majority of individuals who follow low carb diets do lose weight and they lose it extremely fast. Nonetheless, most of the weight loss happens from loss of water as well as muscle tissue, not fat which one requires to lose to avoid the surplus weight.

In addition, if an individual is attempting to lose weight on a permanent basis, losing valuable lean muscle tissue is similar to damaging one's own body. Even when an individual is relaxing, muscle tissue is metabolically active, and burns calories. A reduction in the quantity of muscle tissue an individual possesses will result in a reduction in the number of calories an individual requires every day to preserve one's weight, making it a great deal tough to keep one's weight under check when one discontinues pursuing the low carb diet. Persons are fascinated by low carb diets since weight loss is extremely fast, and individuals love to observe immediate results on the weighing machine. However, low carb diet is not a very healthy choice. Crucial vitamins and nutrients are obtained from a balanced diet and low carbohydrate diets are definitely not balanced.

One can simply obtain a lot of vital nutrients from fruit, vegetables and grains and low carb diets merely permit extremely small quantities of fruit and vegetables which is certainly not sufficient to offer an individual his or her suggested every day allowance. The crucial point these low carb diets expresses is that carbohydrates advance insulin production, which in the process leads to weight gain. Hence by decreasing carbohydrate ingestion, individuals will shed weight. The reality is that by consuming a low carb diet, individuals do not offer sufficient carbohydrates to his or her body for every day function. Consequently it will begin burning the stored carbohydrates known as glycogen for energy. When a person's body commences burning glycogen, water is discharged. Consequently the severe early drop of weight at the start is merely water one loses as a consequence of burning glycogen.

Safe Sweeteners

Widespread obesity and diabetes promoted the expansion of the artificial sweetener industry. Increasing number of people are endeavoring to shed weight or trying to preserve a healthy weight. Sweeteners can be discovered in nearly all chewing gum, diet pop as well as drinks, light yogurt in addition to various frozen ice cream. If a product is labelled sugar free, it is extremely probable that sweeteners are added to them.

Types of sweeteness are:

- Nutritive Sweeteners make available calories to the diet at approximately four calories for every gm., akin to the usual carbohydrate individuals acquire from food.
- Instances of nutritive sweeteners comprise white and brown table sugars as well as molasses, honey in addition to syrups.
- Besides, sugar alcohols obtained from fruits or commercially prepared are as well nutritive sweeteners.
- The majority of widespread sugar alcohols comprise sorbitol, mannitol, xylitol as well as maltitol.
- Every nutritive sweetener supplies calories to the body and may well have an effect on one's blood glucose.
- Non-nutritive sweeteners are the real artificial sweeteners.
- They do not supply calories and will not affect blood glucose.

The safest thing to do is to keep away from all synthetic and chemical sweetener substitutes. They boast of no food value, deceive the body into believing it is consuming something sweet, and they have by-products of damaging poisonous side effects.

Foods having saccharin no more carry a warning maintaining that the utilization of this product may perhaps be dangerous to one's health accompanied by the assertion that such foods have saccharin which has been revealed to trigger cancer in laboratory animals. This caution was removed following indications that saccharin no longer has been associated with cancer in human beings.

Saccharin may possibly be there in drugs in large amounts. Intake of the suggested every day dosage of chewable aspirin or acetaminophen tablets in a child of school going age would make available roughly the similar quantity of saccharin enclosed in one can of a diet soft drink. This quantity, comparative to the body weight of a child younger than 9 or 10 years and consumed for extended duration would be regarded as excessive use, as characterized in a key scientific report.

In this report, heavy utilization of artificial sweeteners was connected with a considerably augmented danger for the growth of bladder cancer. Acesulfame Potassium which was permitted for utilization as a harmless artificial sweetener is an offshoot of acetoacetic acid. Regrettably, a number of probable troubles connected with the application of acesulfame have been brought up. They are centred mainly on animal studies because experiments on humans continue to be limited. Aspartame, a dipeptide of aspartic acid and a methyl ester of phenylalanine, is permitted for utilization in pharmaceutical products and is being employed more and more in chewable tablets and sugar-free formulations.

Fat Burners

Ripped Fuel, ProBURN, Thermo-Cuts, Metabolift, OptiBurn and Hydroxycut are promoted as fat-burning supplements that will enable an individual acquire a lean shape in a rapid manner. In reality, these fat burners do have a propensity to augment the pace at which a person uses up calories, but as with every product that promises marvel, it is essential for an individual to exercise caution prior to use and care should be taken while using them.

A fat burner that an individual selects will more or less at all times have two basic ingredients, namely, ephedrine and caffeine. Ephedrine is a bronchodilator, which is available as asthma medicine or cold medication to augment the body's capacity to carry oxygen into the bloodstream. Additional oxygen in the bloodstream offers individuals the capability to generate more energy in the cells.

More significantly for fat burning, ephedrine is a stimulant that enhances heart rate and blood pressure, thereby stimulating the body during workouts at the gym. In addition, ephedrine has a propensity to hinder appetite and perform as a diuretic. Synephrine, norephedrine, and pseudoephedrine are all related to ephedrine that offers comparable results. Individuals who drink coffee are aware of caffeine's invigourating ability, and packing caffeine collectively with ephedrine augments the thermogenic or heat-producing effect inside the body.

Caffeine in addition shows on labels as kola nut extract, guarana paste, and maté leaves. Studies have revealed that adding aspirin to the ephedrine, caffeine pile additionally boosts the thermogenic effect, thus advancing improved weight loss.

Whenever the internal temperature of the body is raised, individuals automatically burn more calories and this characteristically leads to weight loss and fat loss in particular. White willow bark is a source of salicin, the primary component of aspirin, and each of these expressions might as well become evident on labels. Products having the ephedrine, caffeine, aspirin stack or its chemical counterparts are time and again described as ECAs.

Lure of fat burners:

- Fat burners are appealing since they have an effect on the body just about straight away.
- When individuals check out these stimulant-based products, they generally experience something immediately and it is the effect of the stimulant.
- This acts as a major reason for people clinging to such products. The trouble is fat burners shouldn't be used simply by everyone. Not every individual reacts positively to stimulants and individuals on aspirin or heart medicine or an additional kind of asthma medicine or people who are caffeine responsive are likely to undergo quick or irregular heart rate. A number of individuals have trouble breathing or experience panic attacks, which liberates endorphins, thus aggravating the effect of the stimulants. Often it has been found that many products contain excessive or reduced amounts of ephedrine than declared on the label.

WEIGHT LOSS AFTER PREGNANCY

- Weight gain in pregnancy is beneficial and normal, but a number of women desire to go back to their pre-pregnancy bodies.
- But one should exercise prudence when losing one's baby weight.
- Clearly as it is ideal to gain weight gradually and progressively during one's pregnancy, one should be slow and stable in losing weight following one's pregnancy.

One excellent manner to shake off pregnancy weight is to breastfeed. One should at all times combine breast-feeding with additional types of post pregnancy weight loss. One of the grounds that an individual's body gains weight during pregnancy is to assist in storing the caloric energy it expends to breastfeed one's baby which is approximately 200 to 500 additional calories every day. Hence one should take the benefit of losing calories in the manner the body naturally planned and that is through breastfeeding.

Benefits of exercise:

- There are numerous advantages of exercising in the aftermath of pregnancy.
- It enables individuals to shed those additional pounds gained during pregnancy, ease post pregnancy complications and, not like dieting; it won't hinder one's breast-feeding.

It's vital that one should work one's way into exercising once more. Exercise should be done six weeks subsequent to a vaginal birth and eight weeks following a c-section. It is suggested that individuals should indulge in low-impact workout, for example, walking, swimming or yoga. Exercise for duration of ten minutes should be attempted initially and subsequently enhanced when an individual feels more certain. One should place a 30-minute curb on one's exercise time and stop instantly if one begins to experience giddiness or runs out of breath. There are numerous exercise schedules ideal for the post birth stage that can be done at home. Yoga activities are ideal for work outs at home.

Besides exercising, a healthful diet is the most excellent manner of losing one's pregnancy weight. One should consult a doctor regarding what foods are vital for the long-lasting health of both the baby and the mother. One should concentrate on nutrition and not on weight-loss diets. Walking is one of the finest exercises available and it doesn't even necessitate particular equipment.

All one requires is a fine pair of shoes, bright weather and one's baby, naturally. This exercise is planned to commence six to eight weeks after giving birth and is centered on the baby's requirements for stimulation. Pregnancy and weight increase are closely linked. They are related to each other and it's useful for the concerned mother. Hence, while making an attempt to shed those additional pounds gained during pregnancy one should be reasonable and should not give thought to extremes such as no junk food splurges and no superstar diets. Stable nutrition together with exercise is the most ideal and beneficial manner of retrieving one's pre-pregnancy body.

EATING TIPS DURING HOLIDAYS

During holidays individuals should concentrate on weight preservation instead of weight loss. If an individual is overweight and desires to shed weight, the holidays are the perfect time for doing so. Preservation of an individual's present weight can go a long way in motivating an individual to make good use of the holiday season.

One should not set impractical goals in this regard and end up in failure. It is imperative not to take vows on dieting. Prospect of food curbs can instigate one to overeat during the holidays. Moreover, restraining diets don't succeed eventually. They augment the loss of lean body mass in contrast to fat, decelerate one's metabolism, enhance worry, dejection, food fixation, and overeating, and make weight re-gain more possible.

Physically active:

- During the holiday season it is crucial for one to be physically active each day.
- Physical exercise, particularly aerobic activities such as vigourous walking, jogging, bicycling, roller blading, and swimming can assist in alleviating stress, control appetite, and burn up additional calories from holiday eating.

One should consume a light snack prior to leaving for holiday parties. It is not a helpful idea to turn up at a party hungry. Not only will an individual be inclined to eat too much, but will also be less likely to refuse to give in to the lure of eating the higher fat and higher calorie foods.

During the holiday season it is vital to chalk out a plan. One should deliberate upon where one will be, the persons who will be there, what foods will be accessible, what foods one actually prefers against those that one could possibly remain without and what are one's individual causes to eat too much and how one can restrict them.

When an individual has taken into consideration all of these things, he or she should create a plan of action. It's much trouble free to cope up with a tricky social eating condition if an individual has previously planned for it.

One should take measures to shun frivolous eating. While several foods are more calorie-intense in comparison to others, no food will make a person put on weight unless one consumes excessive amounts of it. One should make an attempt to diminish the fat in holiday recipes.

There are an abundance of low fat and low calorie alternates that are astonishingly delicious. One can attempt employing applesauce instead of oil in one's preferred holiday breads or utilize egg alternates instead of whole eggs. One should select one's beverages prudently. Alcohol is high in calories. Liquors, sweet wines as well as sweet mixed drinks have 150-450 calories in every glass. In comparison, water and diet sodas are calorie-free.

If an individual prefers to drink, he or she should opt for light wines and beers, and utilize non-alcoholic mixers for example water and diet soda. One should get pleasure from good friends and family. Even though food can be a big component of the season, it doesn't have to be the focal point. One can afford to eat in excess for a day or two since overeating in a day or two won't make or cut into one's eating plan.

TIPS FOR EASY WEIGHT LOSS

For numerous individuals weight loss is a prolonged attempt.

The following tips will help individuals in reducing their weight in an effective manner:

- It's nothing novel, but exercise is possibly the most vital indicator whether an individual will be successful at long-term weight loss and weight loss preservation. In order for exercise to be useful in weight loss, one should plan no less than five-30 minute sessions every week.
- There is considerable weight loss advantages associated with weight lifting. The greater muscle tissue an individual possesses, the greater calories he or she will burn. Unlike fat, muscle is an active tissue. day for its own preservation.
- Food diary

  – Maintenance of a food diary can be an immense advantage in successful weight loss.

  – One should dedicate some time each day to note down what one has consumed together with it its quantity, one's level of hunger before eating, and any thoughts or feeling prevailing at the time.
- A food record can offer a substantial degree of self- awareness. It can recognize feelings and behaviours that prompt overeating, promote greater consciousness of portion sizes, and assist an individual in determining his or her individual food triggers. One may examine any pattern that surfaces from one's food diary and distinguish where one might be capable of making more beneficial alterations. A food diary makes available an additional advantage of keeping an individual alert and dedicated to his or her objectives.
- Numerous individuals achieve greater success at long term weight loss when their purpose alters from desiring to be thinner to desiring to be in good health. One should alter one's attitude to dwell on choosing foods that will assist one's body's health rather than be concerned about foods that will have an effect on one's body's weight.

- Frequently overeating is prompted by strain, monotony, isolation, irritation, dejection and additional emotions. One should find out means to cope up with emotions devoid of food and is a considerable ability that will greatly assist long-term weight control.
- A considerable solution in long term weight control arrives from getting support and assistance from others.
- An individual should be careful of the quantities of food he or she eats at a sitting. One should be able to focus on one's hunger level and discontinue eating when one feels contentedly full, not overfed.
- It is vital to understand that the more rapidly weight is lost, the more probable the loss is occurring from water and muscle, not fat. As muscle tissue is vital in keeping the metabolism high, losing it in reality results in a reduction in the quantity of calories individuals can lose every day without putting on weight. Fat loss is ideally accomplished when weight is lost gradually. One should attempt for a weight loss of just 1-2 pounds every week.
- Eating unhurriedly is one technique that can assist individuals in losing weight. That's for the reason that from the time one starts eating it takes the brain 20 minutes to initiate signaling feelings of completeness. Rapid eaters frequently consume further than their right level of fullness prior to the 20 minute signal has had an opportunity to develop.

HEALTHY EATING GUIDELINES

Eating is a vital component in the life of individuals. Food should be pleasant in addition to offering a suitable equilibrium of nutrients as unconsumed food will supply no nourishment by any means. All foods make available a number of nutrients and add to the taste, smell, colour, texture and delight of a meal. Taking time to unwind while eating and to split a meal with acquaintances and family is a significant part of getting pleasure from meals.

Combination of foods:

- No single food makes available all the nutrients necessary for the body to stay healthy.
- A combination of dissimilar foods is crucial to be eaten all through life.
- Choosing foods for a beneficial diet doesn't imply that one has to give up one's preferred foods.

Diversity is vital also in making fruit in addition to vegetables, as well as foods akin to bread, breakfast cereals, rice, pasta and potatoes the major part of the meal. Snacks in addition to meals add up towards the balance.

Food supplies the energy required to keep the body energetic and working properly. Every individual requires a dissimilar quantity of energy and hence every person is different in the quantity of food he or she should consume. Women are likely to require less energy than men.

Older adults are likely to require a lesser quantity of energy than adolescents and young adults. The more dynamic an individual, the greater is his or energy requirements. A beneficial weight is best accomplished and preserved by both being actually active and by not consuming additional calories than those that are expended.

Not consuming sufficiently for the body's requirements could result in underweight and weakness. Eating too much can trigger overweight, which can cause ill health together with heart disease, high blood pressure or diabetes. One should consume abundance of foods rich in starch and fibre. Foods akin to bread, additional cereals as well as potatoes are full of starch and can be excellent sources of fibre. Starches as well as fibre are names for clusters of carbohydrates.

There are diverse kinds of starch as well as fibre and these are obtained only from plants or foods made from plants. The majority of people do not consume an adequate amount of the starchy, fibre-rich foods similar to bread, potatoes, rice and pasta and require eating them in proper quantities.

Whole-grain cereal foods are predominantly high in insoluble fibre, which assists in checking constipation. Soluble fibre in fruit, pulses in addition to vegetables is capable of assisting in the decrease in the quantity of cholesterol in the blood. One should consume lots of fruit and vegetables in order to ensure good health. There is ample proof that diets high in fruits as well as vegetables diminish the danger of developing chronic ailments, for example, coronary heart disease and perhaps some cancers, in life later on.

FOOD ITEMS

How healthy you are depends on what food items you eat. In fact, it is the combination of foods, that makes your diet, and in turn health. So what you eat should be chosen very carefully. If you don't realise what you are eating, then you don't realise what you are inviting into your body.

Fish

It is called sea vegetable in India, and is consumed even by practicing Brahmins. Fish is one of the best foods, offering variety in your food, gives you good taste and health as well. Fish Oil, Omega 3 Fatty Acids are one of the most important nutrients that fish give you. If you are missing out on fish, you should either be advised by a doctor, or else you've never tasted it.

Seeds and Nuts

Fish, seeds and nuts will compete with all the meats in the world to give all the requisite nutrients to your body. Actually nuts and seeds can be called as a vegetarian's meat. Apart from offer enough fibre, they give your body disease fighting energy, improving your immune system.

Garlic

Think medicinal herb, think garlic. Garlic has been used over ages and eons as a medicine. Induce it into your food, you are fighting accumulation in your arteries and cholesterol as well. But if you are taking it too much, it results in a stomach upset. So use it, but carefully.

Tea And Coffee

Ah! Who doesn't love them. Every body knows that tea and coffee taken daily will help you enjoy your life, keep you active. However, keep a check on the amount of coffee you take.

Chocolates and Others

Chocolate has been called a delicious sin. So indulge with it carefully and make sure you use it only for the best purposes. Of course, give it to some one you love because chocolates contain flavanoids that turn on your moods. Just check out each food, and the next time you have them, you know what you are taking.

Flax Seed Benefits for Heart Disease Patients

Flax is cultivated both for seed as well as for fibre. Different portions of the plant have been utilized to produce fabric, medicines, paper, dye, fishing nets in addition to soap. A vegetable oil known as linseed oil or flaxseed oil is produced by the seeds.

Flax seeds are somewhat bigger than sesame seeds and contain a rigid shell that is smooth and glossy. Their colour varies from deep amber to reddish brown conditional on whether the flax is of the golden or brown type. While whole flaxseeds include a soft crunch, the nutrients in grounded seeds are more effortlessly assimilated.

Health advantages:

- There are numerous health advantages to be achieved when eating flax seed as part of a healthy diet.
- A large number of individuals are preferring to incorporate flax seed in their diet due to its role in combating health conditions, for example, diabetes, cancer, menopause and arthritis.
- Possibly the most remarkable of these health advantages is the role of flax seed in effectively combating heart disease.

Flax seed has excessive quantities of the essential fatty acid Alpha-Linolenic Acid or ALA. Essential fatty acids are necessary for human health but cannot be produced by the body and ought to be acquired from food. ALA fits in to a cluster of fatty acids referred to as omega-3 fatty acids. Omega-3 fatty acids are normally obtained from fatty fish such as salmon. Omega-3 fatty acids help the heart by presenting some level of defence against coronary heart disease. Omega-3 fatty acids are as well vital since they are building blocks of human cell membranes and they play a vital part in a number of functions inside the body. Omega-3 fatty acids also aid in diminishing inflammation. Flax seed and flax seed oil have been revealed to assist increase HDL-cholesterol or the "good" cholesterol while reducing LDL-cholesterol or the Bad cholesterol levels. Other advantages demonstrate that flax seed may as well assist in reducing blood triglyceride and blood pressure. It may in addition keep platelets from turning out to be sticky hence diminishing the possibility of a heart attack

Flax seed is principally a good source of lignans. Lignan is a kind of antioxidant obtained from a diversity of plants. These potent antioxidants work all over the human body to eliminate free radicals. Free radicals can harm tissue and are considered to play a part in the pathology of numerous ailments. Lignans also make available an excellent source of fibre. Since the external hull of the flax seed is exceedingly hard to digest, it is usually suggested that one should crush or mill the whole flax seed to obtain the maximum nutritional advantage. Flax seed can be crushed with a reasonably priced coffee grinder or obtained pre-ground or milled. Flax seed is recognizable by the nutty flavour it imparts to a range of dishes. The seeds can be supplemented with almost every food.

Nuts in Diet

Individuals who are averse to eating nuts because of their excessive fat content may be encouraged by recent studies on nuts which show that though nuts are rich in calories and approximately 80 per cent of their calories come from fat, nuts are nutrient intense.

Nuts have the essential fatty acids, linoleic and linolenic acids, which are crucial for development, blood pressure control, healthy skin as well as hair, immune response in addition to blood clotting. Besides, the fats in nuts generally have unsaturated fats, particularly monounsaturated fat. This kind of fat does not increase blood cholesterol intensity like saturated fats. Monounsaturated fats have the extra advantage of increasing high-density lipoprotein, the "good" cholesterol. Nuts also make available one of the most excellent natural sources of Vitamin E, an antioxidant, and are high in protein, magnesium, dietary fibre, copper, potassium, phosphorus, selenium as well as folate.

Nuts are helpful in Reducing heart disease threat:

- It's long been acknowledged that dietary practice influences the threat factors of heart disease.
- A number of major nutrition studies have linked frequent nut use, particularly almonds, walnuts, hazelnuts in addition to macadamias, with a diminished threat of heart disease of 30-50 per cent
- It is believed that nuts can assist in decreasing the build-up of plaque in blood vessels by reducing the "bad" cholesterol levels.
- The antioxidant traits of nuts rich in vitamin E content may also have a say in the decrease of heart disease.
- Besides cholesterol, nuts can be useful in controlling high blood pressure.

Nuts can be utilized in combination with vegetable dishes as well as salads or added to pastas and casseroles for a crispy touch. The most significant point to keep in mind is that nuts should be eaten with restraint. The following are a few guidelines on how to integrate nuts into one's diet without having to bother about the calories: One can diminish the serving size by slicing or cutting the nuts into pieces. Nuts can be roasted at 350° F for 5 to 10 minutes to draw out the flavour. One can extract the cheese from pasta while utilizing nuts. It is advisable to opt for diminished quantities of lean meants, poultry and fish when nuts are being used with them. It is preferable to select fat-free dressing for the salad while utilizing nuts.

One can mix nuts with cereals or dried fruits to prepare a healthful snack that is wonderful to savor. It is recommended that one should opt for pre- portion nutty snacks instead of consuming them from a big jar or bag.

When incorporating nuts in one's diet, one should make certain to consider them as ingredient of the meat, fish, poultry, dry beans, eggs and nuts group. As far as portion size is concerned 1/3 cup of nuts is equivalent to one ounce of meat.

Benefits of Garlic in Heart Disease Patient

Garlic has been utilized as a medication for ages. Numerous researches have in addition confirmed the utilization of garlic for well-being and health. A number of studies imply that garlic may decrease levels of cholesterol, triglycerides or fatty materials and plaque accumulation in the arteries.

If individuals are fond of including additional garlic to their diet, there are definite tactics for cooking it to obtain its utmost advantage. Individuals are advised to be cautious of garlic supplements that are available in the market. Even though consumption of moderate amounts of garlic in food is not likely to be detrimental to health, taking excessive garlic in the shape of supplements can give rise to indications, for example, giddiness or fainting, stomach pain and sickness. In addition, garlic supplements may not be a prudent selection for everybody. Like every vitamin, mineral or herbal supplements, garlic supplements too can trigger adverse reactions if taken with other medicines.

Hence it is advisable for individuals to seek the help of a doctor before using garlic supplements for enhancing their garlic ingestion. The precise procedure by which garlic may be benefiting the body is yet to be comprehended. A number of the substances present in garlic, for example, sulfur-containing compounds, have been connected with definite health advantages.

- Garlic contains adenosine which may help in the deterrence of blood clots.
- Garlic is also known to contain certain substances that assist in the deterrence of blood clots and also aids in reducing cholesterol.
- Organic sulfide compounds present in garlic may aid in reducing cholesterol and thwart cancer.
- Sulfur-containing amino acids such as S-allylcysteine in garlic may assist in reducing cholesterol.
- It is believed that nuts can assist in decreasing the build-up of plaque in blood vessels by reducing the "bad" cholesterol levels.
- Certain studies have indicated considerable heart- linked advantagesofgarlic.Garlichastheantioxidants Vitamin A, Vitamin C as well as selenium and the use of garlic helps in the decline in plaque and deterrence of additional plaque accumulation which in turn diminishes the threat of atherosclerosis or hardening of the arteries.

Studies have revealed that garlic helps in maintaining elasticity or flexibility of the major artery, i.e., the aorta that pumps blood from the heart to the other parts of the body. Garlic seems to present the utmost health benefits when it has been permitted to remain in the crushed state for 10 to 15 minutes after being squashed or crushed. Throughout this time, sulfur-containing compounds are formed. Preferably, garlic is then ingested as an unprocessed flavouring on food. A number of health specialists even advocate that garlic cloves be chewed raw for maximum result. Nonetheless, other experts caution that consumption of excessive garlic can result in stomach trouble or heartburn. Consequently, cooking the garlic lightly after it has been preserved in a crushed state for a while could be the most excellent tactic.

Benefits of Soy

A considerable number of studies back the assertion that soy ingestion can assist an individual in losing weight. Soy protein makes available low-fat high-quality protein in comparison to several additional protein sources. It can assist individuals in developing lean muscle mass. In conjunction with exercise and a beneficial diet, soy protein makes an outstanding collaborator in a profitable weight loss plan. Soy protein assists an individual in feeling fuller for an extended period. New medical researches confirm soy protein assists individuals in feeling less hungry, and aids individuals in feeling full for a greater duration of time. Consumption of soy might work by triggering one's stomach to transmit a message to the brain indicating that one is full. This aids in diminishing the desire to snack between meals and late at night which are the two main reasons of weight gain.

Soy has more protein than carbs:

- Soybeans are the lone vegetable that has more protein than carbs.
- As a low-carb food that occurs naturally, soy is the ideal supplement to any weight loss plan, incorporating well-liked "low-carb" as well as "high-protein" diets.

Not only is soy protein depleted in carbs and fat, but it in addition has a low-glycemic index which implies it won't trigger a fast increase in blood sugar levels after ingestion.

This averts excess discharge of insulin that results in the unnecessary consequence of amassing additional sugar in one's bloodstream as body fat. Steady blood sugar and insulin levels signify fewer hunger yearning and fewer calories being accumulated as fat implies it contains all nine essential amino acids in the correct balance to cater to the body's requirements. This signifies that individuals obtain the top quality protein accessible, with less fat and fewer calories than the majority of meats. Soy protein has important nutritional traits that sustain energy, stamina, and sports activities. Soy protein is plentiful in "branched-chain amino acids" which the body can utilize as "fuel" to generate energy. As an absolute protein, soy assists in developing and preserving lean muscle mass. Soy may aid promote the discharge of specific anabolic hormones that advance muscle formation. Soy may assist in prolonging stamina levels for the duration of exercise.

Soy is also known to assist in enhancing recuperation time and decrease post-exercise exhaustion. Soy is in addition is useful in promoting a healthy cardiovascular system that is vital for exercising or an energetic lifestyle. Studies confirm that soy reduces total cholesterol, the "bad" LDL cholesterol, triglycerides, and might in addition increase good HDL cholesterol levels. Research indicates that diets at a low level in saturated fat and cholesterol that comprise 25 gm. of soy protein daily may diminish the threat of heart disease.

Pomegranate Juice and its Benefits

The pomegranate is approximately the size of a normal orange or apple. It is dark red to brownish in shade with a hard skin. The parts of the fruit that can be eaten are the seeds and the succulent transparent scarlet red pulp. Generally the pomegranate's flavour is covered in the seeds. The essence of these juicy seeds is subtle, sweet, and strong. The seeds are sheathed in the membrane which is white and malleable with an exceedingly unpleasant taste. The pomegranate has been recognized since long as the "jewel of winter".

Health advantages:

- Pomegranates have as well been in recent times preferred for their health advantages.
- The pomegranate has a great possibility for disease-combating antioxidants.
- Latest studies imply that pomegranate juice may possibly have nearly three times the antioxidant capability compared with the similar amount of green tea or red wine.
- It is in addition fairly rich in potassium as well as fibre, and has Vitamin C and niacin.
- Pomegranate juice has been utilized to deal with swelling, painful throats, in addition to rheumatism.
- One garden-fresh pomegranate has 0.1 gm. of saturated, monounsaturated, and polyunsaturated fats, 105 calories, 27 gm. of carbohydrates, 0 cholesterol, 0.9 gm. of dietary fibre, 5 mg. of sodium, 0.9 mg. of manganese, 0.5 gm. of fat, and 2 gm. of protein. Researchers have discovered that pomegranate juice is effective in treating prostate cancer cells. The juice is acknowledged to be plentiful in antioxidants that give rise to the vibrant colours of fruits and vegetables. These antioxidants also destroy cells that causes cancer and additional such ailments. One more study implies that pomegranate juice may perhaps in addition assist in combating heart disease. At present, there is scientific proof for the wild fruit's curative potential.

The antioxidants in the juice may as well aid in reducing the development of fat accumulation on artery walls. The pink or red-flowered sort incorporates the majority of the widespread and popular commercial types of pomegranates. In shape the fruit is round oblate or obviate. The external skin differs in depth. The external and internal colour too differs from off-white to a purplish or lively crimson colour. The seeds of the pomegranate in addition differ in size as well as hardness. Some fruits more or less appear to be seedless, while others are approximately unfit for human consumption since the seeds are very big and hard. Nonetheless, individuals in search of a wonderful tasting, sweet, and juicy pomegranate, should opt for ones that are white or pinkish in colour. The dark red to brownish fruits are frequently bitterer and contain bigger, harder seeds. Wonderful is certainly the most extensively grown pomegranate in the U.S. This type is big and intense purplish-red with a shiny look.

Tea and its Health Benefits

Tea prevents heart disease, reduces cholesterol as well as prevents a number of kinds of cancer while defending skin in addition to fortifying bones and teeth. What's more tea contains almost no calories; no fat and no salt and two cups of genuine tea are as plentiful in flavonoids as a helping of vegetables. One should drink tea that is strong and newly prepared, since studies confirm that bottled in addition to powdered types can be less helpful. An everyday quantity of four to six cups can yield immense benefits for the human body.

Benefits of tea are:

- Several of the most convincing studies related to tea links tea to reduced threat of stroke, high cholesterol and heart disease.
- A number of clinical experiments in addition to sizeable population studies have established that habitual tea drinkers are 44 per cent less expected to experience a heart attack than the common population, and those who have suffered attacks have greater chances of revival.
- Studies indicate that black tea seems to restore blood-vessel harm in individuals who have coronary-artery disease.
- Studies also reveal that regular tea-drinking considerably reduced LDL cholestrol or the bad type without diminishing useful HDL cholesterol.

Tea aids in checking sunburn as well as skin cancer. Researches indicate that consumption of hot black tea seems to defend against squamous-cell carcinoma. Putting on tea could be truly as helpful since studies reveal that green-tea compounds in skin lotions may defend against, and even undo sun harm.

Both experimental and large-population surveys imply black or green tea diminishes the threat of a numbers of cancers, especially, stomach and colorectal. Further studies indicate improved bone-density capacity among tea drinkers, perhaps because of the fluoride in tea, together with the catechins. Tea has been revealed to curb bacterial increase in the mouth, and it aids in checking cavities.

Green tea was the initial tea analysed for its cancer-combating advantages. New studies reveal that any tea obtained from the leaf of a warm-weather perennial referred to as Camellia sinensis has comparable cancer-combating traits. This consists of all green, black as well as red or oolong teas. The leaves of this tree have chemicals named polyphenols, which provide tea its antioxidant characteristics. The amount of processing decides whether a tea will be green, black or red. Green tea is slightly processed. They are just steamed swiftly prior to packaging. Black as well as red teas are moderately dried, compressed and fermented. The duration of fermentation, which causes the leaves to blacken, decides whether the tea will be red or black. No matter what the processing technique is, all teas have polyphenols.

Polyphenols, like additional antioxidants, assist in safeguarding cells from the usual, but harmful, physiological procedure referred to as "oxidative stress". even though oxygen is central to life, it's in addition integrated into reactive substances identified as free radicals. These can harm the cells in the body and have been concerned with the sluggish chain reaction of harm causing heart disease in addition to cancer.

Coffee-Antioxidants and Health Benefits

An individual's daily cup of coffee could in reality be of immense benefit to his or her health. The tannins in addition to antioxidants that occur naturally in coffee are recognized to combat free radicals and additional attacks on the body. Coffee which contains a number of defensive antioxidants is also known to diminish the threat of asthma attacks. Antioxidants are chemical compounds that defend the body's cells from the harmful consequences of oxidation. They assist in sustaining the immune system, and as a result, may reduce the threat of both cancer as well as heart disease. It is thought that the caffeine in coffee assists in enhancing the blood circulation inside the heart and arteries. One study demonstrates that in an evaluation among a variety of food groups, coffee had 64 per cent of the overall antioxidant ingestion. Coffee could in addition decrease the threat of gallstones by 45 per cent and cirrhosis of the liver by 80 per cent. A new study corroborates the presence of an inverse association between coffee ingestion and liver cirrhosis; even though studies have not been able to conclude which element in the coffee is responsible for generating the defensive effect.

Coffee is Helping asthma victims:

- An additional advantage of coffee is a 25 per cent decrease in the commencement of bouts among asthma victims.
- This recurring disease causes the airways to shut because of swelling, resulting in shortness of breath, coughing, tightness in the chest in addition to wheezing.

- One of the compounds in coffee, named theophylline, functions as a bronchodilator, which reduces these hazardous symptoms.
- Individuals with a headache continuing all through the day will find coffee extremely useful in relieving them of their discomfort.
- The caffeine in coffee has been acknowledged to assist in curing such types of headaches.

Generally, doctors suggest consumption of 2 to 4 cups of coffee every day, which is regarded as a sensible and reasonable quantity. Certainly, individuals are all dissimilar, and a number of them may prefer to drink more and several may wish to drink less, according to their personal way of life, routine, and health concerns. An 8 ounce cup of coffee contains roughly 75mg. of caffeine.

As large amounts of caffeine in coffee can be harmful for one's health, it is vital not to go beyond the suggested 300mg. of caffeine every day. Researches indicate that the ingestion of coffee is connected with diminished threat of specific cancers, Parkinson's disease, kidney stones and hepatic diseases. As far has health hazards of coffee consumption is concerned, nothing by any means has been established against coffee when consumed in an amount not in excess of four cups on a daily basis.

Health Benefits of Reishi

Reishi is a type of mushroom generally found in the coastal regions of China. It is also grown in Taiwan, Korea, North America, and Japan. Reishi is known as the "herb of spiritual potency", or hing zhi. They are usually discovered on the bases of fallen trees and decaying logs.

Reishi can be found in six different types of colour, but red mushrooms are commonly utilized for medicinal purposes in Asia and North America. The fruiting portion of the mushroom is generally used for medicinal purposes. Reishi is made use of to cure asthma, coughs, debility and exhaustion, along with sleeplessness. Polysaccharides, coumarin, sterols, mannitol, and triterpenoids labelled ganoderic acids are the chief elements of the mushroom.

Ganoderic acids can be capable of reducing cholesterol and blood pressure apart from hindering blood platelets from joining together. Although it has not yet been established, these acids may also aid in the treatment of hepatitis B that is chronic in nature, sickness associated with altitude, cancer, and diabetes mellitus. It flourishes in thickly wooded mountains where humidity is high and sunlight is not particularly strong. It is not often found because it grows chiefly on the parched trunks of dead plum, guercus serrata or pasonia trees.

Among 10,000 such mature trees, possibly 2 or 3 will have Reishi development. Consequently it is exceedingly in short supply. Its scarcity can be attributed to the hard outer husks of its spores that make germination almost impracticable.

There are several types of Reishi, namely, Akashiba (red reishi), Kuroshiba (black reishi), Aoshiba (blue reishi), Shiroshiba (white reishi), Kishiba (yellow reishi), Murasakishiba (purple reishi). Reishi is considered as an ideal medicine since its wide-ranging qualities can be effective for healing as well as precautionary purposes. It yields outstanding results when made use of by a person who is vulnerable to ailment in the pre-ailment phase. Reishi mushroom is specifically helpful for persons with asthma in addition to other respiratory ailments. Reishi is known to have a curing effect on the lungs and is beneficial for respiratory power in addition to coughing.

Benefits of Reishi are:

- Reishi is known to expand longevity, enhance youthful energy and vigour.
- It also helps in improving blood circulation by eradicating thrombi in the blood streams.
- This accounts for improved vigour of a person. Use of Reishi checks degeneration of body and mind.
- Reishi is indeed well known for its versatility.
- It has also been found that Reishi possesses traits that help in dealing with cholesterosis and coronary deficiency along with effectively enhancing the nervous system.
- The use of Reishi has also proved beneficial in treating chronic bronchitis and hepatitis.
- Reishi also assists in developing the leukocytopenia and reticuloendothelial system.

As far as Reishi is concerned the success rate of healing a number of ailments are highly impressive. For instance, allergy associated with chronic bronchitis, which is among the toughest to heal, has a recuperation rate of 60 per cent to 97.7 per cent when treated with Reishi.

Chocolates—Are they Good for Health ?

Since centuries, chocolate has been extremely appreciated by individuals of all ages because of its unique taste. Several experts have observed that chocolates are harmful and excessive consumption frequently leads to tooth decay. A number of medical professionals have affirmed that chocolates have sugar substances and therefore enhance the level of calories in the body and augment the sugar concentration in the blood.

But, it has been in recent times established that chocolates are beneficial for the health since they have numerous advantages. Chocolates have antioxidants. Consequently they destroy the free radicals and hinder the oxidization of lipids into the body. The antioxidants are a condensed type of flavonoids.

Benefits of chocolates are:

- The antioxidants in chocolate assist in the anti-ageing procedure.
- As indicated by recent studies if individuals eat chocolates he or she is diminishing the possibility of heart troubles.
- Chocolate is an anti-inflammatory means as well.
- Chocolate has cocoa butter to a certain degree and these aids in salvaging the exhausted elasticity in the body.
- In addition to these traits, chocolate functions as a remarkable medicine for depression. Many advocate that individuals eat a chocolate any time he or she feels like consuming it. One can actually spend one's time in an exceedingly attractive manner and stop thinking about all the tribulations of life when one savors tasty chocolate.

Chocolate has in excess of 300 chemicals, and has been the focus of several studies by universities as well as other scientific institutes

Some of the Beneficial Effects of Chocolates

Cacao, the main ingredient of chocolate, has antibacterial agents that combat tooth decay. Obviously, this is neutralized by the excessive amount of sugar present in milk chocolate. The aroma of chocolate may augment theta brain waves, giving rise to relaxation. Chocolate has phenyl ethylamine, a docile mood elevator. The cocoa butter in chocolate has oleic acid, a mono- unsaturated fat which may possibly increase good cholesterol.

It has been found that consumption of a cup of hot chocolate prior to meals may in reality reduce appetite. It has been observed that people who consume chocolate live a year longer in comparison to those who don't. The flavanoids in chocolate may assist in keeping blood vessels elastic. It has been revealed that chocolate augments antioxidant levels in the blood. The carbohydrates in chocolate increase serotonin concentrations in the brain leading to a feeling of happiness. There are numerous misconceptions about the effects of chocolate on the human body. Contrary to popular perception studies confirm that chocolate is not a contributing factor in acne. The stimulants caffeine and bromine are present in cacao in such little amounts that they don't result in nervous excitability. Unlike widespread belief chocolate is not addictive. Chocolate has stearic acid, a neutral fat which doesn't increase bad cholesterol.

Health Benefits of Yogurt

Consumption of yogurt on a daily basis is exceedingly beneficial for the body. For individuals trying to increase their protein, calcium and dairy intake, yogurt is a nourishing alternative. Yogurt is not only a delicious snack including fruits on the bottom, it has immense health advantages.

It is an outstanding source of calcium, protein, riboflavin and vitamin B 12. When yogurt is contrasted to milk, yogurt has greater amounts of calcium as well as protein because of the additional cultures in the yogurt. Yogurt ought to have active and living cultures in order to be yogurt. Cultures are made up of distinctive living microorganisms which are responsible for numerous health as well as nutritional advantages of yogurt.

Yogurts are wed for enhancing natural resistance:

- It enhances natural resistance and contains a good quantity of phosphorus as well as 88 per cent water.
- Individuals with a threat of osteoporosis ought to consume no less than one helping of yogurt every day.
- It has as well been asserted that yogurt may defend against certain kinds of cancer but more studies have to be conducted.

There are three kinds of yogurt, namely regular or whole milk, low-fat and skim. Low-fat and skim yogurt are beneficial for individuals who are on a cholesterol reducing diet or simply trying to maintain their weights. These types of yogurt do not increase blood cholesterol concentrations.

A number of individuals have problems digesting lactose, a carbohydrate in milk as well as milk products, due to the lack of enzyme lactase in the body. Live yogurt cultures yield lactase and split down the lactose.

Yogurt is a beneficial way to obtain the calcium the body requires, for the individuals who can not endure milk products.Additional advantages of live as well as active cultures in the yogurt are that they may assist in improving the immune system.

They promote the appropriate type of bacteria to grow in the gut. These bacteria aid in digesting food and foil stomach infections. In addition, they facilitate to offer respite from vaginal infections.

Yogurt must be stocked in the refrigerator since it is a fresh dairy product. Yogurt treated with heat has a greater shelf life but it does not provide the nutritional advantages akin to the yogurt with live cultures since heat processing damages the cultures.

To obtain the maximum health advantages from yogurt, there ought to be a live and active cultures stamp on the label. Yogurt is quite popular and ingested in nearly all areas of the world. People in several regions utilize lots of yogurt in their food. In certain countries people generally consume yogurt, plain devoid of sugar together with major dishes akin to stuffed cabbage as well as spinach. Some people also make yogurt drinks made with plain yogurt, salt and water. Many people eat yogurt with fried vegetables for example eggplant or zucchini.

KEYS TO A HEALTHY DIET

Developing healthy eating habits isn't as confusing or as restrictive as many people imagine. The first principle of a healthy diet is simply to eat a wide variety of foods. This is important because different foods make different nutritional contributions. Secondly, fruits, vegetables, grains, and legumes— foods high in complex carbohydrates, fibre, vitamins, and minerals, low in fat, and free of cholesterol—should make up the bulk of the calories you consume.

The rest should come from low-fat dairy products, lean meat and poultry, and fish. You should also try to maintain a balance between calorie intake and calorie expenditure—that is, don't eat more food than your body can utilize. Otherwise, you will gain weight. The more active you are, therefore, the more you can eat and still maintain this balance. Following these three basic steps doesn't mean that you have to give up your favourite foods. As long as your overall diet is balanced and rich in nutrients and fibre, there is nothing wrong with an occasional cheeseburger. Just be sure to limit how frequently you eat such foods, and try to eat small portions of them.

You can also view healthy eating as an opportunity to expand your range of choices by trying foods—especially vegetables, whole grains, or fruits— that you don't normally eat. A healthy diet doesn't have to mean eating foods that are bland or unappealing.

The following basic guidelines are what you need to know to construct a healthy diet:

- Eat plenty of high-fibre foods—that is, fruits, vegetables, beans, and whole grains. These are the"good" carbohydrates-nutritious, filling, and relatively low in calories. They should supply the 20 to 30 gm. of dietary fibre you need each day, which slows the absorption of carbohydrates, so there's less effect on insulin and blood sugar, and provides other health benefits as well. Such foods also provide important vitamins, minerals, and phytochemicals.

  The antioxidants and other nutrients in these foods may help protect against developing certain types of cancer and other diseases. Eat five or more servings a day.
- Limit your intake of sugary foods, refined-grain products such as white bread, and salty snack foods. Sugar, our No.1 additive, is added to a vast array of foods. Just one daily 12-ounce can of soda can add up to 16 pounds over the course of a year. Many sugary foods are also high in fat, so they're calorie-dense.

- Cut down on animal fat. It's rich in saturated fat, which boosts blood cholesterol levels and has other adverse health effects. Choose lean meats, skinless poultry, and non-fat or low-fat or non-fat dairy products.
- Cut way down on trans fats, supplied by hydrogenated vegetable oils used in most processed foods in the supermarket and in many fast foods.
- Eat more fish and nuts, which contain healthy unsaturated fats. Substitute olive or canola oil for butter or stick margarine.
- Keep portions moderate, especially of high-calorie foods. In recent years serving sizes have ballooned, particularly in restaurants. Choose a starter instead of an entrée, split a dish with a friend, and don't order supersized anything.
- Keep your cholesterol intake below 300 mg. per day. Cholesterol is found only in animal products, such as meats, poultry, dairy products, and egg yolks.
- Eat a variety of foods. Don't try to fill your nutrient requirements by eating the same foods day in, day out. It is possible that not every essential nutrient has been identified, and so eating a wide assortment of foods helps to ensure that you will get all the necessary nutrients. In addition, this will limit your exposure to any pesticides or toxic substances that may be present in one particular food.
- Maintain an adequate calcium intake. Calcium is essential for strong bones and teeth. Get your calcium from low-fat sources, such as skim milk and low-fat yogurt. If you can't get the optimal amount from foods, take supplements.
- Try to get your vitamins and minerals from foods, not from supplements. Supplements cannot substitute for a healthy diet, which supplies nutrients and other compounds besides vitamins and minerals. Foods also provide the "synergy" that many nutrients require to be efficiently used in the body.
- Maintain a desirable weight. Balance energy intake with energy output. Exercise and other physical activity are essential.
- If you drink alcohol, do so in moderation. That is one drink a day for women, two a day for men. A drink is defined as 12 ounces of beer, 4 ounces of wine, or 1.5 ounces of 80-proof spirits. Excess alcohol consumption leads to a variety of health problems. And alcoholic beverages can add many calories to your diet without supplying nutrients.

□

6

Carbohydrates

INTRODUCTION

A carbohydrate is an organic compound with the empirical formula Cm(H2O)n, that is, consists only of carbon, hydrogen and oxygen, with the last two in the 2:1 atom ratio. Carbohydrates can be viewed as hydrates of carbon, hence their name.

Structurally however, it is more accurate to view them as polyhydroxy aldehydes and ketones. The term is most common in biochemistry, where it is a synonym of saccharide. The carbohydrates (saccharides) are divided into four chemical groupings: monosaccharides, disaccharides, oligosaccharides, and polysaccharides.

In general, the monosaccharides and disaccharides, which are smaller (lower molecular weight) carbohydrates, are commonly referred to as sugars. The word saccharide comes from the Greek word sakkharon meaning "sugar". While the scientific nomenclature of carbohydrates is complex, the names of the monosaccharides and disaccharides very often end in the suffix -ose. For example, blood sugar is the monosaccharide glucose, table sugar is the disaccharide sucrose, and milk sugar is the disaccharide lactose.

Carbohydratesperformnumerousrolesinlivingthings.Polysaccharides serve for the storage of energy and as structural components. The 5-carbon monosaccharide ribose is an important component of coenzymes and the backbone of the genetic molecule known as RNA. The related deoxyribose is a component of DNA. Saccharides and their derivatives include many other important biomolecules that play key roles in the immune system, fertilization, preventing pathogenesis, blood clotting, and development. In food science and in many informal contexts, the term carbohydrate often means any food that is particularly rich in starch (such as cereals, bread and pasta) or sugar (such as candy, jams and desserts).

STRUCTURE AND FORMS

Formerly the name "carbohydrate" was used in chemistry for any compound with the formula $C_m(H_2O)_n$. Following this definition, some chemists considered formaldehyde CH_2O to be the simplest carbohydrate, while others claimed that title for glycolaldehyde. Today the term is generally understood in the biochemistry sense, which excludes compounds with only one or two carbons. Natural saccharides are generally built of simple carbohydrates called monosaccharides with general formula $(CH_2O)_n$ where n is three or more. A typical monosaccharide has the structure H- $(CHOH)_x(C=O)-(CHOH)_y$-H, that is, an aldehyde or ketone with many hydroxyl groups added, usually one on each carbon atom that is not part of the aldehyde or ketone functional group. Examples of monosaccharides are glucose, fructose, and glyceraldehyde.

However, some biological substances commonly called "monosaccharides" do not conform to this formula (e.g., uronic acids and deoxy-sugars such as fucose), and there are many chemicals that do conform to this formula but are not considered to be monosaccharides (e.g., formaldehyde CH_2O and inositol $(CH_2O)_6$).

The open-chain form of a monosaccharide often coexists with a closed ring form where the aldehyde/ketone carbonyl group carbon (C=O) and hydroxyl group (-OH) react forming a hemiacetal with a new C-O-C bridge. Monosaccharides can be linked together into what are called polysaccharides (or oligosaccharides) in a large variety of ways. Many carbohydrates contain one or more modified monosaccharide units that have had one or more groups replaced or removed. For example, deoxyribose, a component of DNA, is a modified version of ribose; chitin is composed of repeating units of N- acetylglucosamine, a nitrogen-containing form of glucose.

Monosaccharides

Monosaccharides are the simplest carbohydrates in that they cannot be hydrolyzed to smaller carbohydrates. They are aldehydes or ketones with two or more hydroxyl groups. The general chemical formula of an unmodified monosaccharide is (CH2O)n, literally a "carbon hydrate". Monosaccharides are important fuel molecules as well as building blocks for nucleic acids. The smallest monosaccharides, for which n = 3, are dihydroxyacetone and D- and L-glyceraldehyde.

Classification of Monosaccharides

Monosaccharides are classified according to three different characteristics: the placement of its carbonyl group, the number of carbon atoms it contains, and its chiral handedness. If the carbonyl group is an aldehyde, the monosaccharide is an aldose; if the carbonyl group is a ketone, the monosaccharide is a ketose.

Monosaccharides with three carbon atoms are called trioses, those with four are called tetroses, five are called pentoses, six are hexoses, and so on. These two systems of classification are often combined. For example, glucose is an aldohexose (a six-carbon aldehyde), ribose is an aldopentose (a five-carbon aldehyde), and fructose is a ketohexose (a six-carbon ketone).

Each carbon atom bearing a hydroxyl group (-OH), with the exception of the first and last carbons, are asymmetric, making them stereocentres with two possible configurations each (R or S). Because of this asymmetry, a number of isomers may exist for any given monosaccharide formula. The aldohexose D-glucose, for example, has the formula $(CH_2O)_6$, of which all but two of its six carbons atoms are stereogenic, making D-glucose one of $2^4 = 16$ possible stereoisomers. In the case of glyceraldehyde, an aldotriose, there is one pair of possible stereoisomers, which are enantiomers and epimers. 1,3- dihydroxyacetone, the ketose corresponding to the aldose glyceraldehyde, is a symmetric molecule with no stereocentres.

The assignment of D or L is made according to the orientation of the asymmetric carbon furthest from the carbonyl group: in a standard Fischer projection if the hydroxyl group is on the right the molecule is a D sugar, otherwise it is an L sugar. The "D-" and "L-" prefixes should not be confused with "d-" or "l-", which indicate the direction that the sugar rotates plane polarized light. This usage of "d-" and "l-" is no longer followed in carbohydrate chemistry.

Ring-straight Chain Isomerism

The aldehyde or ketone group of a straight-chain monosaccharide will react reversibly with a hydroxyl group on a different carbon atom to form a hemiacetal or hemiketal, forming a heterocyclic ring with an oxygen bridge between two carbon atoms.

Rings with five and six atoms are called furanose and pyranose forms, respectively, and exist in equilibrium with the straight-chain form. During the conversion from straight-chain form to cyclic form, the carbon atom containing the carbonyl oxygen, called the anomeric carbon, becomes a stereogenic centre with two possible configurations: The oxygen atom may take a position either above or below the plane of the ring.

The resulting possible pair of stereoisomers are called anomers. In the α anomer, the -OH substituent on the anomeric carbon rests on the opposite side (trans) of the ring from the CH_2OH side branch.

The alternative form, in which the CH_2OH substituent and the anomeric hydroxyl are on the same side (cis) of the plane of the ring, is called the β anomer. You can remember that the β anomer is cis by the mnemonic, "It's always better to βe up." Because the ring and straight-chain forms readily interconvert, both anomers exist in equilibrium. In a Fischer Projection, the α anomer is represented with the anomeric hydroxyl group trans to the CH_2OH and cis in the β anomer.

Use in Living Organisms

Monosaccharides are the major source of fuel for metabolism, being used both as an energy source (glucose being the most important in nature) and in biosynthesis. When monosaccharides are not immediately needed by many cells they are often converted to more space efficient forms, often polysaccharides. In many animals, including humans, this storage form is glycogen, especially in liver and muscle cells. In plants, starch is used for the same purpose.

Disaccharides

Two joined monosaccharides are called a disaccharide and these are the simplest polysaccharides. Examples include sucrose and lactose. They are composed of two monosaccharide units bound together by a covalent bond known as a glycosidic linkage formed via a dehydration reaction, resulting in the loss of a hydrogen atom from one monosaccharide and a hydroxyl group from the other. The formula of unmodified disaccharides is $C_{12}H_{22}O_{11}$.

Although there are numerous kinds of disaccharides, a handful of disaccharides are particularly notable. Sucrose, pictured to the right, is the most abundant disaccharide, and the main form in which carbohydrates are transported in plants. It is composed of one D-glucose molecule and one D-fructose molecule.

The systematic name for sucrose, O-α-D-glucopyranosyl-(1 → 2)-D-fructofuranoside, indicates four things:

- Its monosaccharides: Glucose and fructose.
- Their ring types: Glucose is a pyranose, and fructose is a furanose.
- How they are linked together: The oxygen on carbon number 1 (C1) of α-D-glucose is linked to the C2 of D-fructose.
- The -oside suffix indicates that the anomeric carbon of both monosaccharides participates in the glycosidic bond.

Lactose, a disaccharide composed of one D-galactose molecule and one D-glucose molecule, occurs naturally in mammalian milk. The systematic name for lactose is O-β-D-galactopyranosyl-(1 → 4)-D-glucopyranose. Other notable disaccharides include maltose (two D-glucoses linked α-1,4) and cellulobiose (two D-glucoses linked β-1,4).

Oligosaccharides and Polysaccharides

Oligosaccharides and polysaccharides are composed of longer chains of monosaccharide units bound together by glycosidic bonds. The distinction between the two is based upon the number of monosaccharide units present in the chain. Oligosaccharides typically contain between three and ten monosaccharide units, and polysaccharides contain greater than ten monosaccharide units. Definitions of how large a carbohydrate must be to fall into each category vary according to personal opinion.

Oligosaccharides are found as a common form of protein post-translational modification. Such post-translational modifications include the Lewis and ABO oligosaccharides responsible for blood group classifications and so of tissue incompatibilities, the alpha-Gal epitope responsible for hyperacute rejection in xenotransplantation, and O-GlcNAc modifications. Polysaccharides represent an important class of biological polymers. Their function in living organisms is usually either structure- or storage-related. Starch (a polymer of glucose) is used as a storage polysaccharide in plants, being found in the form of both amylose and the branched amylopectin. In animals, the structurally similar glucose polymer is the more densely branched glycogen, sometimes called "animal starch". Glycogen's properties allow it to be metabolized more quickly, which suits the active lives of moving animals.

Cellulose and chitin are examples of structural polysaccharides. Cellulose is used in the cell walls of plants and other organisms, and is claimed to be the most abundant organic molecule on earth. It has many uses such as a significant role in the paper and textile industries, and is used as a feedstock for the production of rayon (via the viscose process), cellulose acetate, celluloid, and nitrocellulose. Chitin has a similar structure, but has nitrogen-containing side branches, increasing its strength. It is found in arthropod exoskeletons and in the cell walls of some fungi. It also has multiple uses, including surgical threads. Other polysa-eccharides include callose or laminarin, chrysolaminarin, xylan, arabinoxylan, mannan, fucoidan, and galactomannan.

Nutrition

Foods high in simple carbohydrates include fruits, sweets and soft drinks. Foods high in complex carbohydrates include breads, pastas, beans, potatoes, bran, rice, and cereals. The most common complex carbohydrate in these foods is starch. Carbohydrates are the most common source of energy in living organisms. Proteins and fat are necessary building components for body tissue and cells, and are also a source of energy for most organisms.

Carbohydrates are not essential nutrients in humans: the body can obtain all its energy from protein and fats. The brain and neurons generally cannot burn fat for energy, but can use glucose or ketones; the body can also synthesize some glucose from a few of the amino acids in protein and also from the glycerol backbone in triglycerides. Carbohydrate contains 15.8 kilojoules (3.75 kilocalories) and proteins 16.8 kilojoules (4 kilocalories) per gm., while fats contain 37.8 kilojoules (9 kilocalories) per gm. In the case of protein, this is somewhat misleading as only some amino acids are usable for fuel. Likewise, in humans, only some carbohydrates are usable for fuel, as in many monosaccharides and some disaccharides. Other carbohydrate types can be used, but only with the assistance of gut bacteria. Ruminants and termites can even process cellulose, which is indigestible to humans.

Based on the effects on risk of heart disease and obesity, the Institute of Medicine recommends that American and Canadian adults get between 45–65 per cent of dietary energy from carbohydrates. The Food and Agriculture Organization and World Health Organization jointly recommend that national dietary guidelines set a goal of 55–75 per cent of total energy from carbohydrates, but only 10 per cent directly from sugars (their term for simple carbohydrates).

Classification

For dietary purposes, carbohydrates can be classified as simple (monosaccharides and disaccharides) or complex (oligosaccharides and polysaccharides). The term complex carbohydrate was first used in the U.S. Senate Select Committee on Nutrition and Human Needs publication Dietary Goals for the United States (1977), where it denoted "fruit, vegetables and whole-grains".

Dietary guidelines generally recommend that complex carbohydrates, and such nutrient-rich simple carbohydrate sources such as fruit (glucose or fructose) and dairy products (lactose) make up the bulk of carbohydrate consumption. This excludes such sources of simple sugars as candy and sugary drinks. The USDA's Dietary Guidelines for Americans 2005 dispensed with the simple/complex distinction, instead recommending fibre-rich foods and whole grains.

The glycemic index and glycemic load concepts have been developed to characterize food behaviour during human digestion. They rank carbohydrate- rich foods based on the rapidity of their effect on blood glucose levels.

The insulin index is a similar, more recent classification method that ranks foods based on their effects on blood insulin levels, which are caused by glucose (or starch) and some amino acids in food. Glycemic index is a measure of how quickly food glucose is absorbed, while glycemic load is a measure of the total absorbable glucose in foods.

Catabolism

Catabolism is the metabolic reaction cells undergo to extract energy. There are two major metabolic pathways of monosaccharide catabolism: glycolysis and the citric acid cycle. In glycolysis, oligo/polysaccharides are cleaved first to smaller monosaccharides by enzymes called glycoside hydrolases. The monosaccharide units can then enter into monosaccharide catabolism. In some cases, as with humans, not all carbohydrate types are usable as the digestive and metabolic enzymes necessary are not present.

THE ROLE OF CARBOHYDRATES IN NUTRITION

Carbohydrates are polyhydroxy aldehydes, ketones, alcohols, acids, their simple derivatives and their polymers having linkages of the acetal type. They may be classified according to their degree of polymerization and may be divided initially into three principal groups, namely sugars, oligosaccharides and polysaccharides.

Table: The Major Dietary Carbohdrates

Class (DP*)	Sub-Group	Components
Sugars (1-2)	Monosaccharides	Glucose, galactose, fructose
	Disaccharides	Sucrose, lactose, trehalose
	Polyols	Sorbitol, mannitol
Oligosaccharides (3-9)	Malto-oligosaccharides	Maltodextrins
	Other oligosaccharides	Raffinose, stachyose, fructo-oligosaccharides
Polisaccharides (>9)	Starch	Amylose, amylopectin, modified starches
	Non-starch polisaccharides	Cellulose, hemicellulose, pectins, hydrocolloids

Note:

DP * = Degree of polymerization

Each of these three groups may be subdivided on the basis of the monosaccharide composition of the individual carbohydrates. Sugars comprise monosaccharides, disacc-harides and polyols (sugar alcohols); oligosaccharides include malto-oligosaccharides, principally those occurring from the hydrolysis of starch, and other oligosaccharides, e.g., a -galactosides (raffinose, stachyose, etc.) and fructo-oligosaccharides; the final group are the polysaccharides which may be divided into starch (a -glucans) and non-starch polysaccharides of which the major components are the polysaccharides of the plant cell wall such as cellulose, hemicellulose and pectin (2,3,4).

Total Carbohydrate

Although the individual components of dietary carbohydrate are readily identifiable, there is some confusion as to what comprises total carbohydrate as reported in food tables. Two principal measures of total carbohydrate are used, firstly, that derived by "difference" and secondly the direct measurement of the individual components which are then combined to give a total. Calculating carbohydrates by "difference" has been used since the turn of the century.

The protein, fat, ash and moisture content of a food are determined, subtracted from the total weight of the food and the remainder, or "difference", is considered to be carbohydrate. There are, however, a number of problems with this approach to total carbohydrate analysis in that the "by difference" figure includes a number of non-carbohydrate components such as lignin, organic acids, tannins, waxes, and some Maillard products. In addition to this error, it combines all of the analytical errors from the other analyses. Finally, a single global figure for carbohydrates in food is uninformative because it fails to identify the many types of carbohydrates in a food and thus to allow some understanding of the potential physiological properties of those carbohydrates.

Terminlogy

In deciding how to classify dietary carbohydrate the principal problem is to reconcile the various chemical divisions of carbohydrate with that which reflects physiology and health. A classification based purely on chemistry does not allow a ready translation into nutritional terms since each of the major classes of carbohydrate have a variety of physiological effects.

However, a classification based on physiological properties also creates a number of problems in that it requires a single effect to be considered as overridingly important and to be used as the basis of the classification. This dichotomy has led to the introduction of a number of terms to describe various fractions and sub-fractions of carbohydrate.

Sugars

The term "sugars" is conventionally used to describe the mono and disaccharides. "Sugar", by contrast, is used to describe purified sucrose as are the terms "refined sugar" and "added sugar".

Extrinsic and Intrinsic Sugars

These terms had their origin in a United Kingdom Department of Health committee in 1989, which was looking at the question of sugars in the diet. The terms were developed to help the consumer choose between what were considered to be healthy sugars and those which were not. Intrinsic sugars were defined as sugars occurring within the cell walls of plants, i.e., naturally occurring, while extrinsic sugars were those which were usually added to foods. Because lactose in milk is also an extrinsic sugar, an additional phrase "non-milk extrinsic sugars" was developed. These terms have not gained wide acceptance either in the U.K. or other countries in the world. There are no current plans to measure these sugars separately in the diet nor to incorporate their use into food tables.

Complex Carbohydrates

This term was first used in the McGovern report, "Dietary Goals for the United States" in 1977. The term was coined largely to distinguish sugars from other carbohydrates and in the report denotes "fruit, vegetables and whole- grains". The term has since come to be used to describe either starch alone, or the combination of all polysaccharides.

It was used to encourage consumption of what were considered to be healthy foods such as whole-grain cereals, etc., but becomes meaningless when used to describe fruit and vegetables which are low in starch. Furthermore, it is now realised that starch, which is by any definition a complex carbohydrate, is variable metabolically with some forms being rapidly absorbed and having a high glycemic index and some being resistant to digestion.

The term "complex carbohydrate" has encompassed, at various times, starch, dietary fibre and non-digestible oligosaccharides. As a substitute term for starch, however, it would seem to have little merit and, in principle, it is better to discuss carbohydrate components by using their common chemical names.

Available and Unavailable Carbohydrate

A major step forward conceptually in our understanding of carbohydrates was made by McCance and Lawrence in 1929 with the division of dietary carbohydrate into available and unavailable. In an attempt to prepare food tables for diabetic diets they realised that not all carbohydrates could be "utilized and metabolized", i.e., provide the body with "carbohydrates for metabolism".

Available carbohydrate was defined as "starch and soluble sugars" and unavailable as "mainly hemicellulose and fibre". This concept proved useful, not the least because it drew attention to the fact that some carbohydrate is not digested and absorbed in the small intestine but rather reaches the large bowel where it is fermented. It suggests that the site of digestion or fermentation in the gut of carbohydrate is of overriding importance. However, it is misleading to talk of carbohydrate as "unavailable" because some indigestible carbohydrate is able to provide the body with energy through fermentation.

There are many properties of carbohydrate of which digestibility and fermentability are only two. A more appropriate substitute for the terms "available" and "unavailable" today would be to describe carbohydrates as either as glycemic or non-glycemic, which is closer to the original concept of McCance and Lawrence.

Resistant Starch

One of the major developments in our understanding of the importance of carbohydrates for health in the past twenty years has been the discovery of resistant starch. Resistant starch is defined as "starch and starch degradation products not absorbed in the small intestine of healthy humans". The main forms of resistant starch are physically enclosed starch, e.g., within intact cell structures (RS_1), some raw starch granules (RS_2) and retrograded amylose (RS_3).

Modified Starch

The proportions of amylose and amylopectin in a starchy food is variable and can be altered by plant breeding. Techniques using genetic engineering are rapidly emerging, enabling starches to be produced for specific purposes by genetically modifying the crop used for their production. High amylose corn starch and high amylopectin (waxy) corn starch have been available for a long time, and display quite different functional as well as nutritional properties.

High amylose starches require higher temperatures for gelatinization and are more prone to retrograde and to form amylose-lipid complexes. Such properties can be utilized in the formulation of foods with low glycemic index and/or high resistant starch content. Physical modifications of starches include pregelatinization and partial hydrolysis (dextrinization).

Chemical modification is mainly the introduction of side groups and cross- linking or oxidation. These modifications may be used to decrease viscosity and to improve gel stability, mouthfeel, appearance and texture, and resistance for heat treatment. The application of modified starches as fat replacers is another important area. Some modified starches may be partly resistant to digestion in the small intestine, thereby adding to resistant starch.

Dietary Fibre

The original description of dietary fibre by Trowell in 1972 was "that portion of food which is derived from cellular walls of plants which is digested very poorly by human beings". This is not an exact description of any carbohydrate in the diet but is more a physiological concept. It was linked by Burkitt and Trowell to the etiology of a number of "Western diseases" and on the basis of this a hypothesis relating fibre to health was developed. The use of the term has, however, caused many difficulties over the years because of controversies regarding definition.

Moreover, the proposal that there are a number of dietary fibre deficiency disorders is an over-simplification and needs to be modified now in the light of new knowledge of diet and disease. The main components of dietary fibre are derived from the cell walls of plant material in the diet and comprise cellulose, hemicellulose and pectin. Lignin, a non-carbohydrate component of the cell wall is also often included. Dietary fibre is a term which is felt to be valuable for the consumer who looks upon this as a healthy component of the diet. At the present time there is no consensus as to which components of carbohydrate should be included as dietary fibre and different authors have variously included non-starch polysaccharides and resistant starch.

More recently it has been suggested that non-digestible oligosaccharides should also be included. Dietary fibre has also been defined by method. While there is general agreement that the non-starch polysaccharides are the principal part of dietary fibre there is currently no consensus as to whether other components should be included in this term. It has been suggested that the use of the term dietary fibre be gradually phased out. Its widespread use and popularity with the consumer has made this difficult in practice and the term has been useful in nutrition education and product development.

Soluble and Insoluble Fibre

These terms developed out of the early chemistry of non-starch polysaccharides which showed that the fractional extraction of these polysaccharides could be controlled by changing the pH of solutions.

They proved very useful in the initial understanding of the physiological properties of dietary fibre, allowing a simple division into those which principally had effects on glucose and lipid absorption from the small intestine and those which were slowly and incompletely fermented and had more pronounced effects on bowel habit. However, the separation of soluble and insoluble fractions is not chemically very distinct being dependent on the conditions of extraction. Moreover, the physiological differences are not, in fact, so distinct with much insoluble fibre being rapidly and completely fermented while not all soluble fibre has effects on glucose and lipid absorption.

Methodology for Dietary Carbohydrate Analysis

Mono- and Disaccharides: They can be analysed specifically by enzymatic, gas-liquid chromatography (GLC) or high performance liquid chromatography (HPLC) methods. Depending on the food matrix to be analysed, extraction of the low molecular weight carbohydrates in aqueous ethanol, usually 80 per cent (v/ v), may be advisable before analysis. The enzymatic procedures are based on specific, highly purified enzymes and have been instrumental in providing means of specific and precise analysis of individual carbohydrates in mixtures without a large investment in instrumentation.

Enzymatic methods are still preferable when one single carbohydrate is to be analysed, e.g., glucose, as the end point of starch analysis. When several different monosaccharides are to be determined simultaneously, HPLC or GLC methods are preferable. HPLC systems using sensitive amperometric detectors are gaining in popularity over GLC, in that the derivatization necessary before the GLC determination is avoided.

Polyols

Polyols are usually determined by GLC using alditol acetate derivatives. HPLC methods are also available.

Oligosaccharides

Oligosaccharides can also be determined by GLC or HPLC methods. These methods work well for purified preparations, but in complex foods or diets, enzymatic hydrolysis and determination of liberated monosaccharides is an alternative for specific determination. Malto-oligosaccharides are recovered as "starch" if not extracted before starch analysis.

Separation of Oligosaccharides from Polysaccharides

By definition, polysaccharides have 10 or more monomeric units, and Oligosaccharides less than 10. Analytically, separation is based on solubility in aqueous ethanol, usually around 80 per cent (v/v). The alcohol solubility of carbohydrates, however, is dependent not only on the degree of polymerization (DP), but also on the molecular structure. For instance, highly branched carbohydrates may be soluble in 80 per cent ethanol in spite of a DP considerably higher than 10. In practice, therefore, the separation of oligosaccharides from polysaccharides is empirical and does not provide an exact division based on DP.

Starch

Quantitative analysis of starch in foods by most current methods is based on enzymatic degradation and specific determination of liberated glucose. Nutritionally, starch can be divided into glucogenic ("available") and resistant starch, which is not absorbed in the small intestine. Resistant starch is poorly soluble in water and methods aiming at a total starch analysis employ an initial 2M potassium hydroxide (KOH) or dimethylsulfoxide solvent (DMSO) treatment to disperse crystalline starch fractions that would otherwise remain unhydrolyzed.

Methods for measuring resistant starch are still in their infancy and have not yet been tested in formal collaborative studies. They aim at simulating normal starch digestion in the small intestine. A key step is to mimic the normal standardized milling/homogenization technique, whereas others employ standardized chewing by volunteers (19,20). Both approaches have been evaluated against human ileostomy experiments with a limited number of food matrices.

Non-starch Polysaccharides (NSP)

The determination of NSP is based on the following steps:

- Degradation of starch by enzymatic hydrolysis after solublization,
- Removal of low molecular weight carbohydrates, including starch hydrolysis products,
- Hydrolysis of the NSP to their constituent monomers, and
- Quantitative determination of those monomers.

The acid hydrolysis step is a critical one, and it has to be designed as an optimal balance between complete hydrolysis and destruction of the liberated monomers. The most widely-used method today for specific determination of the liberated monomers is GLC with alditol acetate derivatives. HPLC detection is an alternative gaining in popularity.

Colourimetric determination is still preferred for uronic acids, which are derived mainly from pectic substances. A colourimetric method is also available for total NSP. Fractions of NSP, such as cellulose and non-cellulosic polysaccharides, can be separated by using sequential extraction and hydrolysis methods. For instance, cellulose is not hydrolyzed by dilute (1-2M) sulphuric acid, unless it has first been dispersed in concentrated acid.

Dietary Fibre

Three methods for dietary fibre analysis have undergone extensive testing in recent years, including collaborative studies satisfactory enough for official approval of bodies such as the AOAC International and the Bureau Communautaire de Reference of the European Community:

- The enzymatic, gravimetric AOAC methods of Prosky and co-workers, and subsequently Lee and co-workers.
- The enzymatic-chemical methods of Englyst and co-workers.
- The enzymatic-chemical method of Theander and co-workers (the Uppsala method).

The enzymatic-gravimetric AOAC methods are derived from methods aiming at simulating the digestion in the human small intestine to isolate an undigested residue as a measure of dietary fibre. This residue is corrected for associated ash and protein. Since no DMSO or KOH dispersion is used, starch that resists the amylases used in the assay will remain as a fibre component. Since the sample has to be milled, and since a heat-stable amylase (termamyl) is used at a temperature close to 100°C, physically enclosed starch (RS_1) and resistant starch granules (RS_2) will not be included.

Retrograded amylose (RS_3) that is included is the main form of resistant starch in processed foods. Lignin, a non-carbohydrate component of the dietary fibre complex is also included, as well as some tannins. These components are a very small proportion of most foods but can be substantial in some unconventional raw materials or special "fibre" preparations. The Englyst method measures the NSP specifically, either as individual monomeric components by GLC or colourimetrically as reducing substances.

Accordingly, DMSO is used initially to ensure a complete removal of starch, and lignin is not determined. The difference between estimates with the gravimetric methods and the Englyst method is mainly due to resistant starch and lignin. The Uppsala method employs hydrolysis conditions and GLC determination of monomers in a similar way as in the Englyst method. However, DMSO is not employed for starch dispersion, and a gravimetric estimate of lignin is added to obtain the dietary fibre. The Uppsala method and the gravimetric AOAC methods give very concordant results.

Labelling

Food labelling has two main aims: to inform the consumer of the composition of the food and to assist them in the selection of a healthy diet. These two aims are not always easy to reconcile because the health benefit of different carbohydrate-containing foods cannot readily be communicated simply from a description of their composition. Labelling should be based on the chemical classification. Analytical methods should be clearly defined and validated. The principal information should be total carbohydrate, measured as the sum of the individual components. Further information on carbohydrate composition could include terms such as sugars, starch and non-starch polysaccharides. Other terms, such as non-digestible oligosaccharides, polyols, resistant starch and dietary fibre may be used, provided the components included in these terms are clearly defined.

Availability And Consumption

Trends in the supply and intake of carbohydrates can be studied by four principal approaches:

1. Production.
2. Food balance sheets.
3. Household surveys.
4. Individual assessments.

Food production statistics, which are available from FAO for every country in the world and for every crop, are useful for examining trends in consumption.

From these data it can be seen that the major sources of carbohydrate in the human diet are:

- Cereals.
- Root crops.
- Sugar crops.
- Pulses.
- Vegetables.
- Fruit.
- Milk products.

Sustainability

Trends over the last 20-30 years indicate growth in world production of cereals, sugarcane, vegetables and fruit. On the other hand, production of root crops, pulses and sugar beet has changed little on a world basis. Marked decreases have actually been seen in pulse production in some countries in Asia, and in root crop production in Europe. This suggests a change in food preference away from roots and pulses and towards cereals.

Examination of eating habits in a number of countries indicates that this is the case. Since root crops are an excellent source of carbohydrate, there is concern about this downward trend in production.

Populations continue to grow in most parts of the world and, overall, food production would seem to be keeping pace with population growth. Increased production is due to improved agricultural ractices rather than increased crop area, the major reason for increases being greater use of fertilizer.

There are, however, specific countries where this is not happening. For the entire continent of Africa, cereal production is inadequate.

A major question is how much more improvement and efficiency in production can be achieved, and whether the amount of carbohydrate will be sufficient for the world's population in the future. Projections for future growth suggest problems ahead, particularly in Africa.

Changing Patterns of Consumption

Both food balance information and results from individual assessments are used to determine carbohydrate intakes. Food balance data is intended to describe food available for consumption. It is unlikely to do so because it does not include home production, which is variable from country to country, and may be considerable in some developing countries. As a reflection of food consumed, food balance data is questionable, since it does not include food wasted or spoiled, or used for purposes other than human food, the proportion of which may change from year to year. As a result, food balance data for individual countries has failed to demonstrate the changes in consumption of carbohydrates which are seen using individual surveys. Data from individual surveys also have limitations. Surveys are carried out by a variety of methodologies. While each has advantages and disadvantages, all suffer from a degree of underreporting. This can be intentional or involuntary, most likely due to individuals forgetting food items or not describing foods thought to be undesirable. There is also the failure to record data or the altering of actual diets.

The difference, then, between food balance data and individual assessments, for energy and nutrient intakes, is not only the form of wastage and spoilage on the food balance side of the equation, but also the under- reporting on the individual intake side. True food intakes therefore lie somewhere between food balance and individual intake estimates.

Another major problem is the varied carbohydrate terminology used in different countries. Many countries express total carbohydrate "by difference", rather than as carbohydrate analysed directly, and this results in overestimates of the per cent energy derived from carbohydrate. There is also a great variety in terms used to describe simple sugars, such as "sugars", "sugar", "refined sugar", "added sugar", "sucrose", and "sugars minus lactose". Often there is no description of what is being reported. There is a need to standardize the terminology for carbohydrate and its components in individual surveys and a need for consistency in both reporting and the description of the terms used. In spite of terminology difficulties, it is possible to gain a picture of carbohydrate intakes and trends.

As a per cent of energy, total carbohydrate ranges from about 40 per cent to over 80 per cent, with the developed countries, such as those in North America, Western Europe and Australia at the low end of the range, and developing countries in Asia and Africa at the high end. Starch accounts for 20 per cent-50 per cent or more of energy where the total carbohydrate intake is in the high range.

Sugars account for 9 per cent-27 per cent of energy intake; where total carbohydrate is high, sugar intake is generally low. Where data are available, intake of carbohydrate as a per cent of energy is higher for children than for adults. Trends in consumption indicate a falling carbohydrate intake in developed countries until the last two decades. During that time some increase has been noted as fat intakes fall.

The major sources of carbohydrate are cereals, representing over 50 per cent of all carbohydrate consumed in both developed and developing countries, with sugar crops the next major source, followed by root crops, fruits, vegetables, pulses and milk products. In some of the developing countries much of the carbohydrate is derived from a single food source such as rice, cassava or maize. Carbohydrate foods are an important vehicle for protein, micronutrients and other food components, like phytochemicals, which have important benefits for health. Individual food sources vary, however, in the provision of these components.

A single food source of carbohydrate is therefore undesirable and populations whose diets are primarily based on a single food can suffer from micronutrient deficiencies due to lack of variety. It is important, therefore, that a number of different carbohydrate sources be consumed and efforts should be made to encourage a wide variety of carbohydrate foods. Data on intake of sources of sugars is only available for developed countries. These data show similar proportions of sugars are derived from cereal products, milk products and beverages, among these countries. There is some variation in the proportions derived from fruit and confectionery, with the U.K. consuming less fruit and higher amounts of confectionery than countries such as the United States and Australia.

Intakes of non-starch polysaccharides range from about 19gm./day in some countries in Europe and North America, to nearly 30gm./day in rural Africa. Cereals are again the major source of this component. Data on intake of dietary fibre, determined by methods such as that of the AOAC and the older Southgate method are about 15-20 gm./day for North America, Europe and Australia, to 25-40 gm./day for countries in Asia and Africa.

Physiology

Carbohydrates have a wide range of physiological effects which may be important to health, such as:

- Provision of energy.
- Effects on satiety/gastric emptying.
- Control of blood glucose and insulin metabolism.
- Protein glycosylation.
- Cholesterol and triglyceride metabolism.
- Bile acid dehydroxylation.
- Fermentation.
- Hydrogen/methane production.
- Short-chain fatty acids production.
- Control of colonic epithelial cell function.
- Bowel habit/laxation/motor activity.
- Effects on large bowel microflora.

Carbohydrate as an Energy Source

Dietary carbohydrates have by convention been given an energy value of 4 kcal/gm. (17 kJ/gm), although where carbohydrates are expressed as monosaccharides, the value of 3.75 kcal/gm. (15.7 kJ/gm.) is used. It is now clear, however, that a number of carbohydrates are only partly or not at all digested in the small intestine and are fermented in the large bowel to short chain fatty acids. These include the non-digestible oligosaccharides, resistant starch and non-starch polysaccharides. The process of fermentation is metabolically less efficient than absorption in the small intestine and these carbohydrates provide the body with less energy. In light of a new understanding of the digestion and metabolism of carbohydrate and developments in methodology, the energy value of all carbohydrates in the diet should be reassessed and more accurate energy factors assigned to each group or sub-group. There are a number of potential approaches to accomplish this.

These include the classic calorimetry experiments similar to those first undertaken by Atwater, as well as human balance studies and ileostomy recovery experiments. Knowledge of the chemistry of individual carbohydrates allows a prediction to be made regarding their digestion or fermentation, and an energy value to be assigned. In vitro models of fermentation can be constructed and from these the fermentation stoichiometry can be deduced. Studies using stable isotope tracer techniques may also be of value. While the energy yield of carbohydrate delivered to the colon will vary according to the extent of colonic fermentation (or the assumptions made in the model used), there may be an argument for assigning a single energy value to all such carbohydrate. Published studies suggest that a caloric value of about 2 kcal/ gm. (8 kJ/gm.) would be a reasonable average figure for carbohydrate which reaches the colon. While individual carbohydrates will have different values, in the range of 1-2 kcal/gm., these differences are unlikely to be of importance to health.

Satiety

The possibility of controlling hunger, satiety and food intake by altering the type of carbohydrate in food has intrigued a number of investigators. At present the variability of the findings and the lack of understanding of a clear relationship to physiologic parametres thought to be involved in the regulation of food intake limit practical application of this approach. It is unlikely that controlling a single dietary component, such as the type of sugar or starch, will lead to significant changes in the amount of food consumed. Also, compensation for small dietary changes made in one meal may often be seen at a subsequent meal. A better approach to controlling hunger and increasing satiety is likely to be associated with changes in the composition of the total diet.

Glucose and Insulin

The digestion of dietary carbohydrates starts in the mouth, where salivary a-amylase initiates starch degradation. The starch fragments thus formed include maltose, some glucose and dextrins containing the 1,6-a -glycosidic branching points of amylopectin. The a-amylase degradation of starch is completed by the pancreatic amylase active in the small intestine. Dietary disaccharides, as well as degradation products of starch, need to be broken down to monosaccharides in order to be absorbed. This final hydrolysis is accomplished by hydrolases attached to the intestinal brush-border membrane, referred to as "disaccharidases". Disaccharidase deficiencies occur as rare genetic defects, causing malabsorption and intolerance of the corresponding disaccharide. Glucose and galactose are transported actively against a concentration gradient into the intestinal mucosal cells by a sodium dependent transporter. Fructose undergoes facilitated transport by another mechanism.

Fructose taken together with other sugars is better absorbed than fructose alone. When delivered to the circulation, the absorbed carbohydrates cause an elevation of the blood glucose concentration. Fructose and galactose have to be converted to glucose mainly in the liver and therefore produce less pronounced blood glucose elevation.

The extent and duration of the blood glucose rise after a meal is dependent upon the rate of absorption, which in turn depends upon factors such as gastric emptying as well as the rate of hydrolysis and diffusion of hydrolysis products in the small intestine. Insulin is secreted as a response to blood glucose elevation but is modified by many neural and endocrine stimuli. Insulin secretion is also influenced by food related factors, especially by the amount and the amino acid composition of dietary proteins. Insulin has important regulatory functions in both carbohydrate and lipid metabolism and is necessary for glucose uptake by most body cells.

Lactose

Lactose, a b -linked disaccharide of glucose and galactose, is the principal sugar in milk. At birth, lactase activity is high in the brush-border of the small bowel of infants, but declines after weaning so that most populations of the world have low activity in adult life.

The exceptions are Caucasian peoples and some other population groups in whom the majority retain a high lactase activity throughout life. During the years since 1980, there has been a major change in the way lactose absorption is viewed and a resultant shift away from the concept that lactose "malabsorption" is a pathological state. Low mucosal lactase activity in adults is the norm throughout most of the world. However, such a state usually allows the drinking of modest quantities of milk spaced throughout the day without adverse symptoms. Milk consumption is therefore now being encouraged in many areas of the world because of its value as a source of protein, calcium and riboflavin.

Fermented milk products, which have lower lactose content and contain enzymes and microorganisms that can assist in lactose digestion, are better tolerated than milk. Technology exists to reduce the lactose level in foods and this should be taken into consideration when milk is included as food aid. Cheese, however, has almost no lactose.

Lactose which is not digested, passes into the colon where it is fermented. In some individuals this causes lactose intolerance, the term used to describe the clinical symptoms of abdominal discomfort, flatulence and diarrhoea, associated with the ingestion of lactose containing foods by persons with low lactase activity.

It also occurs as a transient phenomenon when the intestinal mucosa is injured following acute infection in children and in protein-energy malnutrition. It is also found in adults, particularly in association with coeliac disease and tropical sprue. In these conditions, lactose malabsorption is said to be "secondary" to intestinal mucosal disease. A small proportion of the Caucasian population also exhibits low lactase activity and lactose intolerance.

Protein Glycosylation

The non-enzymatic glycation of proteins is dependent on the concentration of glucose and fructose in blood and the half-life of the protein. The initial reaction is between the monosaccharide and the amino group of an amino acid, usually lysine, to form a Shiff base which undergoes rearrangement and formation of Amadori products.

As the reaction progresses, increasingly complex Maillard products are formed with the eventual production of Advanced Glycation End-products or AGEs which are associated with irreversible loss of protein function. The extent of glycation of specific proteins, such as Haemoglobin Ale in diabetics serves as an indication of medium term control of blood glucose.

Examples of functional changes induced by glycation include lens proteins in the eye with resultant cataract formation, increased microvascular complications, abnormal fibrin network formation and impaired fibrinolysis. These changes are most clearly seen in diabetic patients.

Lipids and Bile Acids

There has been concern that a substantial increase in carbohydrate-containing food at the expense of fat, might result in a decrease in high-density lipoprotein and a corresponding increase in very low-density lipoprotein and triglycerides in the blood. However, there is no evidence that this happens when the increase in carbohydrates occurs as a result of increased consumption of vegetables, fruits and appropriately processed cereals over prolonged periods.

Polysaccharides like oat b-glucan, guar gum and those from psyllium have been repeatedly shown to lower serum cholesterol levels in those with elevated levels, with little change if serum levels are normal. Proposed mechanisms include impaired bile acid and cholesterol reabsorption through physical entrapment in the small intestine, or inhibitory effects on cholesterol synthesis by products of lower bowel fermentation, particularly propionic acid. Not all fermentable polysaccharides are effective, however, and recent studies have indicated that neither oligosaccharides nor resistant starch have a significant effect on serum lipids in young normolipidemic subjects.

Fermentation

Fermentation is the colonic phase of the digestive process and describes the breakdown in the large intestine of carbohydrates not digested and absorbed in the upper gut. This process involves gut microflora and is unique to the colon of humans because it occurs without the availability of oxygen. It thus results in the formation of the gases hydrogen, methane and carbon dioxide, as well as short chain fatty acids (SCFA) (acetate, propionate and butyrate), and stimulates bacterial growth (biomass).

The gases are either absorbed and excreted in breath, or passed out via the rectum. The major products of such fermentation are the SCFA which are rapidly absorbed and metabolized by the body. Acetate passes primarily into the blood and is taken up by liver, muscle and other tissues. Propionate is a major glucose precursor in ruminant animals such as the cow and sheep, but this is not an important pathway in humans.

Butyrate is metabolized primarily by colonocytes and has been shown to regulate cell growth, and to induce differentiation and apoptosis.

Bowel Habit

It has long been known that non-starch polysaccharides are the principal dietary component affecting laxation. This occurs through increases in bowel content bulk and a speeding up of intestinal transit time. The extent of the effect depends on the chemical and physical nature of the polysaccharides and the extent to which they are fermented in the colon. Fermentable polysaccharides stimulate increases in microbial biomass in the colon, resulting in some increase in fecal weight, but not to the extent of non-fermentable polysaccharides.

The latter are not significantly degraded in the colon and become consituents of the stool. In so doing, they hold water and produce a marked increase in fecal weight. Similarly, resistant starch can increase fecal weight, but this again depends on the extent of fermentation.

Microflora

Carbohydrate which is fermented stimulates the growth of bacteria in the large gut. This is a generalized effect which leads to an increase in the total number of bacteria or biomass. When bacterial growth occurs, the microflora synthesize protein actively from preformed amino acids and peptides as well as some de-novo synthesis using ammonia as the source of nitrogen. The additional biomass is excreted in faeces and is one of the mechanisms whereby carbohydrate influences bowel habit. The increased biomass excretion is accompanied by increased nitrogen excretion.

The efficiency of conversion of carbohydrate to biomass is determined principally by the type of substrate, the rate of breakdown and the transit time through the large intestine. One of the more significant developments in recent years with regard to the gut microflora has been the demonstration that specific dietary carbohydrates selectively stimulate the growth of individual groups or species of bacteria.

An example of this is the effect of fructo-oligosaccharides on the growth of bifidobacteria. The importance of bifidobacteria is that they may be one of the major contributors to colonization resistance in the colon, thereby protecting the host from invasion by pathogenic species. Foods which selectively stimulate the growth of gut bacteria are known as pre-biotics.

THE ROLE OF CARBOHYDRATES IN MAINTENANCE OF HEALTH

Carbohydrates In The Diet

While the amount of carbohydrate required to avoid ketosis is very small carbohydrate provides the majority of energy in the diets of most people. There are many reasons why this is desirable. In addition to providing easily available energy for oxidative metabolism, carbohydrate-containing foods are vehicles for important micronutrients and phytochemicals.

Dietary carbohydrate is important to maintain glycemic homeostasis and for gastrointestinal integrity and function. Unlike fat and protein, high levels of dietary carbohydrate, provided it is obtained from a variety of sources, is not associated with adverse health effects. Finally, diets high in carbohydrate as compared to those high in fat, reduce the likelihood of developing obesity and its co-morbid conditions. An optimum diet should consist of at least 55 per cent of total energy coming from carbohydrate obtained from a variety of food sources.

The consultation agreed that when carbohydrate consumption levels are at or above 75 per cent of total energy there could be significant adverse effects on nutritional status by the exclusion of adequate quantities of protein, fat and other essential nutrients.

In arriving at its recommendation of a minimum of 55 per cent of total energy from carbohydrate, the consultation realised that a significant percentage of total energy needs to be provided by protein and fat, but that their contribution to total energy intakes will vary from one country to another on the basis of food consumption patterns and food availability.

Energy Balance

In adults, it is important that the amount of energy ingested be matched to the amount of energy expended. Maintenance of energy balance is important in order to avoid obesity and its associated co-morbidities such as diabetes and cardiovascular disease. Positive energy balance and obesity occur when total energy intake exceeds total energy expenditure, regardless of composition of the excess energy. However, the composition of the diet can affect whether and to what extent positive energy balance occurs. The composition of the diet can also affect the ability to maintain energy balance. In particular, diets containing at least 55 per cent of energy from a variety of carbohydrate sources, as compared to high fat diets, reduce the likelihood that body fat accumulation will occur. Substantial data suggest that diets high in fat content tend to promote consumption of more total energy than diets high in carbohydrates.

This effect may be due to the low energy density of high carbohydrate diets, since total volume of food consumed appears to provide an important satiety cue. There are no data to suggest that different types of carbohydrates differentially affect total energy intake. In addition to affecting the chance of having excess energy available, the composition of the diet also affects the proportion of excess energy that will be stored as body fat.

The body has a large fat storage capacity and excess dietary fat is stored very efficiently in adipose tissue. Alternatively, the body's capacity to store carbohydrate is limited and excess carbohydrate is not efficiently stored as body fat. Instead, excess carbohydrate tends to be oxidized, leading to indirect fat accumulation via reductions in fat oxidation. Excess fat and carbohydrate were previously thought to be equally fattening. This was due to the assumption that de novo lipogenesis was a commonly used pathway for disposal of excess carbohydrate.

The available data suggest, however, that this process occurs rarely in human subjects and only in situations of appreciable carbohydrate overfeeding. In most usual circumstances, accumulation of body fat via de novo lipogenesis is quantitatively very low. While noting the low overall contribution of de novo lipogenesis to body fat accumulation, it should be noted that de novo lipogenesis is increased with insulin resistance and with extremely high consumption of sucrose or fructose.

Physical Activity

Maintenance of energy balance is dependent both on energy intake and energy expenditure. Maintaining regular physical activity greatly reduces the likelihood of creating positive energy balance, regardless of the composition of the diet. There is agreement that the combination of a high carbohydrate diet and regular physical activity is the optimal arrangement to avoid positive energy balance and obesity.

The increased energy needs of physical activity can be supplied by carbohydrate or fat. The importance of carbohydrate in the diet becomes more critical as the amount and intensity of physical activity increases. In many developing countries, the major challenge is to meet daily energy needs created by high levels of daily physical labour. In such cases, any combination of carbohydrate and fat which provides sufficient energy is to be encouraged. Many countries recommend increasing leisure time physical activity. While increased physical activity would clearly increase energy needs, these do not create needs for specific macronutrients.

Rather, the optimum diet identified is considered sufficient to provide for such physical activity. There is substantial evidence that supplemental carbohydrate can improve performance for the elite endurance-trained athlete. A high carbohydrate diet during a few days preceding an endurance event, carbohydrate loading, a high carbohydrate pre-event meal and carbohydrate supplementation in the form of carbohydrate-containing beverages have all been shown to enhance performance during long-distance cycling and running.

There is, however, no evidence that such carbohydrate supplementation would improve performance for the majority of people who engage in recreational physical activity of lower intensity and duration. On the other hand, carbohydrate intake following exercise can help to quickly replenish depleted glycogen stores.

Carbohydrate and Behaviour

It has been suggested that food intake could have important effects on behaviour. While providing breakfast to children who do not typically eat breakfast can increase cognitive performance, it is less clear that the overall composition of the diet can affect behaviour. It has been suggested that sugar consumption leads to hyperactivity in children. However, an extensive review of the literature in this area concluded that there is no evidence to support the claim that refined sugar intake has any significant influence on either behaviour or cognitive performance in children. Because glucose is an essential fuel for the central nervous system, carbohydrate has also been suggested to play a role in memory and cognitive function. While there appears to be a relationship between glucose levels and memory processing, the clinical significance of this relationship remains unclear.

Carbohydrate Through the Life Cycle

Energy and nutrient needs are increased in pregnancy and lactation, and the primary challenge for pregnant women is to meet these increased energy needs in order to ensure healthy offspring. It has been observed that where variety in the food supply is low and carbohydrate intake is high, a low birth weight is more common.

This raises concerns about the adequacy of high carbohydrate diets to meet the energy and nutrient needs of pregnancy when food variety is limited. Energy and nutrient needs should be met by consumption of a wide variety of carbohydrate foods. There is also some concern about excessive fat intake in pregnancy since it may be associated with risk of obesity in the mother. In many countries, infants receive 45-55 per cent of energy from fat through breastmilk or formulas and 35-45 per cent of energy from carbohydrate. While specific reductions in fat intake are not recommended below the age of two years, infants in many countries consume lower fat diets. This does not present a problem as long as energy requirements are fulfilled.

From the age of two and on, the optimum diet should be gradually introduced. During the first four to six months of life, exclusive breast feeding is recommended as this tailors the concentration of lactose to the maturing neo-natal and infant gut, particularly while colonic microflora and pancreatic amylase production are developing. For infants fed on formula, the carbohydrate and other nutrient components should usually mimic breastmilk to the extent possible and in accordance with standards of the Codex Alimentarius. Carbohydrate digestion in the neo-nate and young infant is significantly influenced by both gastrointestinal maturation and the chemical nature of the carbohydrate ingested.

The establishment of colonic microflora is responsible for colonic carbohydrate scavenging, converting any carbohydrate entering the colon into short chain fatty acids. Any disturbances or inappropriate development of this microflora (incorrect infant formula, antibiotics, infection) leads to colonic carbohydrate overloading and diarrhoea.

Lactose from dairy products can be a major source of carbohydrate for young children. In addition, milk represents an excellent source of high quality protein, calcium, and riboflavin. In most populations, even those with low lactase activity, milk can be ingested in small amounts, especially after meals with dilution by co-ingestion.

Fermented dairy products can be valuable items in the diet of most people irrespective of intestinal lactase status. Often the transition from childhood to adulthood is associated with changes in dietary pattern. In developing countries, children frequently consume very high carbohydrate intakes from a single or a small number of sources, while adults have greater variety. In such cases, the adult diet is preferred. In developed countries, on the other hand, surveys indicate that children have higher intakes of carbohydrate from more sources than adults. In those countries, the diet consumed by children would seem to be more beneficial. In both situations, at least 55 per cent of carbohydrate energy from a variety of sources is the optimum.

Individualization of carbohydrate intake is necessary for elderly populations. Elderly individuals in many countries are at risk as regards both malnutrition and obesity. Food intake patterns can be altered by changes in taste perception, chronic disease and medication use.

While a high carbohydrate diet is recommended for prevention of weight gain and obesity, it should be recognized that some individuals may need diets higher in energy density (e.g., fats) in order to prevent malnutrition. Optimizing intake of carbohydrate to minimize glucose intolerance in later life is a consideration in countries where such intolerance is a problem.

DIETARY CARBOHYDRATE AND DISEASE

Carbohydrates may directly influence human diseases by affecting physiological and metabolic processes, thereby reducing risk factors for the disease or the disease process itself. Carbohydrates may also have indirect effects on diseases, for example, by displacing other nutrients or facilitating increased intakes of a wide range of other substances frequently found in carbohydrate-containing foods. Evidence of associations between carbohydrates and diseases comes from epidemiological and clinical studies.

There are relatively few examples in which direct causal links between carbohydrates and diseases have been proven. Thus the nutrient-disease or food-disease associations discussed must be considered in terms of the strength of evidence from a range of observational studies and clinical experiments and the existence of plausible hypotheses.

Obesity

The frequency of obesity has increased dramatically in many developed and developing countries. This is of profound public health importance because of the clearly defined negative effect of obesity, especially when centrally distributed, in relation to diabetes, coronary heart disease and other chronic diseases of lifestyle. Genetic and environmental factors play a role in determining the propensity for obesity in populations and individuals. Lack of physical activity is believed to contribute to the increasing rates of obesity observed in many countries and may be a factor in whether an individual who is at risk will become overweight or obese.

High carbohydrate foods promote satiety in the short term. As fat is stored more efficiently than excess carbohydrate, use of high carbohydrate foods is likely to reduce the risk of obesity in the long term. Much controversy surrounds the extent to which sugars and starch promote obesity. There is no direct evidence to implicate either of these groups of carbohydrates in the etiology of obesity, based on data derived from studies in affluent societies. Nevertheless, it is important to reiterate that excess energy in any form will promote body fat accumulation and that excess consumption of low fat foods, while not as obesity-producing as excess consumption of high fat products, will lead to obesity if energy expenditure is not increased. While high carbohydrate diets may help reduce the risk of obesity by preventing overconsumption of energy, there is no evidence to suggest that the macronutrient composition of a low energy diet influences the rate and extent of weight loss in the treatment of obese patients.

Non-Insulin Dependent Diabetes Mellitus (Niddm)

High rates of NIDDM in all population groups are associated with rapid cultural changes in populations previously consuming traditional diets, and also with increasing obesity, especially when centrally distributed. Although the precise mode of inheritance has not been established, there is no doubt that genetic factors are involved. Certain populations appear to have a strong predisposition to the development of NIDDM to the extent that in some groups about half the adult population have the disease. Within all populations a family history of NIDDM is an important predisposing factor.

Diet and lifestyle-related conditions which may lead to obesity will clearly influence the risk of developing NIDDM in populations and individuals who are susceptible to this condition. Foods rich in non-starch polysaccharides and carbohydrate-containing foods with a low glycemic index appear to protect against diabetes, the effect being independent of body mass index.

In terms of disease prevention, it is not possible on the basis of current data to distinguish the relative merits of different types of non-starch polysaccharides. Some epidemiological evidence suggests particular benefit of appropriately processed cereal foods, while other epidemiological and clinical studies suggest benefits of non-starch polysaccharide from legumes and pectin-rich foods. Thus, avoiding obesity and increasing intakes of a wide range of foods rich in non-starch polysaccharide and carbohydrate-containing foods with a low glycemic index offers the best means of reducing the rapidly increasing rates of NIDDM in many countries. Consuming a wide range of carbohydrate foods is now regarded as acceptable in the nutritional management of people who have already developed NIDDM. It has been suggested that between 60 and 70 per cent of total energy should be derived from a mix of mono-unsaturated fatty acids and carbohydrates. Carbohydrates should principally be derived from a wide range of appropriately processed cereals, vegetables & fruits, with particular emphasis on those foods which have a low glycemic index.

The goal to achieve and maintain ideal body weight remains paramount, ensuring that foods high in fat which might predispose to obesity are not encouraged, even though they might have a low glycemic index. Sucrose and other sugars have not been directly implicated in the etiology of diabetes and recommendations concerning intake relate primarily to the avoidance of all energy-dense foods in order to reduce obesity.

Most recommendations for the management of diabetes permit modest (30-50 gm./day) intakes of sucrose and other added sugars in the diabetic dietary prescription provided these are:

- Consumed within the context of total energy allowance;
- Nutrient-dense foods and foods rich in non-starch polysaccharides are not displaced; and,
- They are incorporated as part of a mixed meal.

In some populations where fat intake is relatively low and sucrose intake high, a reduced intake of sucrose may be considered in the diabetic dietary prescription. Increased meal frequency under iso-energetic conditions does not, in the long term, appear to be associated with any alteration in glycemic control. This suggests that personal preference is the key determinant of meal frequency, provided that body weight and daily (as well as long-term) glycemic control are not adversely influenced. Special diabetic food products are not generally recommended and fructose is not regarded as having any particular merits as a sweetener when compared with other added sugars.

However, low-energy beverages containing alternative non-nutritive sweeteners may be useful for people with diabetes. Dietary factors have not been conclusively shown to be risk factors for insulin-dependent diabetes and the key advice concerning carbohydrates in the management of this condition concerns distribution of intake of carbohydrates during the day. Carbohydrate intake needs to be regularly distributed and balanced with injected insulin. The general principles of the diabetic dietary approach to non-insulin dependent diabetes may also be applied to those with insulin-dependent diabetes.

Cardiovascular Disease

Many genetic and lifestyle factors are involved in the etiology of coronary heart disease and influence both the atherosclerotic and thrombotic processes underlying the clinical manifestations of this disease. Dietary factors may influence these processes directly or via a range of cardiovascular disease risk factors. Obesity, particularly when centrally distributed, is associated with an appreciable increase in the risk of coronary heart disease. There is also evidence implicating specific nutrients and, in particular, high intakes of some saturated fatty acids appear to be important promoters of coronary heart disease.

On the other hand, there is increasing evidence of a strong protective effect by a range of antioxidant nutrients. Increasing carbohydrate intake can assist in the reduction of saturated fat and many fruits and vegetables rich in carbohydrates are also rich in several antioxidants. Cereal foods rich in non-starch polysaccharides have been shown to be protective against coronary heart disease in a series of prospective studies.

There is no evidence for a causal role of sucrose in the etiology of coronary heart disease. The cornerstone of dietary advice aimed at reducing coronary heart disease risk is to increase the intake of carbohydrate-rich foods, especially cereals, vegetables and fruits rich in non-starch polysaccharide, at the expense of fat. Among those who are overweight or obese it is more important to reduce total fat intake and to encourage the consumption of the most appropriate carbohydrate-containing foods.

There has been concern that a substantial increase in carbohydrate-containing food at the expense of fat, might result in a decrease in high-density lipoprotein and an increase in very low-density lipoprotein and triglycerides in the blood. There is, however, no evidence that this occurs when the increase in carbohydrates results from increased consumption of vegetables, fruits and appropriately processed cereals, over prolonged periods.

Certain non-starch polysaccharides (for example b-glucans) have been shown to have an appreciable effect in lowering serum cholesterol when consumed in naturally occurring foods, or foods which have been enriched by purified forms, or even when fed as dietary supplements. Such polysaccharides may be used in the management of patients with existing hypercholesterolemia but their role, if any, in the prevention of coronary heart disease remains to be established.

Less information is available concerning the role of carbohydrates in other cardiovascular diseases. Plant foods are good sources of potassium and reducing the sodium to potassium ratio may help to reduce the risk of hypertension.

Limited data suggest a protective effect of vegetables and fruit in cerebrovascular disease. There has been considerable debate in many developed countries which have high rates of coronary heart disease regarding the age at which children should start to reduce fat intake towards the recommended level for adults.

Clearly children require an adequate intake of energy for growth, and it is important that this does not include an excessive intake of carbohydrates at a very young age. It is generally accepted that dietary carbohydrate should gradually be increased and fat reduced after the age of two years, so that by the age of five years children should have reached a diet in the range of that recommended for adults.

This advice should, of course, include the key dietary guidelines for children and adolescents, which suggest that nutritional adequacy should be achieved by eating a wide variety of foods and that energy intake should be adequate to promote growth and development, and to reach and maintain desirable body weight.

Cancer

Diet is widely regarded as important in the etiology of colorectal cancer with meat and fat considered the primary risk factors, and fruit, vegetable and cereal foods considered to be protective. Cancer is a disease associated with well-recognized genetic abnormalities and for colorectal cancer in particular, defects in a number of genes have been clearly defined. These genes mostly code for proteins responsible for the control of either cell growth, cell- to-cell communication or DNA repair. They are mainly oncogenes or tumour suppressor genes.

For the development of colorectal cancer an individual must acquire several of these genetic abnormalities in the same cell. The acquisition of gene defects in somatic cells is thought to be through DNA damage and a resultant failure of the DNA repair system (or of apoptosis). Dietary carbohydrate is thought to be protective through mechanisms involving arrest of cell growth, differentiation and selection of damaged cells for cell death (apoptosis).

This is probably achieved primarily through the action of butyric acid which is formed in the colon from fermentation of carbohydrates such as resistant starch and non-starch polysaccharides. Such carbohydrates are found mostly in cereals, fruit and vegetables.

The process of fermentation may protect the colorectal area against the genetic damage that leads to colorectal cancer through other mechanisms which include:

- The dilution of potential carcinogens;
- The reduction of products of protein fermentation through stimulation of bacterial growth;
- pH effects;
- Maintenance of the gut mucosal barrier; and,
- Effects on bile acid degradation.

These mechanisms, however, are much less well-established. Carbohydrate staple foods are a source of phytoestrogens which may be protective for breast cancer. Cancer risk is increased for the obese. This applies especially to cancers of the breast and uterus. However, this is a general effect of total energy intake and not specifically of carbohydrates.

Dietary carbohydrates do not have a known role in the etiology of lung, breast, stomach, prostate, pancreas, oesophagus, liver or cervical cancers. There is, however, some evidence that there is an increased risk of ovarian cancer in women with mild galactosemia.

Gastrointestinal Diseases other than Cancer

Intakes of non-starch polysaccharides and resistant starch are the most important contributors to stool weight. Therefore, increasing consumption of foods rich in these carbohydrates is a very effective means of preventing and treating constipation, as well as haemorrhoids and anal fissures. Bran and other cereal sources containing non-starch polysaccharide also appear to protect against diverticular disease and have an important role in the treatment of this condition. Obesity is an important risk factor for gallstones. High intakes of carbohydrate may facilitate the colonization of bifidobacteria and lactobacilli in the gut and thus reduce the risk of acute infective gastrointestinal illnesses.

50gm. Carbohydrate Portion

The portion of food tested should contain 50gm. of glycemic (available) carbohydrate. In practice, glycemic carbohydrate is often measured as total carbohydrate minus dietary fibre, as determined by the AOAC method. Since this method does not include RS 1 and RS2 when they are present, they will be mistakenly included as glycemic carbohydrate.

Blood Glucose Response

This is normally measured in capillary whole blood. Plasma glucose can be used to determine the glycemic index and gives similar values.

However, capillary blood is preferred because it is easier to obtain, the rise in blood glucose is greater than in venous plasma and the results for capillary blood glucose are less variable than those for venous plasma glucose. Thus, differences between foods are larger and easier to detect statistically using capillary blood glucose. An illustration of the difference between glucose as measured in simultaneously-obtained venous plasma and capillary whole blood is shown in Table below.

Table: Glucose Response from Capillary Blood and Venous Plasma

	0 min	15 min	30 min	45 min	60 min	90 min	120 min	IAUC
Capillary blood	4.1	6.3	9.0	8.7	6.7	5.7	3.9	279
Venous plasma	5.0	7.1	8.8	8.0	5.6	5.4	4.2	155

Standard Food

Either white bread or glucose can be used as the standard food. The GI values obtained if white bread is used are about 1.4 times those obtained if glucose is the standard food. Other standard foods could be used, but to enable comparison with data in the literature, the GI of the new standard food relative to standardized white bread or glucose should be established.

FACTORS INFLUENCING THE BLOOD GLUCOSE RESPONSES OF FOODS

Starchy foods with a low GI are digested and absorbed more slowly than foods with a high GI. Some factors that influence glycemic properties of foods are listed in Table below.

Table: Food Factors Influencing Glycemic Responses

Amount of carbohydrate
• Nature of the monosaccharide components: – Glucose – Fructose – Galactose
• Nature of the starch: – Amylose – Amylopectin – Starch-nutrient interaction – Resistant starch
• Cooking/food processing: – Degree of starch gelatinization – Particle size – Food form – Cellular structure
• Other food components: – Fat and protein – Dietary fibre – Antinutrients – Organic acids

Calculation of Glycemic Index of Meals or Diets

The GI can be applied in a detailed fashion to mixed meals or whole diets by calculating the weighted GI value of the meal or diet. For example, the way to calculate the GI of a meal containing bread, cereal, sucrose, milk and orange juice is shown in Table below.

Table: Calculation of the Glycemic Index of Meals

Food	Grams Glycemic Carbohydrate	Proportion of total Glycemic Carbohydrate	Food Glycemic Index	Meal Glycemic Index *
Bread	25	0.342	100	34.2
Cereal	25	0.342	72	24.6
Milk	6	0.082	39	3.2
Sucrose	5	0.068	87	5.9
Orange juice	12	0.164	74	12.1
Total	73			80.0

Note:

*Values for each food equals the proportion of total glycemic carbohydrate multiplied by the food GI. The sum of these values is the meal GI.

Using this type of calculation, there is a good correlation between meal GI and the observed glycemic responses of meals of equal nutrient composition.

Blood glucose responses are also influenced by the amount of carbohydrate in the meal. To compare the expected glycemic load of meals with different carbohydrate contents, a non-linear adjustment can be applied but this has only been tested in normal subjects. For detailed application of the GI, a value of the GI for every food in the diet or meal needs to have been assigned (for many foods the value has to be estimated). The accuracy of the calculation depends upon the accuracy of the GI values ascribed to foods, which may vary from place to place due to local factors such as variety, cooking, processing, etc. Foods particularly prone to such variation include rice, potatoes and bananas.

Practical Application of the Glycemic Index

The glycemic index can be used, in conjunction with information about food composition, to guide food choices. For practical application, the glycemic index is useful to rank foods by developing exchange lists of categories of low glycemic index foods, such as legumes, pearled barley, lightly refined grains (e.g., whole grain pumpernickel bread, or breads made from coarse flour), pasta, etc. Specific local foods should be included in such lists where information is available (e.g. green bananas in the Caribbean and specific rice varieties in Southeast Asia).

In choosing carbohydrate foods, both glycemic index and food composition must be considered. Some low GI foods may not always be a good choice because they are high in fat. Conversely, some high GI foods may be a good choice because of convenience or because they have low energy and high nutrient content. It is not necessary or desirable to exclude or avoid all high GI foods.

Physiologic and Therapeutic Effects of Low Glycemic Index Foods

Meals containing low GI foods reduce both postpr-andial blood glucose and insulin responses. Animal studies suggest that incorporating slowly digested starch into the diet delays the onset of insulin resistance. Some epidemiologic studies suggest that a low GI diet is associated with reduced risk of developing non-insulin diabetes in men and women. Clinical trials in normal, diabetic and hyperlipidemic subjects show that low GI diets reduce mean blood glucose concentrations, reduce insulin secretion and reduce serum triglycerides in individuals with hypertrigly-ceridemia.

In addition, the digestibility of the carbohydrate in low GI foods is generally less than that of high GI foods. Thus, low GI foods increase the amount of carbohydrate entering the colon and increase colonic fermentation and short chain fatty acid production. This has implications for systemic nitrogen and lipid metabolism, and for local events within the colon.

GOALS AND GUIDELINES FOR CARBOHYDRATE FOOD CHOICES

Rationale and Framework

Although the scientific basis for dietary guidelines requires an understanding of physiology and health relationships, the guidance most helpful to consumers uses food-based terms. In preparing such guidelines, food traditions and beliefs must be taken into account and the total food intake should reflect practical issues, such as meal patterns, food status, celebratory or usual role, seasonal availability, affordability and sustainability. These, including the health priorities, are matters for national policy makers.

Principles Of Carbohydrate Food Choices

The principles are:

- To acknowledge the socio-cultural context, lifestyle and stage of life-cycle, in food carbohydrate choice;
- To give preference to food choices rather than to nutrient goals in carbohydrate food choices, and in so doing:
  - use food categories as a guide to chemically defined carbohydrate type.
  - use numbers of portions (serving sizes) of foods from designated food categories in order to provide semi-quantitative food-based advice. This may imply that meal frequency would need to increase in some cultures, because the accommodation of enough carbohydrate food in the course of the day, without an excessive amount on any one occasion, requires more frequent servings and consumption;

- To appreciate that many of the world's health problems are associated with inadequate carbo-hydrate intake, and potentially also associated with inappropriate carbohydrate intake;
- To ensure the acceptability and practicality of any recommended change in carbohydrate food intake;
- To acknowledge that there may be unintended consequences involved in carbohydrate food intake change, and also to ensure that risks involved in dietary changes from traditional diets is considered;
- To monitor the intake of carbohydrate foods and, wherever possible, of chemically defined carbohydrate components of those foods in relation to health issues; and
- To ascertain whether food carbohydrate choices encourage biodiversity and are sustainable.

Carbohydrate Nutrient And Food Goals

Nutrient Goals: The minimum amount of carbohydrate in the human diet that is needed to avoid ketosis is of the order of 50 g/day in adults. Beyond this, additional energy needs are best met by nutrient-dense carbohydrate foods. There must, of course, be adequate intakes of protein (with essential amino acids) and essential fatty acids from fat. Moderate intake of sugar-rich foods can also provide for a palatable and nutritious diet.

Food Goals

There are a number of approaches to translating nutrient recommendations to food goals:

- Recommending the total weight of food groups to be consumed. Various national food guides have suggested quantities of specific foods to be consumed, such as fruits and vegetables, and pulses, nuts and seeds.
- Examining sources of carbohydrate foods in various diets, particularly diets which have desirable total carbohydrate intakes or from countries where the incidence of lifestyle diseases is low. Recommen-dations can then be made on the basis of intakes.
- Examining major food groups which contain carbohydrate foods and recommending numbers of servings of those food groups. Numerous countries around the world, both developed and developing, have produced food guides with such groupings, and considering the level of agreement that exists for carbohydrate as a per cent energy, these food guides are remarkably consistent in their advice.

- Examining indices which exist to describe various physiological properties of carbohydrate-containing foods, such as glycemic index values and values from other indices which are presently being developed.

On the basis of the approaches, and taking into account the principles for carbohydrate food choice, the following recommendations can be made:

- A variety of foods should provide the carbohydrate in the diet, not a single or small number of sources.
- Cereals, roots, pulses, fruit and vegetables are all components of a healthy diet throughout the world.
- Cereal foods or root crops, where this is the main staple, should provide the major source of carbohydrate energy.
- Intake of fruits and vegetables (including potatoes in developed countries) should be high. As well as being a valuable source of carbohydrate, fruit and vegetables are an important source of antioxidant vitamins and other food components.
- Consumption of pulses, nuts and seeds should be encouraged. While this group often represents only a small amount of carbohydrate energy, these foods are a good source of protein and micronutrients. They should be consumed with cereals to optimize protein quality.
- At least small quantities of milk products are desirable, even when low lactase activity exists, since these are a good source of protein and micro-nutrients.
- These recommendations apply to all individuals over the age of two years, with adjustments as necessary for growth and the increased demand of pregnancy and lactation.

Translation from Carbohydrate Nutrients to Foods

Achieving goals for intake of carbohydrates does not ensure nutritional adequacy. Carbohydrate foods provide a range of nutrients and other substances essential for health in addition to energy. It is therefore essential to consume a variety of foods in order to derive the full benefits of a high carbohydrate diet. Nutrients from foods require monitoring. For example, in Iran carbohydrate foods include vegetables (250 gm./day), fruits (210 gm./ day), pulses (20 gm./day) and cereals (wheat at about 250 gm./day and rice 110 gm./day, uncooked). Wheat has mostly been consumed as bread with traditional pastries being festive foods. Recently, consumption of the latter has increased substantially with potential reduction of nutritionally useful food groups traditionally accompanying bread.

This may not significantly impact on total carbohydrate intake, but could influence nutritional adequacy. Traditional methods of food preparation and preservation facilitate food choice variety, and promote nutritional benefits. Alteration of traditional practices may compromise such benefits. Ongoing monitoring may be required to guard against nutritional inadequacy.

Considerations for Target Audiences

Planners and policy makers need to:

- Recognize dietary goals of at least 55 per cent of total energy from a variety of carbohydrate sources.
- Recognize the extent of change necessary in order to meet these goals (e.g. it may take considerable change in food production and consumption to meet goals in Western countries).
- Understand that there must be a gradual transition in meeting new dietary guidelines and that new terminology will need to be gradually accepted.
- Consider the effects of economic and cultural factors in achieving dietary goals.
- Develop clear guides about the types and quantities of food recommended.
- Develop methods to monitor food consumption to meet dietary goals.

Primary producers and processors need to:

- Consider how existing and new technologies can be used to help meet dietary goals regarding the quantity and nutritional properties of food carbohydrates, as well as levels of micronutrients and other desirable food components.
- Provide foods, such as breakfast cereals and snack foods that are high in NSP, low in energy density, and with a low glycemic index.
- Increase the availability and convenience of fruits and vegetables.
- Provide appropriate information to the consumer on food labels. To facilitate individual choice:
- Provide easily understandable food-based guides for the consumer.

□

7

Understanding the Nutrition

Nutrition (also called nourishment or aliment) is the provision, to cells and organisms, of the materials necessary (in the form of food) to support life. Many common health problems can be prevented or alleviated with a healthy diet. The diet of an organism is what it eats, which is largely determined by the perceived palatability of foods. Dietitians are health professionals who specialize in human nutrition, meal planning, economics, and preparation.

They are trained to provide safe, evidence-based dietary advice and management to individuals (in health and disease), as well as to institutions. A poor diet can have an injurious impact on health, causing deficiency diseases such as scurvy, beriberi, and kwashiorkor; health-threatening conditions like obesity and metabolic syndrome; and such common chronic systemic diseases as cardiovascular disease, diabetes, and osteoporosis.

Nutrition science investigates the metabolic and physiological responses of the body to diet. With advances in the fields of molecular biology, biochemistry, and genetics, the study of nutrition is increasingly concerned with metabolism and metabolic pathways: the sequences of biochemical steps through which substances in living things change from one form to another. Nitrogen is needed by animals to build proteins. Carnivore and herbivore diets vary in their source of nitrogen, which is a limiting nutrient for both. Herbivores consume plants to get nitrogen and carnivores consume other animals to obtain nitrogen. Nitrogen is a common element in the atmosphere but exists in a state that is not usable by most living organisms, certain fungi and bacteria are able to convert atmospheric nitrogen into a form plants can adsorb and utilize.

The human body contains chemical compounds, such as water, carbohydrates (sugar, starch, and fibre), amino acids (in proteins), fatty acids (in lipids), and nucleic acids (DNA and RNA). These compounds in turn consist of elements such as carbon, hydrogen, oxygen, nitrogen, phosphorus, calcium, and elements occur in various forms and combinations (e.g., hormones, vitamins, phospholipids, hydroxyapatite), both in the human body and in the plant and animal organisms that humans eat.

The human body consists of elements and compounds ingested, digested, absorbed, and circulated through the bloodstream to feed the cells of the body. Except in the unborn foetus, which receive processed nutrients from the mother, the digestive system is the first system involved in breaking down food prior to further digestion.

Digestive juices, excreted into the lumen of the gastrointestinal tract, break chemical bonds in ingested molecules, and modulate their conformations and energy states. Though some molecules are absorbed into the bloodstream unchanged, digestive processes release them from the matrix of foods. Unabsorbed matter, along with some waste products of metabolism, is eliminated from the body in the feces. Studies of nutritional status must take into account the state of the body before and after experiments, as well as the chemical composition of the whole diet and of all material excreted and eliminated from the body (in urine and foeces).

Comparing the food to the waste can help determine the specific compounds and elements absorbed and metabolized in the body. The effects of nutrients may only be discernible over an extended period, during which all food and waste must be analysed. The number of variables involved in such experiments is high, making nutritional studies time-consuming and expensive, which explains why the science of human nutrition is still slowly evolving. In general, eating a wide variety of fresh, whole (unprocessed), foods has proven favourable for one's health compared to monotonous diets based on processed foods. In particular, the consumption of whole-plant foods slows digestion and allows better absorption, and a more favourable balance of essential nutrients per Calorie, resulting in better management of cell growth, maintenance, and mitosis (cell division), as well as better regulation of appetite and blood sugar. Regularly scheduled meals (every few hours) have also proven more wholesome than infrequent or haphazard ones, although a recent study has also linked more frequent meals with a higher risk of colon cancer in men.

There are six major classes of nutrients: carbohydrates, fats, minerals, protein, vitamins, and water. These nutrient classes can be categorized as either macronutrients (needed in relatively large amounts) or micronutrients (needed in smaller quantities). The macronutrients include carbohydrates, fats, protein, and water. The micronutrients are minerals and vitamins. The macronutrients (excluding water) provide structural material (amino acids from which proteins are built, and lipids from which cell membranes and some signaling molecules are built), energy.

Some of the structural material can be used to generate energy internally, and in either case it is measured in Joules or kilocalories (often called "Calories" and written with a capital C to distinguish them from little 'c' calories). Carbohydrates and proteins provide 17 kJ approximately (4 kcal) of energy per gram, while fats provide 37 kJ (9 kcal) per gm., though the net energy from either depends on such factors as absorption and digestive effort, which vary substantially from instance to instance.

Vitamins, minerals, fibre, and water do not provide energy, but are required for other reasons. A third class of dietary material, fibre (i.e., non-digestible material such as cellulose), is also required, for both mechanical and biochemical reasons, although the exact reasons remain unclear.

Molecules of carbohydrates and fats consist of carbon, hydrogen, and oxygen atoms. Carbohydrates range from simple monosaccharides (glucose, fructose, galactose) to complex polysaccharides (starch). Fats are triglycerides, made of assorted fatty acid monomers bound to glycerol backbone. Some fatty acids, but not all, are essential in the diet: they cannot be synthesized in the body. Protein molecules contain nitrogen atoms in addition to carbon, oxygen, and hydrogen. The fundamental components of protein are nitrogen- containing amino acids, some of which are essential in the sense that humans cannot make them internally. Some of the amino acids are convertible (with the expenditure of energy) to glucose and can be used for energy production just as ordinary glucose in a process known as gluconeogenesis.

By breaking down existing protein, some glucose can be produced internally; the remaining amino acids are discarded, primarily as urea in urine. This occurs normally only during prolonged starvation. Other micronutrients include antioxidants and phytochemicals, which are said to influence (or protect) some body systems. Their necessity is not as well established as in the case of, for instance, vitamins.

Most foods contain a mix of some or all of the nutrient classes, together with other substances, such as toxins of various sorts. Some nutrients can be stored internally (e.g., the fat soluble vitamins), while others are required more or less continuously. Poor health can be caused by a lack of required nutrients or, in extreme cases, too much of a required nutrient. For example, both salt and water (both absolutely required) will cause illness or even death in excessive amounts.

CARBOHYDRATES

Carbohydrates include sugars, starches and fibre. They constitute a large part of foods such as rice, noodles, bread, and other grain-based products. Carbohydrates may be classified chemically as monosaccharides, disaccharides, or polysaccharides depending on the number of monomer (saccharide or sugar) units they contain and three or more sugar units, respectively. Polysaccharides are often referred to as complex carbohydrates because they consist of long, sometimes branched chains of single sugar units. Mono- and disaccharides are called simple carbohydrates. Dietary advice frequently but erroneously suggests that complex carbohydrates are superior to simple because they take longer to digest and absorb. Simple carbohydrates, on the other hand, are said to cause a spike in blood glucose levels rapidly after ingestion. These traditional claims are false. In fact, many digestible polysaccharides are processed as rapidly and simple sugars in the human body.

On the other hand, some simple carbohydrates (fructose, for example) are processed in a different way and do not spike blood sugar. Thus the distinction between "complex" and "simple" does not predict the nutritional value or impact of carbohydrates. A better way of determining what effect particular foods may have on blood sugar and ultimately on health in general is the glycemic index.

Carbohydrates are not essential nutrients (with the likely exception of fibre), but are typically an important part of the human diet. While it would not be accurate to categorize all carbohydrates as "bad" nutritionally, some carbohydrate sources may well have deleterious effects on health, especially when consumed in large quantities. Highly processed carbohydrates (sugars and starches) as well as fructose consumed in large quantities have been implicated in negative.

Fibre

Dietary fibre is a carbohydrate (or a polysaccharide) that is incompletely absorbed in humans and in some animals. Like all carbohydrates, when it is metabolized it can produce four Calories (kilocalories) of energy per gm. However, in most circumstances it accounts for less than that because of its limited absorption and digestibility. Dietary fibre consists mainly of cellulose, a large carbohydrate polymer that is indigestible because humans do not have the required enzymes to disassemble it.

There are two subcategories: soluble and insoluble fibre. Whole grains, fruits (especially plums, prunes, and figs), and vegetables are good sources of dietary fibre. There are many health benefits of a high-fibre diet. Dietary fibre helps reduce the chance of gastrointestinal problems such as constipation and diarrhoea by increasing the weight and size of stool and softening it. Insoluble fibre, found in whole-wheat flour, nuts and vegetables, especially stimulates peristalsis—the rhythmic muscular contractions of the intestines which move digesta along the digestive tract. Soluble fibre, found in oats, peas, beans, and many fruits, dissolves in water in the intestinal tract to produce a gel which slows the movement of food through the intestines. This may help lower blood glucose levels because it can slow the absorption of sugar. Additionally, fibre, perhaps especially that from whole grains, is thought to possibly help lessen insulin spikes, and therefore reduce the risk of type 2 diabetes. The link between increased fibre consumption and a decreased risk of colorectal cancer is still uncertain.

FAT

A molecule of dietary fat typically consists of several fatty acids (containing long chains of carbon and hydrogen atoms), bonded to a glycerol. They are typically found as triglycerides (three fatty acids attached to one glycerol backbone). Fats may be classified as saturated or unsaturated depending on the detailed structure of the fatty acids involved.

Saturated fats have all of the carbon atoms in their fatty acid chains bonded to hydrogen atoms, whereas unsaturated fats have some of these carbon atoms double-bonded, so their molecules have relatively fewer hydrogen atoms than a saturated fatty acid of the same length. Unsaturated fats may be further classified as monounsaturated (one double-bond) or polyunsaturated (many double-bonds).

Furthermore, depending on the location of the double-bond in the fatty acid chain, unsaturated fatty acids are classified as omega-3 or omega-6 fatty acids. Trans fats are a type of unsaturated fat with trans-isomer bonds; these are rare in nature and in foods from natural sources; they are typically created in an industrial process called (partial) hydrogenation. There are nine kilocalories in each gm. of fat. Saturated fats (typically from animal sources) have been a staple in many world cultures for millennia. Unsaturated fats (e. g., vegetable oil) are considered healthier while trans fats are to be avoided.

Saturated and some trans fats are typically solid at room temperature (such as butter or lard), while unsaturated fats are typically liquids (such as olive oil or flaxseed oil). Trans fats are very rare in nature, and have been shown to be highly detrimental to human health, but have properties useful in the food processing industry, such as rancidity resistance.

Essential Fatty Acids

Most fatty acids are non-essential, meaning the body can produce them as needed, generally from other fatty acids and always by expending energy to do so. However, in humans, at least two fatty acids are essential and must be included in the diet. An appropriate balance of essential fatty acids—omega-3 and omega-6 fatty acids—seems also important for health, although definitive experimental demonstration has been elusive.

Both of these "omega" long-chain polyunsaturated fatty acids are substrates for a class of eicosanoids known as prostaglandins, which have roles throughout the human body. They are hormones, in some respects. The omega-3 eicosapentaenoic acid (EPA), which can be made in the human body from the omega-3 essential fatty acid alpha-linolenic acid (LNA), or taken in through marine food sources, serves as a building block for series 3 prostaglandins (e.g., weakly inflammatory PGE3). The omega-6 dihomo- gamma-linolenic acid (DGLA) serves as a building block for series 1 prostaglandins (e.g., anti-inflammatory PGE1), whereas arachidonic acid (AA) serves as a building block for series 2 prostaglandins (e.g., pro-inflammatory PGE 2). Both DGLA and AA can be made from the omega-6 linoleic acid (LA) in the human body, or can be taken in directly through food.

An appropriately balanced intake of omega-3 and omega-6 partly determines the relative production of different prostaglandins, which is one reason why a balance between omega-3 and omega-6 is believed important for cardiovascular health.

In industrialized societies, people typically consume large amounts of processed vegetable oils, which have reduced amounts of the essential fatty acids along with too much of omega-6 fatty acids relative to omega-3 fatty acids. The conversion rate of omega-6 DGLA to AA largely determines the production of the prostaglandins PGE1 and PGE2.

Omega-3 EPA prevents AA from being released from membranes, thereby skewing prostaglandin balance away from pro-inflammatory PGE2 (made from AA) towards anti-inflammatory PGE1 (made from DGLA). Moreover, the conversion (desaturation) of DGLA to AA is controlled by the enzyme delta-5-desaturase, which in turn is controlled by hormones such as insulin (up-regulation) and glucagon (down-regulation).

The amount and type of carbohydrates consumed, along with some types of amino acid, can influence processes involving insulin, glucagon, and other hormones; therefore the ratio of omega-3 versus omega-6 has wide effects on general health, and specific effects on immune function and inflammation, and mitosis (i.e., cell division).

PROTEIN

Proteins are the basis of many animal body structures (e.g., muscles, skin, and hair). They also form the enzymes that control chemical reactions throughout the body. Each molecule is composed of amino acids, which are characterized by inclusion of nitrogen and sometimes sulphur (these components are responsible for the distinctive smell of burning protein, such as the keratin in hair).

The body requires amino acids to produce new proteins (protein retention) and to replace damaged proteins (maintenance). As there is no protein or amino acid storage provision, amino acids must be present in the diet. Excess amino acids are discarded, typically in the urine. For all animals, some amino acids are essential (an animal cannot produce them internally) and some are non- essential (the animal can produce them from other nitrogen-containing compounds). Twenty-one proteinogenic amino acids are found in the human body, along with non-proteinogenic amino acids (e.g., gamma-aminobutyric acid).

Ten of the proteinogenic amino acids are essential and, therefore, must be included in the diet. A diet that contains adequate amounts of amino acids (especially those that are essential) is particularly important in some situations: during early development and maturation, pregnancy, lactation, or injury (a burn, for instance). A complete protein source contains all the essential amino acids; an incomplete protein source lacks one or more of the essential amino acids.

It is possible to combine two incomplete protein sources (e.g., rice and beans) to make a complete protein source, and characteristic combinations are the basis of distinct cultural cooking traditions. Sources of dietary protein include meats, tofu and other soy-products, eggs, legumes, and dairy products such as milk and cheese.

Excess amino acids from protein can be converted into glucose and used for fuel through a process called gluconeogenesis. The amino acids remaining after such conversion are discarded.

MINERALS

Dietary minerals are the chemical elements required by living organisms, other than the four elements carbon, hydrogen, nitrogen, and oxygen that are present in nearly all organic molecules. The term "mineral" is archaic, since the intent is to describe simply the less common elements in the diet. Some are heavier than the four just mentioned, including several metals, which often occur as ions in the body.

Some dietitians recommend that these be supplied from foods in which they occur naturally, or at least as complex compounds, or sometimes even from natural inorganic sources (such as calcium carbonate from ground oyster shells). Some minerals are absorbed much more readily in the ionic forms found in such sources. On the other hand, minerals are often artificially added to the diet as supplements; the most famous is likely iodine in iodized salt which prevents goiter.

Macrominerals

Many elements are essential in relative quantity; they are usually called "bulk minerals". Some are structural, but many play a role as electrolytes. Elements with recommended dietary allowance (RDA) greater than 200 mg/day are, in alphabetical order (with informal or folk-medicine perspectives in parentheses):

- Calcium, a common electrolyte, but also needed structurally (for muscle and digestive system health, bone strength, some forms neutralize acidity, may help clear toxins, provides signaling ions for nerve and membrane functions).
- Chlorine as chloride ions; very common electrolyte;
- Magnesium, required for processing ATP and related reactions (builds bone, causes strong peristalsis, increases flexibility, increases alkalinity).
- Phosphorus, required component of bones; essential for energy processing.
- Potassium, a very common electrolyte (heart and nerve health).
- Sodium, a very common electrolyte; not generally found in dietary supplements, despite being needed in large quantities, because the ion is very common in food: typically as sodium chloride, or common salt. Excessive sodium consumption can deplete calcium and magnesium, leading to high blood pressure and osteoporosis (Note: Some sources suggest high blood pressure is due to high water retention per osmosis).
- Sulfur, for three essential amino acids and therefore many proteins (skin, hair, nails, liver, and pancreas). Sulfur is not consumed alone, but in the form of sulfur-containing amino acids.

Trace Minerals

Many elements are required in trace amounts, usually because they play a catalytic role in enzymes.

Some trace mineral elements (RDA < 200 mg/day) are, in alphabetical order:

- Cobalt required for biosynthesis of vitamin B12 family of coenzymes. Animals cannot biosynthesize B12, and must obtain this cobalt-containing vitamin in the diet.
- Copper required component of many redox enzymes, including cytochrome c oxidase.
- Chromium required for sugar metabolism.
- Iodine required not only for the biosynthesis of thyroxine, but probably, for other important organs as breast, stomach, salivary glands, thymus, etc.; for this reason iodine is needed in larger quantities than others in this list, and sometimes classified with the macrominerals.

- Iron required for many enzymes, and for haemoglobin and some other proteins.
- Manganese (processing of oxygen).
- Molybdenum required for xanthine oxidase and related oxidases.
- Nickel present in urease.
- Selenium required for peroxidase (antioxidant proteins).
- Vanadium (Speculative: there is no established RDA for vanadium. No specific biochemical function has been identified for it in humans, although vanadium is required for some lower organisms.)
- Zinc required for several enzymes such as carboxypeptidase, liver alcohol dehydrogenase, and carbonic anhydrase.

VITAMINS

Some vitamins are recognized as essential nutrients, necessary in the diet for good health. (Vitamin D is the exception: it can be synthesized in the skin, in the presence of UVB radiation.) Certain vitamin-like compounds that are recommended in the diet, such as carnitine, are thought useful for survival and health, but these are not "essential" dietary nutrients because the human body has some capacity to produce them from other compounds.

Moreover, thousands of different phytochemicals have recently been discovered in food (particularly in fresh vegetables), which may have desirable properties including antioxidant activity, however, experimental demonstration has been suggestive but inconclusive. Other essential nutrients that are not classified as vitamins include essential amino acids, choline, essential fatty acids, and the minerals discussed in the preceding part.

Vitamin deficiencies may result in disease conditions, including goitre, scurvy, osteoporosis, impaired immune system, disorders of cell metabolism, certain forms of cancer, symptoms of premature aging, and poor psychological health (including eating disorders), among many others. Excess levels of some vitamins are also dangerous to health (notably vitamin A), and for at least one vitamin, B6, toxicity begins at levels not far the required amount. Deficient or excess levels of minerals can also have serious health consequences.

WATER

It is not fully clear how much water intake is needed by healthy people, although some assert that 6–8 glasses of water daily is the minimum to maintain proper hydration. The notion that a person should consume eight glasses of water per day cannot be traced to a credible scientific source. The effect of, greater or lesser, water intake on weight loss and on constipation is also still unclear. The original water intake recommendation in 1945 by the Food and Nutrition Board of the National Research Council read: "An ordinary standard for diverse persons is 1 milliliter for each calorie of food.

Most of this quantity is contained in prepared foods." The latest dietary reference intake report by the United States National Research Council recommended, generally, (including food sources): 2.7 litres of water total for women and 3.7 litres for men. Specifically, pregnant and breastfeeding women need additional fluids to stay hydrated. According to the Institute of Medicine—who recommend that, on average, women consume 2.2 litres and men 3.0 litres—this is recommended to be 2.4 litres (approx. 9 cups) for pregnant women and 3 litres (approx. 12.5 cups) for breastfeeding women because an especially large amount of fluid is lost during nursing.

For those who have healthy kidneys, it is somewhat difficult to drink too much water, but (especially in warm humid weather and while exercising) it is dangerous to drink too little. People can drink far more water than necessary while exercising, however, putting them at risk of water intoxication, which can be fatal.

In particular, large amounts of de-ionized water are dangerous. Normally, about 20 per cent of water intake comes in food, while the rest comes from drinking water and assorted beverages (caffeinated included). Water is excreted from the body in multiple forms; including urine and faeces, sweating, and by water vapour in the exhaled breath.

ANTIOXIDANTS

As cellular metabolism/energy production requires oxygen, potentially damaging (e.g., mutation causing) compounds known as free radicals can form. Most of these are oxidizers (i.e., acceptors of electrons) and some react very strongly. For the continued normal cellular maintenance, growth, and division, these free radicals must be sufficiently neutralized by antioxidant compounds.

Some are produced by the human body with adequate precursors (glutathione, Vitamin C), and those the body cannot produce may only be obtained in the diet via direct sources (Vitamin C in humans, Vitamin A, Vitamin K) or produced by the body from other compounds (Beta-carotene converted to Vitamin A by the body, Vitamin D synthesized from cholesterol by sunlight).

Phytochemicals and their subgroup, polyphenols, make up the majority of antioxidants; about 4,000 are known. Different antioxidants are now known to function in a cooperative network. For example, Vitamin C can reactivate free radical-containing glutathione or Vitamin E by accepting the free radical itself. Some antioxidants are more effective than others at neutralizing different free radicals.

Some cannot neutralize certain free radicals. Some cannot be present in certain areas of free radical development (Vitamin A is fat-soluble and protects fat areas, Vitamin C is water soluble and protects those areas).

When interacting with a free radical, some antioxidants produce a different free radical compound that is less dangerous or more dangerous than the previous compound.

Having a variety of antioxidants allows any byproducts to be safely dealt with by more efficient antioxidants in neutralizing a free radical's butterfly effect. Although initial studies suggested that antioxidant supplements might promote health, later large clinical trials did not detect any benefit and suggested instead that excess supplementation may be harmful.

Phytochemicals

A growing area of interest is the effect upon human health of trace chemicals, collectively called phytochemicals. These nutrients are typically found in edible plants, especially colourful fruits and vegetables, but also other organisms including seafood, algae, and fungi. The effects of phytochemicals increasingly survive rigourous testing by prominent health organizations. One of the principal classes of phytochemicals are polyphenol antioxidants, chemicals that are known to provide certain health benefits to the cardiovascular system and immune system.

These chemicals are known to down-regulate the formation of reactive oxygen species, key chemicals in cardiovascular disease. Perhaps the most rigourously tested phytochemical is zeaxanthin, a yellow-pigmented carotenoid present in many yellow and orange fruits and vegetables. Repeated studies have shown a strong correlation between ingestion of zeaxanthin and the prevention and treatment of age-related macular degeneration (AMD).

Less rigourous studies have proposed a correlation between zeaxanthin intake and cataracts. A second carotenoid, lutein, has also been shown to lower the risk of contracting AMD. Both compounds have been observed to collect in the retina when ingested orally, and they serve to protect the rods and cones against the destructive effects of light. Another carotenoid, beta- cryptoxanthin, appears to protect against chronic joint inflammatory diseases, such as arthritis.

While the association between serum blood levels of beta-cryptoxanthin and substantially decreased joint disease has been established, neither a convincing mechanism for such protection nor a cause-and-effect have been rigourously studied. Similarly, a red phytochemical, lycopene, has substantial credible evidence of negative association with development of prostate cancer.

Some of the correlations between the ingestion of certain phytochemicals and the prevention of disease are, in some cases, enormous in magnitude. Yet, even when the evidence is obtained, translating it to practical dietary advice can be difficult and counter-intuitive. Lutein, for example, occurs in many yellow and orange fruits and vegetables and protects the eyes against various diseases. However, it does not protect the eye nearly as well as zeaxanthin, and the presence of lutein in the retina will prevent zeaxanthin uptake. Additionally, evidence has shown that the lutein present in egg yolk is more readily absorbed than the lutein from vegetable sources, possibly because of fat solubility. At the most basic level, the question "should you eat eggs?" is complex to the point of dismay, including misperceptions about the health effects of cholesterol in egg yolk, and its saturated fat content.

As another example, lycopene is prevalent in tomatoes (and actually is the chemical that gives tomatoes their red colour). It is more highly concentrated, however, in processed tomato products such as commercial pasta sauce, or tomato soup, than in fresh "healthy" tomatoes. Yet, such sauces tend to have high amounts of salt, sugar, other substances a person may wish or even need to avoid.

The following table presents phytochemical groups and common sources, arranged by family:

Family	Sources	Possible Benefits
Flavonoids	Berries, herbs, vegetables, wine, grapes, tea	General antioxidant, oxidation of LDLs, prevention of arteriosclerosis and heart disease
Isoflavones (phytoestrogens)	Soy, red clover, kudzu root	General antioxidant, prevention of arteriosclerosis and heart disease, easing symptoms of menopause, cancer prevention
Isothiocyanates	Cruciferous vegetables	cancer prevention
monoterpenes	Citrus peels, essential oils, herbs, spices, green plants, atmosphere	Cancer prevention, treating gallstones
Organosulfur compounds	Chives, garlic, onions	Cancer prevention, lowered LDLs, assistance to the immune system
Saponins	Beans, cereals, herbs	Hypercholesterolemia, Hyperglycemia, Antioxidant, cancer prevention, Anti-inflammatory
Capsaicinoids	All capiscum (chile) peppers	Topical pain relief, cancer prevention, cancer cell apoptosis

INTESTINAL BACTERIAL FLORA

It is now also known that animal intestines contain a large population of gut flora. In humans, these include species such as Bacteroides, L. acidophilus, and E. coli, among many others. They are essential to digestion, and are also affected by the food we eat. Bacteria in the gut perform many important functions for humans, including breaking down and aiding in the absorption of otherwise indigestible food; stimulating cell growth; repressing the growth of harmful bacteria, training the immune system to respond only to pathogens; producing vitamin B12, and defending against some infectious diseases.

NUTRITION: WHAT, WHEN AND HOW TO EAT?

What to Eat?

It is very important to eat the right kind of food, but it is even more important to be balanced and use common sense. Those who are moderate in their habits and cheerful can eat almost anything with good results. Of course, people who live almost entirely on such denatured foods as polished rice, finely bolted wheat flour products, sterilized milk and meat spoiled in the cooking, refined sugar and potatoes deprived of most of their salts through being soaked and cooked will suffer.

There are many different diet systems, and some of them are very good. If their advocates say that their way is the only way, they are wrong. Many try to force their ideas upon others. They find their happiness in making others miserable. They are afflicted with the proselyting zeal that makes fools of people. This is the wrong way to solve the food problem. Let each individual choose his own way and allow those who differ to continue in the old way.

Many have changed their dietary habits to their own great benefit. After this they become so enthused and anxious for others to do likewise that they wear themselves and others out exhorting them to share in the new discovery. This does no good, but it often does harm, for it leads the zealot to think too much of and about himself, and it annoys others. Many are like my friend who lunched daily on zwieback and raw carrots. "I think everybody ought to eat some raw carrots every day; don't you?" she said. We cannot mold everybody to our liking, and we should not try. If we conquer ourselves, we have about all we can do. If we succeed in this great work, as suggested, evolve enough tolerance to be willing to allow others to shape their own ends. To volunteer undesired information does no good, for it creates opposition in the mind of the hearers. If the information is sought, the chances are that it may in time do good. It is well enough to indicate how and where better knowledge may be obtained. We should at all times attempt to conserve our energy and use it only when and where it is helpful. Such conduct leads to peace of mind, effectiveness, happiness and health.

The tendency to become too enthusiastic about a dietary regime that has brought personal benefit is to be avoided, for it brings unnecessary odium upon the important subject of food reform. People do not like to change old habits, even if the change would be for the better, and when an enthusiast tries to force the change his actions are resented. He makes no real converts, but as pay for his efforts he gains the reputation of being a crank.

Those who wish to be helpful in an educational way should be patient. The race has been in the making for ages. Its good habits, as well as its bad ones, have been acquired gradually. If we ever get rid of our bad habits it will be through gradual evolution, not through a hasty revolution. We need a change in dietary habits, but those who become food cranks, insisting that others be as they, retard this movement. Only a few will change physical and mental habits suddenly.

If those who know are content to show the benefits more in results than in words, their influence for good will be great. What shall we eat? How are we to know the truth among so many conflicting ideas? We can know the truth because it leads to health. Error leads to suffering, degeneration and premature death. As the homely saying goes, "The proof of the pudding is in the eating." Let us look into some of the diet theories before the public and give them thoughtful consideration. The late Dr. J.H. Salisbury advocated the use of water to drink and meat to eat, and nothing else. The water was to be taken warm and in copious quantities, but not at or near meal time. The meat, preferably beef, was to be scraped or minced, made into cakes and cooked in a very warm skillet until the cakes turned grey within. These meat cakes were to be eaten three times a day, seasoned with salt and a little pepper.

The doctor had a very successful practice, which is attested by many who were benefited when ordinary medical skill failed. His diet was not well balanced. In meats there is a lack of the cell salts and force food. Especially are the cell salts lacking when the flesh is drained of its blood. The animals of prey drink the blood and crunch many of the bones of their victims, thus getting nearly all the salts. But in spite of his giving such an unbalanced diet, the doctor had a satisfactory practice and good success. Why? Because his patients had to quit using narcotics and stimulants and they were compelled to consume such simple food that they ceased overeating. It is a well known fact that a mono-diet forces moderation, for there is no desire to overeat, as there is when living on a very varied diet.

Another fact that the Salisbury plan brings to mind is that starch and sugar are not necessary for the feeding of adults, although they are convenient and cheap foods and ordinarily consumed in large quantities. The fat in the meat takes the place of the starch and sugar. Atomically, starch, sugar and fat are almost identical, and they can be substituted one for the other. Nature makes broad provisions.

Dr. Salisbury's career also serves to remind us that a mixed diet is not necessary for the physical welfare of those who eat to live. Vegetarians dwell upon the toxicity of meat. But Dr. Salisbury fed his patients on nothing but meat and water, and the percentage of recoveries in chronic diseases was considered remarkable. Meat is very easy to digest and when prepared in the simple manner prescribed by the doctor and eaten by itself it will agree with nearly everybody. But when eaten with soup, bread, potatoes, vegetables, cooked and raw, fish, pudding, fruit, coffee, crackers and cheese, there will be overeating followed by indigestion and its consequent train of ills. However, it is not fair to blame the meat entirely, for the whole mixture goes into decomposition and poisons the body.

The cures resulting from Dr. Salisbury's plan also help to disprove the much heralded theory of Dr. Haig, that uric acid from meat eating is the cause of rheumatism. Overeating of meat is often a contributory cause. We are told that the rheumatics who followed Dr. Salisbury's plan got well. They regained physical tone. They lost their gout and rheumatism. They parted company with their pimples and blotches. All of which would indicate that the blood became clean.

The chief part derived from Dr. Salisbury's plan and experience is the helpfulness of simple living and moderation. An exclusive diet of meat is not well balanced. Energy produced from flesh food is too expensive. The good results came from substituting habits of simplicity and moderation for the habit of overeating of too great variety of food. The same results may be obtained by putting a patient on bread and milk.

Dr. Salisbury's patients had unsatisfied longings, doubtless for various tissue salts. The addition of fresh raw fruits or vegetables would improve his diet, for apples, peaches, pears, lettuce, celery and cabbage are rich in the salts in which meats are deficient.

Dr. Emmet Densmore recommended omitting the starches entirely, that is, to avoid such foods as cereals, tubers and legumes. He believed that it is best to live on fruits and nuts. He recommended the sweet fruits—figs, dates, raisins, prunes—instead of the starchy foods. The doctor did much good, as everyone does who gets his patients to simplify. He also had good results before discovering that starch is a harmful food, when he fed his patients bread and milk. Starch must be converted into sugar before it can be used by the body. The sugar is what is known as dextrose, not the refined sugar of commerce. The sweet fruits contain this sugar in the form of fruit sugar, which needs but little preparation to be absorbed by the blood. Dr. Densmore reasons thus: Only birds are furnished with mills; hence the grains are fit food for them only. Other starches should be avoided because they are difficult to digest, the doctor wrote.

Raw starches are difficult to digest, but when they are properly cooked they are digested in a reasonable time without overburdening the system, provided they are well masticated and the amount eaten is not too great and the combining is correct. Rice, which contains much starch, digests in a short time. We can do very nicely without starch. We can also thrive on it if we do not abuse it. The two chief starch-bearing staples, rice and wheat, contain considerable protein and salts in their natural state.

In fact, the natural wheat will sustain life for a long time. Man has improved on nature by polishing the rice and making finely bolted, bleached wheat flour, deprived of nearly all the salts in the wheat berry. The result is that both of them have become very poor foods.

The more we eat of these refined products the worse off we are, unless we partake freely of other foods rich in mineral salts. Not long ago a lady died in England who was a prominent advocate of a "brainy diet". Her brainy diet consisted largely of excessive quantities of meat, pork being a favourite. She died comparatively young, her friends say from overwork. Such a diet doubtless had a large part in wearing her out. To overeat of meat is dangerous. A gentleman is now advocating a diet of nothing but cocoanuts. This is a fad, for they are not a balanced food. He has published a book on the subject. Perhaps his advocacy is influenced by his interest in the sale of cocoanuts.

The vegetarians condemn the use of meat. Some of them are called fruitarians. It is very difficult to decide who are the most representative of them. Some advocate the use of nothing but fruit and nuts. Others add cereals to this. Others use vegetables in addition. Some even allow the use of dairy products and eggs, that is, all foods except flesh. They say that meat is an unnatural food for man and condemn its use on moral grounds. It is difficult to decide what is natural, for we find that man is very adaptable, being able to live on fruits in the tropics and almost exclusively on flesh food, largely fat, in the arctic regions.

In nature the strong live on the weak and the intelligent on the dull. There is no sentiment in nature. In her domain might, physical or mental, makes right. Sentiments of right and justice are not highly developed except among human beings, and even there they are so weakly implanted that it takes but little provocation for civilized man to bare his teeth in a wolfish snarl. With some vegetarianism is largely a matter of aesthetics, ethics and morality.

Morality is based on expediency, so it really is a question whether meat is an advantageous food or not. Another vegetarian argument is that man's anatomy proves that he was not intended by nature to eat meat. Good arguments have been used on both sides, but they are not very convincing nor are they conclusive. It is hard to draw any lines fairly. Another objection to meat is that it is unclean and full of poisons, that these poisons produce various diseases, such as cancer.

We are also informed that refined sugar causes cancer, and the belief in tomatoes as a causative factor is not dead. Cancer is without doubt caused principally by dietary indiscretions but it is impossible to single out any one food. No matter what foods we eat, we are compelled to be careful or they will be unclean. Those who wish clean meat can obtain it. The amount of poison or waste in a proper portion of meat is so small that we need give it no thought.

Those who eat in moderation can take meat once a day during cold weather and enjoy splendid health. During warm weather it should be eaten more seldom. On the other hand, meat is not necessary. We need a certain amount of protein, which we can obtain from nuts, eggs, milk, cheese, peanuts, peas, beans, lentils, cereals and from other food in smaller amounts. The amount of protein needed is small—about one-fifth of what the physiologists used to recommend. Those who think meat eating is wrong should not partake of it. They can get along very well without it. The organism can stand it if the life is active in the fresh air, but it will not do for people who are housed. Much meat eating causes physical degeneration. The body loses tone.

Experiments have shown that vegetarians have more resistance and endurance than the meat eaters, but the meat eaters get so much stimulation from their food that they can speed up in spurts. The excretions of meat eaters are more poisonous than those of vegetarians.

Eggs produced by hens fed largely on meat scraps do not keep as well as those laid by hens feeding more on grains. In short, meat eating leads to instability or degeneration, if carried to excess. Young children should have none of it and it would be a very easy matter for the rising generation to develop without using meat, and we believe this would be better than our present plan of eating.

However, let us give flesh food the credit due it. When meat eaters are debilitated no other food seems to act as kindly as meat, given with fruits or vegetables. When properly prepared and taken in moderation meat digests easily and is quite completely assimilated. Many make the mistake of living too exclusively on starch and taking it in excess. The result is fermentation and an acid state of the alimentary tract. Dr. Daniel S. Sager says that, "About all that we have to fear in eating is excessive use of proteids."

Experience and observation do not bear out this statement, for it is as easy to find people injured by starch as by protein. One form of poisoning is as bad as the other. The doctor also warns against nearly all the succulent vegetables, saying that on account of the indigestible fibre, most of them are unfit for human consumption. Dr. E.H. Dewey condemned the apple as a disease-producer, and inferentially, other fruits. Dr. Charles E. Page objects to the use of milk by adults, on the ground that it is fit food only for the calves for whom nature intended it. Many writers have repeated this opinion. Most of the regular physicians have a very vague idea of dietetics and proper feeding. When asked what to eat they commonly say, "Eat plenty nourishing food of the kinds that agree with you." They do not point out the fundamentals to their patients. Sometimes they advise avoiding combinations of milk and fruits. Sometimes they say that all starches should be avoided and in the next breath prescribe toast, one of the starchiest of foods. At times they proscribe pork and pickles but they are seldom able to give a good diet prescription. What people need is a fair knowledge of what to do and the don'ts will take care of themselves. All foods have been condemned as unfit for human consumption by people who should know.

However, those who look at these matters with open eyes and open minds will come to the cease that man is a very adaptable animal; that if necessary he can get along without almost all foods, being able to subsist on a very small variety; that he can live for a long period on animal food entirely; that he can live all his life without tasting flesh; that he can live on a mixed diet; that he can adopt a great many plans of eating and live in health and comfort on nearly all of them, provided he does not deprive himself of the natural salts and gets some protein; and finally and most important, that moderation is the chief factor in keeping well, for the best foods produce disease in time if taken in excess.

Those who object to flesh, dairy products, cereals, tubers, legumes, refined sugars, fruits or vegetables, should do without the class which they find objectionable, for it is easy to substitute from other classes. Eggs, milk or legumes may be taken in place of flesh foods. The salts contained in fruits may be obtained from vegetables. The starch, which is the chief ingredient of cereals, is easily obtained from tubers and legumes; fats and sugars will take its place. Commercial sugar is not a necessity. The force and heat derived from it can be obtained from starches and fats.

Outside of milk in infancy, there is not a single indispensable food. Some people have peculiarities which prevent them from eating certain foods, such as pork, eggs, milk and strawberries, but with these exceptions a healthy person can eat any food he pleases, provided he is moderate. We eat too much flesh, sugar and starch and we suffer for it.

This does not prove that these foods are harmful, but that overeating is. Sometimes the food question becomes a very trying one in the home.

One individual has learned the fact that good results are obtained by using good sense and judgement in combining and consuming food, and he tries to force others to do as he does. This is unfortunate, for most people object to such actions, and though the intention is good, it accomplishes nothing, but prejudices others against sensible living.

The best way is to do right yourself and let others sin against themselves and suffer until they are weary. Then, seeing how you got out of your trouble, perhaps they will come to you and accept what you have to offer. The attempt to force people to be good or to be healthy is merely wasted effort.

When to Eat?

Three meals a day is the common plan. This is a matter of habit. Three meals a day are sufficient and should not be exceeded by man, woman or child.

Lunching or "piecing" should never be indulged in. Children who are fed on plain, nutritious foods that contain the necessary food elements do not need lunches. Lunching is also a matter of habit, and we can safely say that it is a bad habit. If three meals a day are taken, two should be light. He who wishes to work efficiently can not eat three hearty meals a day. If it is brain work, the digestive organs will take so much of the blood supply that an insufficient amount of blood will be left to nourish the brain. The worker feels the lack of energy. He is not inclined to do thorough work, that is, to go to the root of matters, and he therefore does indifferent work.

One rule to which there is no exception is that the brain can not do its best when the digestive organs are working hard. If there is a piece of work to be done or a problem to be solved that requires all of one's powers it is best to tackle it with an empty stomach, or after a very light meal. If the work is physical, it is not necessary to draw the line so fine. But it is well to remember that hard physical work prevents digestion.

All experiments prove this. So if the labour is very trying, the eating should be light. Those who eat much because they work hard will soon wear themselves out, for hard work retards digestion, and with weakened digestion the more that is eaten, the less nourishment is extracted from it. Those who labour hard should take a light breakfast and the same kind of a noon meal. After the day's work is done, take a hearty meal. Those who perform hard physical labour, as well as those who work chiefly with their brains, should relax a while after the noon meal. A nap lasting ten to twenty minutes is very beneficial, but not necessary if relaxation is taken.

During sleep the activities of the body slow down. Most people who take a heavy meal and retire immediately thereafter feel uncomfortable when they wake in the morning. The reason is that the food did not digest well. It is always well to remain up at least two hours after eating a hearty meal. Most people would be better off if they took but two meals a day. Those who have sedentary occupations need less fuel than manual labourers, and could get along very well on two meals a day. However, if moderation is practiced, no harm will come from eating three times a day.

In olden times many people lived on one meal a day. Some do so today and get along very well. It is easy to get plenty of nourishment from one meal, and it has the advantage of not taking so much time. Most of us spend too much time preparing for meals and eating. Once when it was rather inconvenient to get more meals, we lived for ten months on one meal a day. We enjoyed our food very much and was well nourished. For twelve years we have lived on two meals a day, one of them often consisting of nothing but some juicy fruit. Many others do likewise, not because they are prejudiced against three meals per day, but they find the two meal plan more convenient and very satisfactory. Meat, potatoes and bread, with other foods, three times a day is a common combination.

No ordinary mortal can live in health on such a diet. Such feeding results in discomfort and disease, and unless it is changed, in premature aging and death. The body needs only a certain amount of material. Sufficient can be taken in two meals. If three meals is the custom less food at a meal should be eaten. However, the general rule is that those who eat three meals per day eat fully as large ones as those who take only two.

As a rule, the meal times should be regular. We need a certain amount of nourishment, and it is well to take it regularly. This reduces friction, and is conducive to health, for the body is easily taught to fall into habits of regularity and works best when these are observed. There should be a period of at least four and one-half to five hours between meals. It takes that long for the body to get a meal out of the way. Stomach digestion is but the beginning of the process, and this alone requires from two to five hours.

On the two-meal plan it makes very little difference whether the breakfast or the lunch is omitted. After going without breakfast for a week or two, one does not miss it. Miss the meal that it is the most troublesome to get. Dr. Dewey revived interest in the no-breakfast plan. He considered it very beneficial.

The doctor did not give credit where credit is due, for he insisted on going without breakfast. Omitting lunch or dinner accomplishes the same thing. He got his beneficial results from reducing the number of meals, and consequently the amount of food taken, but it is immaterial which meal is omitted.

Heavy breakfasts are very common in England and in our country. On the European continent they do not eat so much for breakfast, a cup of coffee and one roll being a favourite morning meal there. To eat nothing in the morning is better than to take coffee and rolls. To eat enough to steal one's brain away is a poor way to begin the day. Much better work could be done on some fruit or a glass of milk, or some cereal and butter than on eggs, steak potatoes, hot bread and coffee, which is not an uncommon breakfast.

When we consider the best time to eat, we come back to our old friend, moderation, and find that it is the best solution of the question, for if the meals are moderate we may with benefit take three meals a day, but no more, for there is not time enough during the day to digest more than three meals. However, it is not necessary to eat three times a day.

How to Eat?

It seems that all of us ought to know how to eat, for we have much practice; yet the individuals who know the true principles of nourishing the body are comparatively few. Very few healers are able to give full and explicit directions on this important subject. Some can give partial instructions, but we need a full working knowledge.

In one period of our racial history there were times when it was difficult to obtain food, as it is now among some savage people. Then it was without doubt customary to gorge, as it is among some savages now when they get a plenteous supply of food, especially of flesh food. Even among so-called civilized people, the distribution of food is so uneven that some are in want somewhere, nearly all the time.

In parts of Russia, we are informed, the peasants go into a state of semi- hibernation during part of the winter, living on very small quantities of inferior food. With rapid transportation and the extensive use of power-propelled machinery, famine should be unheard of in civilized countries. In our land there is a sufficient quantity of food and people seldom suffer because they have not enough, but considerable suffering is due to excessive intake and to poor quality of food.

Weight for weight, white bread is not as valuable as whole-wheat bread, though it contains as much starch. Measure for measure, boiled milk is inferior as a food to untreated milk, either fresh or clabbered. Such facts make it necessary for us to know how to eat.

The correct principles of taking nourishment to the best advantage have been fairly well known for a long time, and perhaps they have been fully discussed years ago by some authors, but so far as we know Dr. E.H. Dewey is the first one who grouped them and gave them the prominence they deserve.

He employed many pages in explaining clearly and forcibly these principles, which can be briefly stated as follows:

- First, be guided by the appetite in eating. Eat only when there is hunger.
- Second, during acute illness fast, that is, live on water.
- Third, be moderate in eating.
- Fourth, masticate your food thoroughly.

Dr. J.H. Tilden teaches his patients the same in these words:

- "Never eat when you feel badly.
- "Never eat when you have no desire.
- "Do not overeat.
- "Thoroughly masticate and insalivate all your food."

Because these true dietetic principles are so important let us give them enough consideration to fix them in the mind. They should be a part of every child's education. They should be so thoroughly learned that they become second nature, for if they are observed disease is practically impossible.

Accidents may happen, but no serious disease can develop and certainly none of a chronic nature if these rules are observed, provided the individual gives himself half a chance in other ways. When the eating is correct, it is difficult to fall into bad habits mentally. Correct eating is a powerful aid to health. Health tends to produce proper thinking, which in turn leads the individual to proper acting.

Eat Only When there is Hunger

Hunger is of two kinds, normal and abnormal. The real or normal hunger was given us by nature to make us active enough to get food. If it were not for hunger, there would be no special incentive for the young to partake of nourishment and consequently many would die comfortably of starvation, perhaps enough to endanger the life of the race. Normal hunger asks for food, but no special kind of food. It is satisfied with anything that is clean and nourishing. It is strong enough to make a decided demand for food, but if there is no food to be had it will be satisfied for the time being with a glass of water and will cause no great inconvenience. Abnormal hunger is entirely different. It is a very insistent craving and if it is not satisfied it produces bodily discomfort, perhaps headache. The gnawing remains and gives the victim no rest. Very often it must be pampered. It calls for beefsteak, or toast and tea, or sweets, or some other special food. If not satisfied the results may be nervousness, weakness or headache or some other disagreeable symptom.

When missing a meal or two brings discomfort, it is always a sign of a degenerating or degenerated body. A healthy person can go a day without food without any inconvenience. He feels a keen desire for food at meal times, but as soon as he has made up his mind that he is unable to get it or that he is not going to take any the hunger leaves. Normal hunger is a servant. Abnormal hunger is a hard master.

A person in good condition does not get weak from missing a few meals. One in poor physical condition does, although this is more apparent than real. In the abnormal person a part of the food is used as nourishment, but on account of the poor working of the digestive organs, a part decomposes and this acts as an irritant or a stimulant. The greater the irritation the more food is demanded. The temporary stimulation is followed by depression and then the sufferer is wretched. This depression is relieved by more food. Please note that it is relieved, not cured. The relief is only temporary.

All food stimulates, but only slightly. It is when the food decomposes that it becomes stimulating enough to cause trouble. It is well to remember that considerable alcoholic fermentation can take place in an abused alimentary tract. The stimulation obtained from too much food is very much like the stimulation derived from alcohol, tobacco or morphine. At first there is a feeling of well-being, which is followed by a miserable feeling of depression that demands food, alcohol, tobacco or morphine for relief, as the case may be, and no matter which habit is obtaining mastery, to indulge it is courting disaster. When a habit begins to assert itself strongly, break it, for later on it will be very difficult, so difficult that most people lack the will power to overcome it.

If there is abnormal hunger, reduce the food intake. Instead of eating five or six times a day, reduce the meals to two or three. It is quite common for such people to take lunches, which may consist of candies, ice cream, cakes, milk or buttermilk and various other things which most people do not look upon as real food. Take two or three meals a day, and let a large part of them be fresh vegetables and fresh fruits. Eat in moderation and the troublesome abnormal hunger will soon leave. By indulging it you increase it. Many people get into trouble because they believe that they have to have protein, starch and fat at every meal. This is not necessary, for the blood takes up enough nourishment to last for quite a while. A supply of the various food elements once a day is sufficient, which means that protein needs be taken but once a day, starch once a day and fat once a day. Starch and fat serve the same purpose and one can be replaced by the other.

Cultivate a normal hunger, then fix two or three periods in which to take nourishment, and partake of nothing but water outside of these periods. If there is no desire for food when meal time comes, eat nothing, but drink all the water desired and wait until next meal time.

During Acute Illness Fast

This is so obviously correct that we should expect every normal individual to be guided by it. Even the lower animals know this and act accordingly. This rule we should go without food when ill, but to do so is contrary to the teachings of medical men. They teach that when people are ill there is much waste, which is true, and that for this reason it is necessary to partake of a generous amount of nourishing food, so they give milk, broth, meat, toast and other foods, together with stimulants. Feeding during illness would be all right if the body could take care of the food, which it cannot. In all severe diseases digestion is almost or quite at a standstill and the food given under the circumstances decomposes in the alimentary tract and furnishes additional poison for the system to excrete.

Food under the circumstances is a detriment and a burden to the body. In fevers, the temperature goes up after feeding. This shows that more poison has entered the blood. In fevers little or none of the digestive fluids is secreted, but the alimentary tract is so warm that the food decomposes quickly. Feeding during acute attacks of disease is one of the most serious and fatal of errors. There is an aversion to food, which is nature's request that none be taken.

When an animal becomes seriously ill, it wants to fast, and does so unless man interferes. Here we could with advantage do as the animals do. Nature made no mistake when she took hunger away in acute diseases, and if we disregard her desires, we invariably suffer for it. We should make it a rule to take no food, either liquid or solid, during acute disease.

Those who have had no opportunity to watch the rapidity with which people recover from serious illness may take the ground that sick people would starve to death if they were to be treated thus, for some of these acute diseases last a long time. Typhoid fever, for instance, occasionally lasts two or three months. It never lasts that long when treated by natural means, and it is very mild, as a rule. The fever will be gone in from seven to fourteen days in the vast majority of cases, and then feeding can be resumed.

Chronic disease is often due to neglected acute disease, at other times to the building of abnormality through errors of life which have not resulted in acute troubles. While acquiring chronic disease, the individual may be fairly comfortable, but he is never up to par. Most chronic diseases can be cured quickly by taking a fast, but usually it is not necessary to take a complete fast. The desire for food is not generally absent and there is usually fair power to digest.

One of the most satisfactory methods, if not the most satisfactory one, of treating chronic disease is to reduce the food intake, and instead of giving so much of the concentrated staples, feed more of the succulent vegetables and the fresh fruits, cooked and raw, using but small quantities of flesh, bread, potatoes and sugar. This gives the body a chance to throw off impurities. There are always many impurities in a deranged body.

Be Moderate in Your Eating

This is often very difficult, for most people do not know what moderation is. In infancy the too frequent feeding and the overfeeding begin. The common belief that infants must be fed every two hours, or oftener, is acted upon. The result is that the child soon loses its normal hunger, which is replaced by abnormal hunger. When food is long withheld it begins to fret.

The mother again feeds and there is peace for an hour or so. When mothers learn to feed their children three times a day and no more there will be a great decrease in infant ills and a falling off in the infant mortality. The healthiest children we have seen are fed but three times a day. They become used to it and expect no more. Another thing that makes it difficult to be moderate is impoverishing the food through refinement and poor cooking.

These processes take away a great part of the mineral salts which are present in foods in organic form. These salts can not be replaced by table salt, for sodium chloride is but one of many salts that the body needs and an excess of table salt does not make up for a deficiency in the others. Children fed on refined, impoverished foods are not satisfied with a reasonable amount. There is something lacking and this makes itself known in cravings, which demand more food than is needed to nourish. We have noticed many times that children are satisfied with less of whole wheat bread than of white bread, and that the brown unpolished rice satisfies them more quickly and completely than the polished rice. In other words, depriving the foods of their salts is one of the factors that leads to overeating. Simplicity is a great aid to moderation.

It is also necessary to exercise the conservative measure, self-control. Some writers suggest to eat all that is desired and then fast at various intervals to overcome the effects of overeating. In other words, they advise to eat enough to become diseased and then fast to cure the trouble. This is better than to continue the eating when the evil results of an excessive food intake make themselves known, but it does not bring the best results. Such people have their spells of sickness, which are unnecessary.

If they stop eating as soon as the disease makes itself known, it does not last long. By exercising self-control sickness will be warded off. By using will power daily it grows stronger and those who force themselves to be moderate at first, are in time rewarded by having moderation become second nature. People should always stop eating before they are full. Those who eat until they are uncomfortable are gluttons. They should be classed with drunkards and drug addicts.

Thoroughly Masticate All Food

Horace Fletcher has written a very enthusiastic book on this subject. Enthusiasm is apt to lead one astray, and even if thorough mastication will not do all that Mr. Fletcher believed, it is very important, and we owe Mr. Fletcher thanks for calling our attention to the subject forcibly. Thorough mastication partially checks overeating. Our foods have to be finely divided and subdivided or they cannot be thoroughly acted upon by the digestive juices.

The stomach is well muscled and churns the food about, helping to comminute it, but it can not take the place of the teeth. All foods should be thoroughly masticated. While the mastication is going on the saliva becomes mixed with the food.

In the saliva is the ptyalin, which begins to digest the starch. Starch that is well masticated is not so liable to ferment as that which gets scant attention in the mouth. Starches and nuts need the most thorough mastication. If thorough mastication were the rule, meat gluttons would be fewer, for when flesh is well chewed large quantities cause nausea.

Milk digests best when it is rolled around in the mouth long enough to be mixed with saliva. To treat milk as a drink is a mistake, for it is a very nourishing food. All kinds of nuts must be well masticated. If they are not they cannot be well digested, for the digestive organs are unable to break down big pieces of the hard nut meats. The succulent vegetables contain considerable starch. If mastication is slighted they often ferment enough to produce considerable gas. Fruits are generally eaten too rapidly, and therefore often produce bad results. Even green fruits can be eaten with impunity if they are very thoroughly masticated. Those who are fond enough of liquors to take an excess should sip their alcoholic beverages very slowly, tasting every drop before swallowing. This would decrease their consumption of liquor greatly. Even water should not be gulped down. It should be taken rather slowly, especially on hot days. During hot weather many drink too much water. This tendency can usually be overcome by avoiding iced water and by drinking slowly.

These four rules should be a part of your vital knowledge. Remember them and try to put them into practice:

1. "Eat only when hungry.
2. During acute illness fast.
3. Be moderate in your eating.
4. Thoroughly masticate all food."

□

Index

R

S

U

□□□